Chemistry
of Space

DAVID E. NEWTON

An imprint of Infobase Publishing

One Last Time . . .
for John McArdle, Lee Nolet, Richard Olson,
David Parr, David Rowand, Jeff Williams, and John D'Emilio
Thanks for the memories!

Chemistry of Space

Facts On File, Inc.
An imprint of Infobase Publishing
132 West 31st Street
New York NY 10001

ISBN-10: 0-8160-5274-3
ISBN-13: 978-0-8160-5274-5

Library of Congress Cataloging-in-Publication Data
Newton, David E.
    Chemistry of space / David E. Newton.
       p. cm. — (The new chemistry)
    Includes bibliographical references and index.
    ISBN: 0-8160-5274-3 (acid-free paper)
    1. Cosmochemistry. 2. Interstellar matter. 3. Stars—Evolution. I. Title.
    QB450.N49 2007
    523'02—dc22   2006037373

Facts On File books are available at special discounts when purchased in bulk quantities for businesses, associations, institutions, or sales promotions. Please call our Special Sales Department in New York at (212) 967-8800 or (800) 322-8755.

You can find Facts On File on the World Wide Web at
http://www.factsonfile.com

Text design by James Scotto-Lavino
Illustrations by DiacriTech, LLC
Project editing by Dorothy Cummings

Printed in the United States of America

MP CGI 10 9 8 7 6 5 4 3 2 1

This book is printed on acid-free paper.

CONTENTS

Preface   vii
Introduction   ix

1   THE BIRTH OF THE UNIVERSE   1
     In the Beginning   1
          Georges Edouard Lemaître (1894–1966)   2
     A Cooling Universe   5
     Particle Decay   7
     The Formation of Compound Particles   8
     And Then There Were Atoms   11
     Is the Theory True?   13
          George Gamow (1904–1968)   16
     Where to Next?   19

2   THE CHEMISTRY OF INTERSTELLAR SPACE   21
     The Composition of the Interstellar Medium   22
     Interstellar Clouds   29
          Robert Julius Trumpler (1886–1956)   30
     Chemistry of the Interstellar Medium   34
     Tools for Studying the Chemical Characteristics
          of the ISM   39
          Hendrik Christoffel van de Hulst (1918–2000)   40

3   FORMATION OF THE HEAVY ELEMENTS   47
     Stellar Evolution   48

Classifying Stars   49
   Annie Jump Cannon (1863–1941)   *50*
A Star Is Born   55
Turning Hydrogen into Helium   61
Helium Burning . . . and Beyond   66
Bigger Stars = More Elements   69
   Margaret Burbidge (1919–   ) and
     Geoffrey Burbidge (1925–   )   *74*

4 THE INNER PLANETS   **81**
Studying the Chemical Composition of a Planet   82
Mercury   90
Venus   94
   The Hubble Space Telescope   *108*
Mars   111
   Asaph Hall (1829–1907)   *122*

5 THE OUTER PLANETS   **126**
Missions to the Outer Planets   127
Jupiter   132
   S. Alan Stern (1957–   )   *134*
The Jovian Moons   143
Saturn   151
Uranus   156
Neptune   161
Pluto   164
   James E. Webb (1906–1992)   *165*
Kuiper Belt Objects   167
   Gerard Peter Kuiper (1905–1973)   *168*

6 COMETS, METEORS, ASTEROIDS, AND THE MOON   **171**
Comets   172
   Edmund Halley (1656–1742)   *176*
Meteors, Meteoroids, and Meteorites   192
Asteroids   202
The Moon   216

CONCLUSION 227

Glossary   229
Further Reading   235
Index   239

PREFACE

The subject matter covered in introductory chemistry classes at the middle and high school levels tends to be fairly traditional and relatively consistent from school to school. Topics that are typically covered in such classes include atomic theory, chemical periodicity, ionic and covalent compounds, equation writing, stoichiometry, and solutions. While these topics are essential for students planning to continue their studies in chemistry or the other sciences and teachers are correct in emphasizing their importance, they usually provide only a limited introduction to the rich and exciting character of research currently being conducted in the field of chemistry. Many students not planning to continue their studies in chemistry or the other sciences may benefit from information about areas of chemistry with immediate impact on their daily lives or of general intellectual interest. Indeed, science majors themselves may also benefit from the study of such subjects.

The New Chemistry is a set of six books intended to provide an overview of some areas of research not typically included in the beginning middle or high school curriculum in chemistry. The six books in the set—*Chemistry of Drugs, Chemistry of New Materials, Forensic Chemistry, Chemistry of the Environment, Food Chemistry,* and *Chemistry of Space*—are designed to provide a broad, general introduction to some fields of chemistry that are less commonly mentioned in standard introductory chemistry courses. They cover topics ranging from the most fundamental fields of chemistry, such as the origins of matter and of the universe, to those with important applications to everyday life, such as the composition of foods and drugs. The set title The New Chemistry has been selected to emphasize the extensive review of recent research and advances in each of the fields of chemistry covered in the set. The books in The New Chemistry set are written for middle school and high school readers. They assume some basic understanding of the principles of chemistry that are generally gained in an introductory middle or high school course in the subject. Every book contains a large amount of material that should be accessible to the interested reader with no more than an introductory understanding of chemistry and a smaller amount of material that may require a more advanced understanding of the subject.

The six books that make up the set are independent of each other. That is, readers may approach all of the books in any sequence whatsoever. To assist the reader in extending his or her understanding of each subject, each book in the set includes a glossary and a list of additional reading sources from both print and Internet sources. Short bibliographic sketches of important figures from each of the six fields are also included in the books.

INTRODUCTION

Space and astronomy is the oldest of all sciences. Long before humans understood the composition of rocks and minerals, knew how chemical reactions take place, or even discovered how their own bodies were constructed and operated, they knew of the existence of bodies beyond the Earth's atmosphere: other planets, stars, and a variety of strange objects for which they had only simple explanations. The knowledge that early astronomers had of the skies was quite remarkable. They were able to predict the motion of stars, the arrival of seasons, the appearance of eclipses, and other astronomical phenomena with an accuracy that is quite astonishing to modern scientists.

Although it qualifies as the oldest of all sciences, space and astronomy has often been called the most difficult. Geologists can pick up and analyze the rocks they would like to study. Chemists can create the conditions under which almost any chemical reaction can be studied. Biologists are able to dissect living organisms and find out how they are composed and how they function, but astronomers have only tiny bits of light with which to study the objects of their field. They must devise ingenious methods for capturing that light and analyzing it in as many ways as possible. The information gained by astronomers using these limited resources is truly amazing.

The challenge faced by astrochemists—scientists who study the chemical composition of astronomical bodies and the chemical changes that take place within them—is at least as daunting as it is to researchers in other fields of astronomy. They must find ways to interpret the information a beam of light gives about the elements and compounds present in its source—a star or a *dust* cloud, for example—where those elements and compounds may have come from originally, and what kinds of chemical changes they are undergoing.

Yet astrochemists have managed to deduce an impressive amount of information about our universe, the events through which it was created, the changes that have taken place during its evolution, and its present composition. Some of that information relates to the most basic questions in all of chemistry; for instance, where did fundamental particles, such as protons and neutrons, come from, and how were the elements created. Although many important facts are still missing, astrochemists are able to respond to these questions and to explain much about how the world we live in has come to be as it is.

Astrochemists can also tell us a great deal about the nature of solar bodies that fascinate and intrigue all of us. What is Venus like? Where did the Moon come from? What is the composition of giant planets like Jupiter and Saturn? Can Mars support life? Questions like these that people with little or no background in astronomy are likely to ask can now be answered, to at least some extent.

The purpose of *Chemistry of Space* is to provide an overview of the latest information about the solar system, the planets, comets, and meteors, and other features of our universe that has become available as a result of research in astrochemistry. This information changes rapidly, however. New space probes are being sent into the solar system and outer space on a regular basis; each such probe sends back new treasure troves of information about astronomical bodies. Interested readers will find useful and recent data in this book but should consider using the bibliographical section at the end of the book to pursue further changes taking place within the field.

1

THE BIRTH OF
THE UNIVERSE

It's "Time Zero" for the universe: Time Zero is the instant in time at which the universe was born. Scientists now believe that Time Zero occurred about 10 billion to 20 billion years ago in a sudden, dramatic explosion known as the big bang. They know nothing at all about the state of the universe before the big bang or in the first few microseconds after that enormous explosion occurred. In fact, some of the most interesting and vigorous debates now taking place among cosmologists (people who study the origin and properties of the universe) are about just what was taking place in the newborn universe during those earliest microseconds.

Most scientists, however, are fairly confident that they understand the changes that took place immediately afterward. It was during those early moments that the chemical building blocks of which the universe, the solar system, and planet Earth and all living things on it, were created.

In the Beginning

Probably the most pronounced feature of the early universe was an all-encompassing flood of energy, which was comparable in its

◄ GEORGES EDOUARD LEMAÎTRE (1894–1966) ►

Some people wonder if the big bang theory is in conflict with religious teachings. In view of such concerns, it is of interest to note that the first big-bang-like theory was proposed by a Belgian priest, Georges Edouard Lemaître.

Lemaître was born in Charleroi, Belgium, on July 17, 1894. He earned a degree in civil engineering from the University of Louvain and then joined the Belgian army during World War I. After the war, he returned to Louvain, intending to work toward a Ph.D., but he soon changed his mind and entered a seminary with the goal of becoming a priest. He was ordained in 1923 but did not abandon his interest in science. He attended the University of Cambridge, where he studied solar physics and met the great English astronomer Arthur Eddington (1882–1944). He also studied at the Massachusetts Institute of Technology, from which he eventually received a Ph.D. in 1927. He then returned to Belgium, where he took a post as professor of astrophysics

In 1927, Lemaître published a paper entitled *Un Univers homogène de masse constante et de rayon croissant rendant compte de la vitesse radiale des nébuleuses extragalactiques (A homogeneous Universe of constant mass and*

characteristics to the various forms of electromagnetic radiation recorded today. Electromagnetic radiation is a form of energy propagated by periodic fluctuations of electrical and magnetic fields in space. Some common forms of electromagnetic radiation are light, X-rays, ultraviolet radiation, infrared radiation, radar, radio waves, and gamma rays. The two most common forms of energy present in the early universe were gamma rays and photons. Gamma rays are very energetic forms of electromagnetic radiation, while photons are the particles by which light is transferred through space. Many types of gamma rays and photons were present, differing from each other in the amount of energy they possessed.

In the young universe there were also present large numbers of neutrinos, very small particles carrying no electrical charge and little or no mass. (A great deal of research is being focused today *growing radius accounting for the radial velocity of extragalactic nebulae),* in which he suggested a mechanism by which the universe might have been created. Suppose we think of the history of the universe as a motion picture that can be played backward. In such a case, the stars and galaxies of which the universe is made would move closer and closer together until they all collapsed into one single region of space at some time in the far distant past. This "thought experiment" suggested to Lemaître that the universe may have originated as a highly compact mass of matter and energy, to which he gave the name of "cosmic egg" or "primal superatom." The universe originated then, according to Lemaître, when the cosmic egg or superatom exploded, sending matter and energy spewing away from the central point, producing the expanding universe we know today. Lemaître estimated the size of the cosmic egg to be about 30 times the size of the Sun and thought that the time of origin was between 20 billion and 60 billion years ago.

Lemaître's theory was largely ignored for some time until it was promoted by his former teacher, Eddington, who provided an English language translation in the journal *Nature* in 1930. With that exposure, Lemaître's theory became widely known and discussed by astronomers worldwide. The theory has been extensively revised and improved in the past 70 years but is now widely regarded as fundamentally correct in its description of the way the universe was formed. Lemaître died in Louvain on June 20, 1966.

on discovering whether neutrinos do have any mass at all and, if so, what that mass is.) The interaction among gamma rays, photons, and neutrinos resulted in the formation of the first particles.

The relationship between energy and mass was first explained by the German-Swiss-American physicist Albert Einstein (1879–1955) in 1905. Einstein said that energy and matter are interconvertible— that is, a certain amount of energy is equivalent to a specific amount of matter, and, conversely, a given quantity of matter is equivalent to a specific amount of energy. He quantified this relationship in a now-famous equation, $E = mc^2$. This equation says that a given quantity of mass (m) has an energy equivalent (E) equal to that mass multiplied by the square of the speed of light (c^2). By using this equation, one can calculate the amount of mass that is equivalent to some given amount of energy, and vice versa.

For example, the interaction of gamma rays, photons, and neutrinos with relatively small amounts of energy may result in the production of relatively light particles. An electron is one of the lightest particles known, with a mass of 9.042×10^{-28} g. It can be formed in the interaction between a gamma ray (γ) and a neutrino (ν) whose total energy is no more than 0.511 MeV. The symbol MeV stands for million electron volts, a measure of energy. A million electron volts is the amount of energy gained or lost by an electron accelerated by a potential difference of one million volts. The reaction in which electrons are formed from the interaction of gamma rays and neutrinos can be represented by the following equation:

$$\gamma_e + \nu_e \rightarrow e^-$$

That is, the interaction of a gamma ray with the correct amount of energy (γ_e) and a neutrino with the correct amount of energy (ν_e) may result in the formation of an electron (e^-).

A common practice among scientists reflects the relationship between mass and energy: They express the mass of a particle in either traditional units (grams, for example) or the energy equivalent of that mass. For example, the mass of an electron can be expressed as 9.042×10^{-28} g or as 0.511 MeV. Similarly, the mass of a proton can be expressed either as 1.660×10^{-24} g or as 938.26 MeV, the energy equivalent of that mass.

Conditions in the universe almost immediately after the big bang were not favorable for the formation of electrons. At that point in time, gamma rays, photons, and neutrinos had very large amounts of energy, much more than was needed to produce electrons. Instead, conditions favored the creation of much more massive particles with large energy equivalents. Among these particles were the muon and the proton. A muon (also known as a mu meson) is a much more massive relative of the electron. It has a mass of 1.870×10^{-25} g, about 2,000 times that of an electron. A proton is even heavier, with a mass of about 1.660×10^{-24} g, nearly 3,000 times that of an electron.

Another group of particles being formed during this period were the quarks, the most elementary of known particles. Six "flavors" (types) of quarks have been identified: up, down, charm, strange, top, and bottom. The masses of these quarks range from slightly more than that of the electron (the up and down quarks) to about that of the proton and muon (strange and charm) to more than 100 times that of the proton and muon (top and bottom).

Like electrons, protons, muons, and quarks are formed by the interaction of gamma rays, photons, and neutrinos with a particular amount of energy. The situation for proton formation, for example, involves the interaction of gamma rays and neutrinos with a total energy of about 1,000 MeV:

$$\gamma_p + \bar{\nu}_p \rightarrow p^+$$

where the energies of gamma rays and neutrinos are much larger than those required for the formation of electrons. The formation of muons can be described by a similar equation:

$$\gamma_\mu + \bar{\nu}_\mu \rightarrow \mu^-$$

In this case, the total energy needed for gamma ray and neutrino is about 100 MeV.

A Cooling Universe

In order to understand the types of reactions taking place in the early universe, scientists need to have some estimates of the amount of energy present. Another way to express that concept is to say that scientists must know the approximate temperature of the universe, since temperature is a measure of the average kinetic energy present. Discussions of the evolution of the young universe are, therefore, often phrased in terms of the temperatures present at various stages of cosmic evolution.

Scientists now believe that the temperature of the universe a few microseconds after the big bang was probably about 10^{14} K. The symbol K stands for degrees kelvin, a measure of absolute temperature. At very high temperatures, the kelvin, centigrade, and Fahrenheit temperatures are roughly the same. By comparison, the temperature at the interior of our Sun is about 10^7 K.

The original fireball created by the big bang expanded and cooled very rapidly. Within a few microseconds, the temperature had dropped to less than 10^{13} K, an environment in which heavy quarks and protons were able to form by the mechanisms just described. At the 10 microsecond mark, the temperature had dropped to less than 10^{12} K, a condition under which muons were able to form. Then, about 10 seconds later, the temperature had fallen even further, to about 4×10^9 K, allowing the formation of electrons. In other words, only 10 seconds after the universe had been created in the big bang, all of the fundamental particles of which matter consists—protons, electrons, muons, and quarks—had been created.

In fact, another category of particles was also being created at the same time, the various forms of antimatter. Antimatter particles are identical to the particles already discussed except for their charge. The antielectron, for example, is identical to the electron except that it carries a positive charge rather than a negative charge. (For this reason, the antielectron is sometimes known as the "positron.") Similarly, the antiproton is identical to the proton, except that it carries a negative charge instead of a positive charge, and the antimuon carries a positive charge rather than the negative charge of a muon.

Antiparticles are formed by reactions similar to those by which protons, muons, and electrons are formed. The only difference is that such reactions involve the use of antineutrinos rather than neutrinos. For example, an antiproton is formed in the following reaction:

$$\gamma_p + \bar{\nu}_p \rightarrow p^-$$

The bar over the neutrino symbol in this equation represents an antineutrino in its reaction with a gamma ray to produce an antiproton. Similarly, an antielectron is formed in the reaction between a gamma ray and an electron antineutrino:

$$\gamma_e + \bar{\nu}_e \rightarrow e^+$$

The creation and ultimate fate of antimatter is one of the most puzzling and intriguing questions in all of *cosmology*. Scientists believe that relatively equal amounts of matter (protons, muons, and electrons) must have been formed in the first few seconds of the universe's life. There appears to be no reason that one form of matter was more likely to form than the other.

The present state of the known universe does not seem to confirm that assumption. Antimatter is virtually absent. Antimatter can be made in the laboratory, and there are reasons to believe that it exists in some parts of the universe, but it is far less common—almost nonexistent—in the universe today. So what happened to all of that antimatter that was created 10 to 20 billion years ago?

One important clue to answering that question is that matter and antimatter do not get along very well with each other. When a particle comes into contact with its antiparticle, a reaction occurs in which both particles are annihilated. The products of that reaction are two gamma rays, a neutrino, and an antineutrino. For example, suppose that a proton and an antiproton interact with each other. The reaction that occurs is:

$$p^+ + p^- \rightarrow 2\gamma + v_p + \bar{v}_p$$

One could argue, then, that a small excess of particles over antiparticles was produced during the creation of the universe. Suppose, for example, that there were a million antiprotons and a million and one protons created in a section of the universe. Then a million of each particle would have been annihilated as they came into contact with each other, leaving an excess of a single proton. Over time, a small irregularity of this kind might explain the dominance of matter over antimatter in the modern universe.

Other scientists think, however, that there may be other explanations for the "missing" antimatter in the universe today. They suspect that at least one other universe may exist, one about which nothing at all is known. That parallel universe, they suggest, may consist of atoms, molecules, ions, and other particles made up of antiprotons and antielectrons. These two universes, our own and that made of antimatter, could well exist at the same time provided that they never came into contact with each other. If they did, of course, both would be annihilated.

Particle Decay

Some particles created in the early moments following the big bang were destroyed by the process of matter/antimatter annihilation just described. Other particles disappeared by other processes. The most common of these processes was nuclear instability. At some point, these particles spontaneously broke apart into two or more other particles. This process is similar to the mechanism of radioactive decay, in which an atomic nucleus breaks apart into two or more smaller particles.

For example, neutrons were also formed very soon after the big bang by the interaction of protons and electrons:

$$p^+ + e^- \rightarrow n^0 + v$$

but free neutrons are inherently unstable and decay with a half-life of 1,013 seconds:

$$n^0 \rightarrow p^+ + e^- + v$$

That means that many neutrons disappeared quite soon after they were produced from protons and electrons. The only neutrons that were able to survive at all were those that came into contact with protons and formed hydrogen nuclei, as described in the next section.

Muons suffered a similar fate to that of neutrons. A mu meson decays into an electron and two neutrinos with a half-life of only 2.2×10^{-6} second:

$$\mu^- \rightarrow e^- + \bar{v}_e + v_\mu$$

The Formation of Compound Particles

The first particles formed following the big bang were quickly dispersed over a very wide space. As with any explosion, the force of expansion was very great indeed. Particles rushed outward, away from each other, with blinding speed.

Within a matter of seconds, however, a new force came into being that challenged the force of expansion. This was gravitation, a force that tends to pull particles toward each other. At first, there was not much of a contest between the forces of expansion and gravity, and the universe expanded rapidly. As temperatures declined after the big bang, gravitation became a more significant force and expansion a relatively less significant force. Eventually it became possible for two of the newly produced particles (such as protons and electrons) to be near each other in space and approach each other closely enough to bond. The first and simplest such reaction was probably that between a single proton and a single neutron, forming a deuteron:

$$p^+ + n^0 \rightarrow D$$

A deuteron is the nucleus of an isotope of hydrogen, deuterium. The nuclear symbol for a deuteron (D) is $_1^2H$. In a nuclear symbol of this kind, the superscript (2, in this case) represents the mass number of the particle (the total number of protons and neutrons), while the subscript (1, in this case) represents the atomic number, or the total number of protons.

Deuterons were relatively unstable during the early moments after the big bang because, when struck by gamma rays, they break apart into their constituent parts:

$$D + \gamma \rightarrow p^+ + n^0$$

So, as long as high-energy gamma rays were widely available, the chances for the survival of deuterons was relatively slight.

The key transition point in this story occurred when the temperature of the young universe fell to less than 10^9 K. At that point, gamma rays with sufficient energy to break apart deuterons (about 0.1 MeV) became much less abundant, and deuterons had a much greater chance of survival. It was then, about 100 seconds after the big bang, that deuterons began to accumulate in space.

At this point, however, a second reaction began to occur. Although deuterons were now beginning to accumulate, they were still very reactive because their nuclei are somewhat unstable. When two such particles collide, they may react to form yet another new particle, the helium-3 nucleus:

$$D + D \rightarrow {}_2^3He + n^0$$

A by-product of this reaction is neutrons, so it began to replenish the supply that was otherwise being depleted by decay.

A second reaction between two deuterons was also producing helium-3. In the first step of this reaction, the deuterons combine to form a hydrogen-3 (tritium), whose nucleus is called a triton:

$$D + D \rightarrow {}_1^3H + p^+$$

Hydrogen-3 is unstable, decaying with a half-life of 12.33 years to form helium-3, an electron, and a neutrino:

$${}_1^3H \rightarrow {}_2^3He + e^- + \bar{\nu}_e$$

As the temperature of the young universe continued to drop, a greater variety of reactions became possible involving primarily protons, neutrons, deuterons, and helium-3 nuclei. One of these is of particular interest because it resulted in the formation of yet another new compound particle, helium-4. In this reaction, two helium-3 nuclei interact to form helium-4, as shown in the following equation:

$${}_2^3He + {}_2^3He \rightarrow {}_2^4He + 2p^+ + \gamma$$

As the universe cooled after the big bang, the concentration of various chemical species varied rapidly and dramatically. The diagram on page 11 shows the relative abundance of the most important of these species. Notice that only the concentration of protons remained relatively constant and very high. As the concentration of neutrons dropped off, the concentrations of more complex species, such as deuterium, tritium, and the two isotopes of helium, increased. Between about 100 and 1,000 seconds after the big bang, the ratio among these particles gradually assumed a relatively constant value, with protons and helium-4 nuclei occupying by far the greatest proportion of that mixture.

Not shown in the graph are three additional isotopes formed after the first 100 seconds of the universe's evolution. They are lithium-6, lithium-7, and beryllium-7. These isotopes were formed by a variety of processes involving simpler nuclei, such as protons, deuterons, and helium nuclei. For example, the lithium-7 nucleus could have been formed by any one (or probably all) of the following reactions:

$${}_1^3H + {}_2^4He \rightarrow {}_3^7Li + \gamma$$

or

$${}_2^4He + {}_2^4He \rightarrow {}_3^7Li + {}_1^1H + \gamma$$

or

$$_2^3\text{He} + _3^7\text{He} \rightarrow _4^7\text{Be} + \gamma$$

followed by

$$_4^7\text{Be} + {}^0\text{e} \rightarrow _3^7\text{Li}$$

The concentrations of these three isotopes was probably very low up to the 1,000th second, ranging from about 10^{-12} for lithium-6 to 10^{-10} for lithium-7 and beryllium-7.

And Then There Were Atoms

After a few minutes of existence, the universe was swarming with fundamental particles: protons, neutrons, electrons, deuterons, and helium nuclei. It might seem that the time had arrived for atoms to

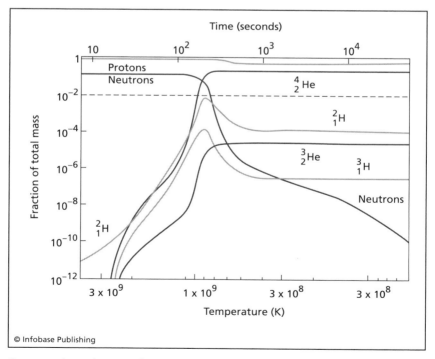

© Infobase Publishing

Concentrations of various chemical species in the early universe start forming. All it would have taken was for a single proton and a single electron to combine to form the first hydrogen atom:

$$p^+ + e^- \rightarrow H^0$$

but such reactions did not occur for millions of years after the big bang. Why not?

The reason involved kinetic energy. The kinetic energy of particles in the first few minutes, months, and years of the universe's existence was very great. When temperatures still ranged in the millions of degrees kelvin, the electrostatic force of attraction between particles was not strong enough for protons and electrons to combine and stay combined. The electrostatic force is the force of attraction between two particles of unlike charges.

In fact, the electrostatic force is so weak relative to other forces in the universe that it did not become effective in drawing particles to each other until the temperature had dropped to less than 10^4 K, about 10 million years after the big bang. At this point, the first neutral atoms began to form: Protons and electrons combined to form hydrogen atoms; deuterons and electrons combined to form deuterium; and helium nuclei and electrons combined to form neutral helium atoms.

Not much later, after the temperature had dropped to less than 10^3 K, the first diatomic atoms began to form when two neutral hydrogen atoms combined to form a hydrogen molecule:

$$H^0 + H^0 \rightarrow H_2$$

At this point, the synthesis of new elements stopped. The reason is that nuclei larger than those of hydrogen and helium can form only when like-charged particles (such as protons or helium nuclei) combine to form heavier nuclei. A hypothetical example is the formation of a beryllium nucleus by the combination of two helium nuclei:

$$^4_2He + {}^4_2He \rightarrow {}^7_4Be + {}^{-1}_0e$$

Such a reaction would require that two nuclei of helium, each carrying a strong positive charge, would combine with each other, but the kinetic energy of those nuclei after a few million years would have been too small to permit this. Consequently, elements heavier than lithium were able to begin forming in any significant amounts only after a new source of energy became available during the formation of stars.

Is the Theory True?

The big bang theory is a well-developed, sophisticated mathematical hypothesis about the creation of the universe that has now been tested for many decades. As with all such theories, the question is whether there is physical evidence to support it. Are there aspects of the modern universe that would tend to support or contradict this theory?

At least three major observational tests can be applied to the big bang theory:

1. Is the universe expanding?

2. What is the abundance of the light elements?

3. Is it possible to detect a cosmic microwave background?

The first of these tests is based on the simple fact that, if the big bang occurred, the universe must now be expanding. That is, if the universe originated at some point in time millions of years ago with an enormous explosion, one would expect that matter formed as a result of that explosion would be expanding outward. The first person to observe this effect was the American astronomer Edwin Powell Hubble (1889–1953), who in 1929 announced that every galaxy outside Earth's own Milky Way that he studied was moving away. Further, the rate of recession for any given galaxy was related to its distance from Earth: The more distant a galaxy was, the faster it was receding. A balloon with a number of dots on its surface illustrates this effect. As one blows up the balloon, the dots move away from the center of the balloon with a speed that depends on their distance from the center.

One of the intriguing questions for cosmologists today is whether the universe's process of expansion is destined to continue forever. Three possibilities exist. First, the universe could keep expanding forever, becoming less and less dense as time passes. Second, the rate of expansion could begin to slow down until stars and galaxies no longer moved away from each other. The force responsible for this change would be gravity, which draws matter together. Thus, in the second possible future for the universe, the outward force of expansion remaining from the big bang and the inward force of attraction produced by gravity eventually become equal. Such conditions result in a "steady-state" universe that eventually reaches a point where it no longer grows larger or smaller but retains some final dimensions. The third possibility is that the force of gravitation among particles and bodies in the universe eventually becomes greater than the outward force of expansion. In this case, the process of expansion would cease and "turn around." Gravitational forces would begin to pull particles and bodies back inward, toward each other, such that the universe would at some point collapse in upon itself in what some scientists have called "the big crunch."

Scientists will be able to determine which of these three scenarios is most likely by finding out what the shape of the universe is. For example, if the universe is found to be spherical, like the balloon in the preceding example, it will eventually stop expanding and begin collapsing, resulting in the big crunch. If the universe has a more complex shape, however, like that of a saddle, it will continue to expand forever. Finally, if the universe is flat, it will eventually achieve the steady-state condition in which it ceases expanding but never begins contracting.

One of the intriguing experimental challenges facing astronomers is to determine the shape of the universe today. While a number of methods can be used to solve this problem, one of the most promising is to determine the distribution of radiation now present in the universe, left over from the original big bang explosion billions of years ago. (Some of the research designed to obtain those data is discussed later in this chapter.)

A second way of testing the big bang theory is by estimating the abundance of certain light elements, particularly hydrogen, helium, and lithium. Astronomers believe that most of the light elements present in the universe today were created in the first few moments following the big bang. They can estimate how much hydrogen, helium, and lithium were formed after the big bang, making only a few simple assumptions about the state of the universe at the time. They can then compare the actual amount of these elements present today with the predicted amounts calculated from the big bang theory. If the two amounts are similar, they can have increased confidence that the big bang theory is correct.

The calculations needed to predict the initial amounts of hydrogen, helium, and lithium are somewhat complex, but they are based primarily on one measurement, the ratio of protons to neutrons at some equilibrium point in the early universe. Once that number has been determined, it is possible to estimate the relative abundance of the light elements that will form. The case of the most common isotope of helium, helium-4, is an example. Using a generally accepted figure of 7 protons for each neutron ($n/p = 1/7$), one can then use the following formula to estimate the abundance of helium-4 in the early universe:

$$A_{He} = \frac{2(n/p)}{1 + (n/p)} = 0.25$$

That is, if the big bang theory is correct, the abundance of helium created during the first few minutes following the big bang ought to be about 25 percent.

Helium was still being formed after the first few moments of the universe's evolution. For example, it is produced as a by-product of nuclear reactions in stars. The amount produced by such reactions is thought to be very small compared with the amount formed as a result of the big bang. Thus, if observers were to examine the abundance of helium in various parts of the universe today, they would expect to find quantities very close to 25 percent.

That is just what happens. The present-day abundance of helium in the Sun, for example, is about 22 percent. It is 28 percent in massive young stars and anywhere from 26 percent to 29 percent in the *interstellar medium.* Averaging the data found in many studies, astronomers suggest that the present-day abundance of helium throughout the universe is about 24 ± 1 percent, in very good agreement with calculations based on the big bang theory.

◄ GEORGE GAMOW (1904–1968) ►

Scientific theories usually do not have a lot of value unless they can be expressed mathematically. This was true of the big bang theory, the model first suggested by Abbé Georges Lemaître in 1927; it attracted relatively little attention at first, at least partly because it did not provide mathematical explanations for the changes that took place in the young universe after the big bang had occurred. That step was taken more than a decade after Lemaître's original paper by the Russian-born American physicist George Gamow.

Gamow was born in Odessa on March 4, 1904. His interest in astronomy began when his father gave him a telescope for his 13th birthday. Gamow studied at Novorossysky University and the University of Leningrad, where he earned his Ph.D. in 1928. Soviet premier Joseph Stalin increasingly tried to control the work of scientists in the 1930s, and Gamow attempted to leave the country for a more open working environment. He was eventually able to defect to the United States while attending the Solvay Conference held in Brussels in 1933. Once in the United States, he served as professor of physics at George Washington University from 1934 until 1956. He then accepted a similar post at the University of Colorado, where he remained until his death on August 20, 1968.

Similar studies have looked at the abundance of lithium in the present-day universe. Calculations based on the big bang theory suggest that the amount of lithium-7 was very small indeed, approaching 10^{-10}, by number of particles. Over the past few decades, studies of more than 100 stars have been made to determine how much lithium they contain. The average obtained for the abundance of lithium in these stars is about $(1.6 \pm 0.1) \times 10^{-10}$, providing good agreement with the theoretical value. Studies of the abundance of helium and lithium in the present-day universe agree well with the amounts calculated for big bang nucleosynthesis and, therefore, strongly support that theory.

A third test of the big bang theory is the search for *cosmic microwave background* (CMB). As early as 1934, the American astrophysicist Richard Tolman (1881–1948) showed that radiation produced

Gamow's research career focused on two major fields, seemingly about as far apart as one can imagine: nuclear physics and astronomy. In his work on nuclear physics, he devised explanations for two ways in which nuclei can decay, by the loss of alpha particles and by the emission of beta particles. During World War II, he was a member of the Manhattan Project, the program for the development of the first atomic (fission) bomb, and he was later involved in work on the first hydrogen (fusion) bomb.

Gamow's research on the big bang was published in 1948 in a joint paper with the German-born American physicist Hans Bethe (1906–2005) and American physicist Ralph Alpher (1921–   ). The paper is often known as the alpha-beta-gamma (for Alpher-Bethe-Gamow) hypothesis of cosmology. Gamow and his colleagues suggested that the universe began in an enormous explosion that resulted in the formation of an incredibly hot mixture of particles (primarily neutrons, protons, and electrons) that they called *ylem* (pronounced "eye-lem"). That term was originally used by the Greek natural philosopher Aristotle for the ultimate form of matter. The alpha-beta-gamma hypothesis went on to explain how more complex particles, such as helium nuclei, were eventually able to form as the temperature of the ylem gradually cooled down. Although this hypothesis has been modified, it provides the fundamental basis for the big bang theory still accepted by most astronomers and physicists today.

as a result of the big bang would continue to exist in the present-day universe. Its temperature would have decreased dramatically over a few billion years, but it should still retain its thermal characteristics.

Between 1948 and 1950 a trio of physicists, George Gamow (1904–68), Ralph Alpher (1921–   ), and Robert Herman (1914–97), worked out a detailed mathematical analysis of this "fossil radiation" and determined that its temperature would be about 5 K (about 2.72 degrees above absolute zero), a very cold temperature indeed, but not zero! That prediction made possible another experimental test of the big bang. The challenge was to search the skies to see if low-level radiation of this temperature could be found.

Interestingly enough, big bang radiation was found some two decades later, but only by accident. In 1963, the German-American physicist Arno Penzias (1933–   ) and his American colleague Robert Woodrow Wilson (1936–   ) had begun a search for radio waves that they thought might be coming from the outer portions of our own galaxy, the Milky Way. During their research, they discovered background noise in the microwave region of the *electromagnetic spectrum* for which they had no explanation. After discussing their observations with American physicist Robert Dicke (1916–97), they concluded that they had found the cosmic microwave background predicted by Gamow, Alpher, and Herman. Penzias and Wilson were awarded the 1978 Nobel Prize in physics for their research.

Some of the most exciting research in astronomy since the mid-1990s has arisen from efforts to develop a better understanding of CMB in the modern universe. An essential part of that research was the 1989 launch of the *Cosmic Background Explorer (COBE)* at NASA's Goddard Space Flight Center. *COBE* carried three instruments designed to measure the universe's microwave and infrared background. It made three important discoveries. First, it confirmed the level of the CMB with a very high precision of 2.725 $\pm$ 0.002 K, corresponding very closely to theoretical predictions of the big bang theory. Second, it discovered the existence of very small "ripples" in the cosmic microwave background. That is, as the satellite's instruments looked out across the universe, it found that the CMB was slightly more intense in some directions and slightly less intense in others.

The intensity of this ripple effect is very small indeed, amounting to only a few parts per 100,000. While this anisotropy (differences in quantity depending on direction) is exceedingly small, it is not at all insignificant. Indeed, astronomers believe that these tiny variations in CMB may be related to differences of distribution of matter in the early universe and are, therefore, a possible key to the later formation of stars and galaxies.

Finally, one of the instruments on *COBE* detected the presence of a cosmic infrared background (CIB), a remnant of the period during which the first stars began to form, many millions of years after the big bang itself. *COBE* was only one, albeit the best-known, of several research programs designed to study the CMB. In 1998, for example, two other research teams made use of balloons released into the stratosphere to study the cosmic microwave background. These

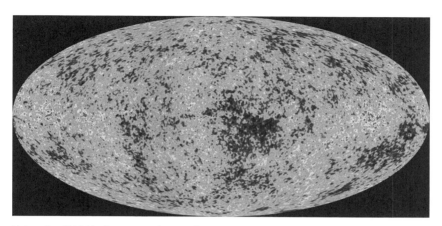

Taken by NASA's *Cosmic Background Explorer,* this photograph shows temperature variations in various parts of the sky surveyed by the satellite. (NASA/Photo Researchers, Inc.)

projects, known as BOOMERANG and MAXIMA, have produced microwave maps of the sky with somewhat different perspectives and orientations from those produced by *COBE.*

Where to Next?

The discovery of CMB anisotropy by *COBE* has whetted the appetite of astronomers for more information about the distribution of microwaves in the present-day universe: It may provide clues about the evolution of the young universe. Additional experiments are now planned to find out more details about CMB anisotropy. The most important of these experiments is NASA's Microwave Anisotropy Probe (MAP) project, first proposed in 1995. MAP is designed to continue a search of the sky for irregularities in the cosmic microwave background, but at a higher resolution than that of *COBE.*

   COBE had an angular resolution of 7 degrees across the sky. Angular resolution is the ability of an instrument to distinguish between two objects. The microwave maps produced by *COBE* were, therefore, relatively coarse and lacking in detail. By contrast, MAP has an angular resolution of 0.3 degrees, allowing it to detect temperature differences as small as 20 μK (microkelvins) within a sector

0.3 degrees on a side. As a result, the sky maps produced by MAP are far more precise than those obtained from *COBE*.

MAP was launched by NASA on June 30, 2001. It arrived at its parking orbit three months later, on October 1, 2001. This parking orbit is located at a distance of about 1,500,000 km (1,000,000 miles) from Earth, on the side of the Earth opposite the Sun. By April 2002, MAP had completed its first full mapping of the sky, and six months later it had completed its second full mapping.

Initial data from these first two mappings were released in January 2003. These data provided a remarkably precise picture of the universe as it looked 379,000 years after it was formed some 13.7 billion years ago. They showed that the first stars were formed far earlier than had long been thought, at an age of about 200 million years. MAP also appears to have found that the universe is essentially flat, with no significant convex or concave shape. When the MAP data are fully processed and studied, scientists expect to have a much better understanding of the cosmic microwave distribution in the universe and to develop an even more refined explanation of the first few seconds, minutes, and hours of the universe's life.

2

THE CHEMISTRY OF
INTERSTELLAR SPACE

Under a set of ideal circumstances, the big bang might have produced a totally homogeneous universe, one where protons, hydrogen atoms, helium atoms, photons, and other particles of matter and energy were equally distributed in space. That scenario, as the anisotropy ("ripples") of the cosmic microwave background (CMB) indicates, did not occur. Instead, particles began to clump together, to a greater or lesser extent, relatively soon after the big bang occurred. Over a very long period of time, that "clumping effect" resulted in the formation of the stars, galaxies, and other characteristic features that make up the universe today.

Such features so dramatically attract one's attention that it is easy to ignore the vast stretches of space between these objects, the interstellar medium (ISM). Indeed, until the first decade of the 20th century, most astronomers thought that the interstellar medium was essentially empty, a massive vacuum, lacking in even the simplest forms of matter. Then, in 1904, the German astronomer Johannes Hartmann (1865–1936) obtained the first evidence that suggested that the ISM is not empty but contains atoms of at least some elements. While the ISM is indeed "empty" by some standards (such as those commonly used on Earth), the particles of matter and energy it does contain give it a critical role in the creation of new matter,

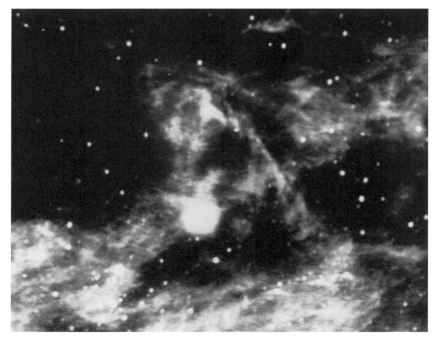

A view of the interstellar medium in the region of the constellation Chamaeleon (NASA/ Photo Researchers, Inc.)

the elements that make up all other astronomical bodies, including the Earth and its inhabitants.

The Composition of the Interstellar Medium

Two forms of matter make up the interstellar medium, gas and dust. The term *gas* refers to substances that are familiar here on Earth, such as hydrogen, helium, oxygen, and nitrogen. By contrast, the term *dust* means something quite different from what people encounter on Earth. It does not refer to the collection of tiny particles one might find in an unused room but rather denotes tiny particles less than a micron (one micron; one micrometer; 10^{-6} m) in diameter. Gases are far more common than dust, making up about 99 percent of the ISM compared to only about 1 percent dust.

Although their concentrations vary in different parts of the ISM, molecules of gas and particles of dust tend to be spread out very thinly. The average density of matter in the ISM is about one atom per cubic centimeter. By contrast, the best vacuums humans are capable of producing on Earth have a concentration of about 10^7 atoms per cubic centimeter, and the density of air on the Earth's surface is about 3×10^{19} atoms per cubic centimeter.

More than 100 different atoms and molecules have been discovered in the ISM in the last 40 years. By far the most abundant of these are the hydrogen and helium remnants of the big bang. About 90 percent of all atoms and molecules in the ISM are made of hydrogen; the remaining 10 percent are molecules of helium. By mass, the ISM is about 75 percent hydrogen and 25 percent helium.

Hydrogen gas may exist in the ISM in any of three forms: as molecular hydrogen (H_2), neutral atomic hydrogen (H), or ionized hydrogen (H^+). The latter two forms of hydrogen are designated as HI ("hydrogen one"; atomic hydrogen) and HII ("hydrogen two"; ionized hydrogen, H^+). This system of nomenclature is used with other atoms and molecules also to indicate the degree of ionization of a particle. Thus, HeI is neutral helium (He^0), HeII is singly-ionized helium (He^+), and HeIII is doubly-ionized helium (He^{2+}). Some writers use a slightly different designation, with the element's symbol and the roman numeral separated by a space, as H I, H II, and He I.

By far the most abundant form of hydrogen in the ISM is neutral hydrogen, H^0. Ionized hydrogen (HI; H^+) and molecular hydrogen (HII; H_2) are found in only certain, specific regions of space known as *clouds*. Gas clouds contain either ionized or molecular hydrogen, but not both, as explained in the next section.

Since Hartmann's 1904 discovery, astronomers have learned that a variety of elements and compounds exist in the interstellar medium, albeit at very low concentrations. In fact, Hartmann's original discovery was based on his observation of the spectrum of calcium in the ISM. Today, astrochemists know of at least 123 interstellar molecules. The chart on page 24 lists some of the more common of these molecules. Notice that some familiar elements and compounds have been identified in the ISM, including ozone (O_3), hydrogen chloride

◀ SOME MOLECULES FOUND IN THE INTERSTELLAR MEDIUM ▶

NUMBER OF ATOMS IN MOLECULE*

2	3	4	5	6	7	8	MORE THAN 8
H_2	O_3	C_3H	CH_4	C_2H_4	C_6H	C_7H	C_8H
HD	H_3^+	NH_3	$c\text{-}C_3H_2$	CH_3OH	CH_3C_2H	C_6H_2	HC_7N
CH	C_2H	C_2H_2	HCOOH	CH_3SH	CH_3CHO	$HCOOCH_3$	HC_9N
OH	C_2O	C_3O	CH_2CN	CH_3NC	$c\text{-}C_2H_4O$	CH_3C_3N	$HC_{11}N$
NH	C_2S	$c\text{-}SiC_3$	C_4H	C_5H	CH_2CHOH	CH_2OHCHO	$(CH_3)_2O$
NO	CH_3	HC_2N	C_4Si	C_5N	HC_4CN	HC_5CN	$(CH_3)_2CO$
NaCl	HNO	HCHO	HC_3N	NH_2CHO	HC_5N		CH_3C_4H
AlCl	HCO	HNCS	CH_2CO	HC_2CHO	CH_3NH_2		$HC_{10}CN$

*The letter c indicates a cyclic substance. Note that most species can exist as neutral or charged particles. Thus, H_2 represents either H_2^0 or H_2^+.

(HCl), sodium chloride (NaCl), formic acid (HCOOH), formaldehyde (HCHO), and methane (CH_4).

Interestingly, this chart includes some molecules that do not occur on Earth! A beginning chemistry student would be hard-pressed to suggest the molecular structure of many of these compounds. They exist in space in the form of long carbon chains with one or two hydrogen atoms and/or an atom of another element, such as oxygen or nitrogen. They often occur as ring compounds with one or more double bonds, and they are often very unsaturated, with multiple double and/or triple bonds. Even the existence of such compounds, in an environment where hydrogen is abundant, poses a puzzle to chemists. One example of these unusual compounds includes the members of the family of cyanoacetylenes, molecules that contain two or more carbon atoms bonded to each other with triple bonds, a hydrogen atom at one end of the chain, and a nitrogen atom at the other end of the chain. The molecules with formulas HC_7N, HC_9N, and $HC_{11}N$ in the above chart are examples of such compounds. Examples of the unusual cyclic compounds found in the ISM are the four-membered ring c-SiC_3 and three-membered ring c-C_3H_2.

The mechanisms by which more complex species in the chart on page 24 are formed are poorly understood. One can imagine the synthesis of a diatomic molecule such as CO rather easily as the result of the collision between an atom of carbon and an atom of oxygen, but a simple two-body collision sequence of this kind would be inadequate to explain the production of more complex molecules, such as methylamine (CH_3NH_2). Scientists now suspect the involvement of dust particles in more complex syntheses of this kind. (See "Chemistry of the Interstellar Medium," page 34.)

Scientists are continuing to search for new chemical species in the interstellar medium. Sometimes that search is simply an effort to learn more about the chemical composition of the ISM, but in other cases, the discovery of a particular chemical species can yield useful information about the evolution of the universe itself. For example, some research teams have been especially interested in determining the distribution of the radioactive isotope aluminum-26 in the ISM. The reason for their interest is that aluminum-26 is produced during certain element-forming reactions in stars. Its presence can provide useful information as to where and how stars are forming elements. Also, aluminum-26 has a relatively short half-life (7.2 $\times$ 10^5 years), providing a timeline over which stellar evolution may be taking place.

The search for new species in the ISM often yields results with interesting connections to Earth-based chemistry. One such discovery was announced in 2001. Researchers at the National Radio Astronomy Observatory in Charlottesville, Virginia, announced the discovery of the vinyl alcohol molecule in space. Vinyl alcohol has the structural formula $CH_2 = CHOH$ and is an important precursor molecule in many organic synthesis reactions in industrial and research operations. Chemists suspect that the vinyl alcohol molecule may play a similar role in the synthesis of complex organic molecules in the ISM.

One class of chemical species of special interest to astrochemists is the group of compounds known as *amino acids*. Amino acids are organic acids that contain the amino group ($-NH_2$); their general formula is RNH_2COOH. Amino acids are important because they are the building blocks of which proteins are made. Over the past few decades, there has been considerable debate among scientists as to whether amino acids could exist in space or whether they occur only on Earth. Amino acids have been found in meteorites, but some researchers argue that they are a remnant of the creation of the solar system and could not exist outside it.

This debate is not without its practical consequences. If amino acids exist only on Earth, then life as we know it may also exist only on our planet. If, on the other hand, amino acids exist in the interstellar medium, then it is at least possible that Earth-like life may exist almost anywhere in the universe.

In March 2002, a team of researchers from the SETI (Search for Extraterrestrial Intelligence) Institute and the National Aeronautics and Space Administration (NASA) reported on an important breakthrough in the search for amino acids in the ISM. These researchers attempted to reproduce in their laboratory the conditions found in the ISM. They enclosed a mixture of molecules already known to exist in the ISM in a container cooled to 15K under a pressure of about 10^{-8} torr (a pressure of 1 torr is equal to 1 mm of mercury), conditions similar to those encountered in the ISM. The mixture was then exposed to ultraviolet radiation, again analogous to conditions in the ISM. Upon analysis of the contents of the container, researchers found that three simple amino acids—glycine, alanine, and serine—had been produced. Their conclusion, according to a spokesman for the research team, was that "amino acids can be made in interstellar clouds suggest[ing] that the Earth may have been seeded with amino acids from space in its earliest days." Furthermore, the spokesman explained, "since new stars and planets are formed with the same clouds in which new amino acids are being created, this probably increases the odds that life has evolved elsewhere."

The concentration of dust in the interstellar medium is far less than that of gas, about one particle per 10^{13} cubic centimeter for dust compared with one atom, molecule, or ion per cubic centimeter for gas. Comparatively little is known about the composition and origin

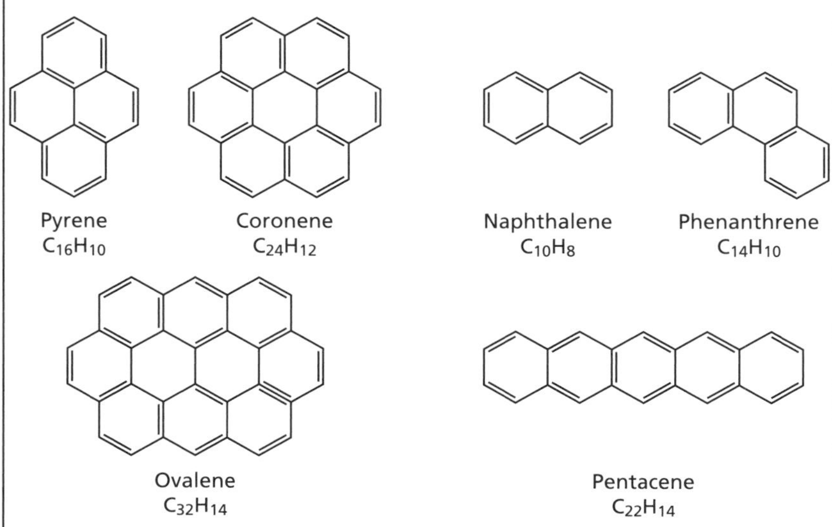

Pyrene
$C_{16}H_{10}$

Coronene
$C_{24}H_{12}$

Naphthalene
$C_{10}H_8$

Phenanthrene
$C_{14}H_{10}$

Ovalene
$C_{32}H_{14}$

Pentacene
$C_{22}H_{14}$

© Infobase Publishing

Examples of polycyclic aromatic hydrocarbons (PAHs) found in space of dust particles compared to that known for gas. Most scientists believe that dust particles have an irregular shape, like very tiny pieces (less than a micron in diameter) of broken rock. The particles appear to be of two general types: carbonaceous (made up primarily of the element carbon) and metal silicates (made up of a metal bonded to a silicate radical such as iron silicate [Fe_2SO_4]). In most cases, the particles seem to be coated with a layer of ice consisting of frozen water, carbon dioxide, carbon monoxide, and/or methane.

The carbonaceous particles, in turn, occur in one of two forms, graphitic and PAH clusters. PAH is an abbreviation for a family of organic compounds, the polycyclic aromatic hydrocarbons, that consist of two or more benzene rings condensed on each other in a variety of ways. The diagrams on page 27 show the structures of some typical PAH molecules.

The graphitic particles consist almost entirely of carbon atoms, probably bonded to each other in a variety of complex forms. PAH clusters have been hypothesized for some time and evidence is accumulating that they occur abundantly in the ISM. No specific PAH molecule, however, has as yet been definitively identified in the interstellar medium. Whatever form they may take, dust particles are now thought to be remnants of stellar explosions, in which a star expels part or all of its mass into the ISM.

Much of our knowledge of dust in the ISM is based on its effects on light. Suppose that light from a star passes through a region of the ISM that contains a certain amount of dust. If the concentration of dust is high enough, it may block off that light entirely. Instead of seeing the star, an observer on Earth would see only a dark spot in the sky. This effect is known as *interstellar extinction*. It can be observed very easily simply by looking at the Milky Way on a moonless night. A prominent feature of the sky is the Horsehead Nebula, an extended area where dust is thick enough to block out all light from behind it.

In regions where dust is less concentrated, light from behind it may be only partially blocked out. In such cases, a band of bright light from millions of stars may be somewhat reduced in intensity ("darker") by the intervening dust particles. The band is also likely to be more reddish in color than the original light.

Dust particles can also reflect the light that passes through them. The type of reflection that occurs depends on two factors, the wavelength of light striking the particle and the particle's size. For example, if the wavelength of the incident light is very much greater than the particle's diameter, it will pass around the particle without interacting with it. The average size of most dust particles, however, is roughly the same as the wavelength of visible light (about 100 to 1,000 nanometers [nm]). Specifically, dust particles have diameters corresponding closely with the wavelength of blue light (about 475 nm) and somewhat less closely to the wavelength of red light (about 650 nm). This means that light striking dust particles will scatter preferentially, with more blue light being produced than red light.

For this reason, dust particles that are not dense enough to cause extinction may, instead, produce a *reflection nebula,* regions of space that have a bluish appearance to observers on Earth because of the light reflected from them off dust particles.

Depending on the orientation of a light source (such as a star or group of stars) and a region of dust particles, the differential scattering of light wavelengths may have another effect also. As blue light is scattered away by a dust cloud, the light that gets through tends to be more red than it was at its source. In this form of interstellar extinction, the star's light is not actually lost but is observed by an Earth-bound observer as more red than it should be. This effect is called *interstellar reddening.*

Interstellar Clouds

The gas and dust that make up the ISM are not distributed uniformly throughout the universe. Instead, they are collected together in "envelopes" or "bubbles" with greater or lesser concentrations of particles or molecules. The reflection nebula described in the preceding section is an example of such a cluster.

Three of the most interesting types of these envelopes are HI clouds, HII clouds, and giant molecular clouds (GMCs). These three regions differ in the types of molecules they contain, their temperature, and their densities.

◄ ROBERT JULIUS TRUMPLER (1886–1956) ►

The 1930s were an exciting period in astronomy. New discoveries showed many beliefs about the composition and structure of the heavens to be inaccurate. One of the most important discoveries during this period was the presence of dust in the interstellar medium. In the late 1920s, Robert Trumpler was studying the distance, size, and distribution of galactic star clusters. His results suggested that these objects were, without exception, much closer than they appeared to be. His explanation for this fact was that the space between stars and galaxies actually contained some kind of material, now known as *dust,* that interfered with the transmission of light from distant portions of the universe. This dust made stars and galaxies appear to be much farther away than they actually were, introducing an important new factor into studies of the universe and opening a new horizon in the study of the interstellar medium.

Robert Julius Trumpler was born in Zurich, Switzerland, on October 2, 1886, the third in a family of 10 children. Robert's father was a successful businessman who was eager for his sons to choose careers in business. He tried to dissuade Robert from pursuing his interest in astronomy because he thought it would not provide an adequate income for his future. As a result, after graduating from the local gymnasium (high school), Trumpler took a

HII clouds are small, spherical regions with very hot, young stars at their centers. Their temperatures are estimated to be about 10^4–10^6K. Ultraviolet radiation emitted by the clouds' core stars is sufficiently energetic to ionize the hydrogen gas around them. As the diagram on page 32 shows, electrons from the lowest (ground) level of hydrogen atoms are raised to higher levels, forming ions of hydrogen. After a brief moment (less than a second), many of these electrons fall back to ground level, releasing radiation.

The radiation thus produced includes a number of *spectral lines,* one of the strongest of which is the Balmer alpha line (λ = 656.3 nm) in the red region of the visible spectrum. The emission of these red lines is responsible for the brilliant reddish color of HII clouds and also for their common name *emission nebulae.* In the photograph on page 33, the famous Horsehead Nebula is visible because the dust of job as a bank clerk. Very soon he found that type of work not to his liking, and he enrolled as an astronomy major at the University of Zurich in 1906. Two years later, he transferred to the University of Göttingen, from which he received his doctoral degree in 1910. After working briefly with the Swiss Geodetic Commission, Trumpler was offered a position with the Allegheny Observatory at the University of Pittsburgh. He was unable to accept that offer immediately because World War broke out and he was conscripted by the Swiss Militia. In the spring of 1915, however, he managed to obtain a release from his military duty and was able to begin work at the Allegheny.

After three years in the Pittsburgh area, Trumpler moved to the Lick Observatory, affiliated with the University of California. One of his most important assignments at the Lick was a test of Einstein's theory of relativity, conducted in the fall of 1922. By detecting the deflection of light around the limb (circumference) of the Sun, Trumpler was able to provide the first experimental proof for Einstein's theory.

In 1938, Trumpler left the Lick Observatory to take on teaching and research responsibilities at the University of California at Berkeley's Department of Astronomy. He remained there until his retirement in 1951. He died in Berkeley on September 10, 1956, after several years of poor health.

which it is composed stands out against the bright emission nebula in the background.

Astronomers classify HII regions into one of six groups depending on their size and the extent to which their hydrogen atoms are ionized. These regions range from the *ultracompact,* no more than a few light-years in diameter, to the *supergiant,* which may stretch to more than 1,000 light-years in diameter. Although they are among the most dramatic sights in the night sky, HII regions actually contain relatively little mass, probably no more than 1 percent of all mass in the universe.

HI clouds and giant molecular clouds (GMCs) are much cooler than HII regions, with temperatures of no more than about 100K and 10K respectively. HI clouds consist of hydrogen atoms, and GMCs almost certainly consist of hydrogen molecules. The total mass of

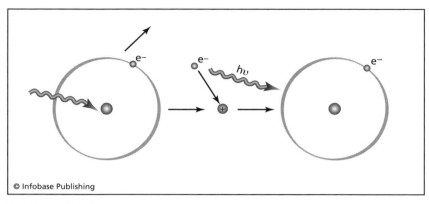

Emission of light from an excited atom

all HI regions is very large, probably about half the total mass of the ISM. GMCs are very compact regions with relatively small volumes but very high concentrations of molecules. They are the regions in which star formation is most likely to begin.

The detection of hydrogen and other elements in HI clouds and GMCs was long a difficult challenge for researchers. Both types of clouds are so cold that hydrogen (and other kinds of atoms) are not ionized. Without ionization, little or no radiation at any wavelength is produced. These clouds, it seemed, left no "footprints" for astronomers to study.

In 1951, however, scientists discovered that this is not quite the case. They found that neutral hydrogen atoms (H^0) *do* emit a distinctive form of radiation by which they can be recognized, the 21-cm spectral line. Here is the way that line is produced: Both the proton and the electron that make up a hydrogen atom are spinning on their axes, like a pair of tops. Either may spin in one direction (clockwise) or the opposite direction (counterclockwise). If both particles are spinning in the *same* direction, the hydrogen atom has some total amount of energy, call it E; but if the two particles are spinning in opposite directions, the atom has somewhat less energy, call it $E - e$.

Electrons in hydrogen atoms naturally intraconvert (switch back and forth) from a condition of like spin with their protons to opposite spin on a regular and predictable basis, about once every 11 million years. When they do so, they give off that excess bit of energy, e, with

The bright emission nebula IC 434 provides a spectacular background for the cold dust of which the Horsehead Nebula is composed. (European Southern Observatory/Photo Researchers, Inc.)

a wavelength of 21 cm. The 21-cm wavelength is one that can easily be detected by Earth-based astronomers, thereby allowing them to locate the presence of an HI cloud. (Although 11 million years may seem like a long time to wait to observe a 21-cm line, recall that HI clouds contain large number of hydrogen atoms, some of which are always intraconverting. Thus, at any one time, enough hydrogen atoms are emitting 21-cm radiation to allow detection of the cloud.)

The detection of giant molecular clouds presents a somewhat different problem for astronomers. The composition of these clouds is similar to that of interstellar matter, about 75 percent hydrogen and 25 percent helium, with smaller amounts of other elements, but in GMCs, as their name suggests, elements tend to occur as molecules rather than atoms. Hence, the 21-cm spectral lines are not emitted by hydrogen in giant molecular clouds, and they cannot be used to detect GMCs. In fact, hydrogen and helium molecules emit essentially no radiation by which GMCs can be detected. Instead, astronomers use a different molecule—carbon monoxide—to find GMCs. Carbon monoxide does emit radiation in the millimeter range of the electromagnetic spectrum because of its rotational motions. Astronomers are able to detect this radiation, and they use it to locate the presence of GMCs.

Two other structures can be identified in the ISM. One of these is called *coronal gas,* consisting of material ejected from stars, novae, supernovae, and other explosive objects in the universe. The temperature of coronal gas is very high, about 10^6 K, and it is composed of a complex mixture of elements contained within or produced by the star or nova. Although coronal gas has a very low density, its volume is very large, the largest of any other single type of structure found in the interstellar medium.

Finally, the space not occupied by coronal gas, by HI or HII clouds, or by giant molecular clouds is occupied by the intercloud medium, consisting primarily of neutral hydrogen atoms. This "filler" space occupies the second largest volume of the interstellar medium.

Chemistry of the Interstellar Medium

A half-century ago, a discussion of the chemistry of the ISM would have been brief indeed, because scientists knew virtually nothing about either the nature of atoms and molecules in the ISM or the kinds of chemical reactions they undergo. Since that time, researchers have learned a great deal about that topic. A large part of this problem depends on understanding the chemical changes that took place in the first few minutes after the big bang. As discussed in chapter 1, most of the hydrogen and helium (the two elements that account for more than 99 percent of all atoms present in the universe today) was formed during this time. Astrochemists suspect that some forms of hydrogen and helium are still being formed today, however, so some research is directed at finding explanations for these processes.

One question on which researchers have focused, for example, is how molecular hydrogen is formed in today's universe from atomic hydrogen produced during the big bang. One tempting answer is to imagine that hydrogen molecules are formed in the simplest possible way, by the collision of two hydrogen atoms with each other:

$$H + H \rightarrow H_2$$

Chemists recognize, however, that this reaction is highly unlikely to occur in the conditions present in the ISM. The concentration of gases in the ISM is such that the chance of two hydrogen atoms finding each other is relatively low. One can calculate that such an event is likely to occur only once in every 10^6 seconds, or about once every two weeks. Further, the mean free path (the distance a particle will travel before it comes into contact with another particle) is estimated to be about 10^5 kilometers.

While both the time scale and the distance scale of such events are large by Earth standards, they are minuscule by astronomical standards. A more compelling problem related to the formation of hydrogen molecules is that, given the environment of the ISM, the reverse reaction of that shown above,

$$H_2 \rightarrow H + H$$

is at least as likely as the forward reaction. The probability is, therefore, that hydrogen molecules will break apart in the ISM almost as quickly as they are formed. What, then, is the mechanism by which these ubiquitous molecules are formed? The answer may involve interstellar dust.

Beginning in the early 1960s, Edwin Salpeter (1924–   ) of Cornell University and his graduate student David Hollenbach wrote a series of papers hypothesizing the process by which hydrogen molecules could form on grains of dust in the ISM. This process begins, they suggested, when a hydrogen atom collides with a grain of dust and sticks to its surface. The attractive force between atom and dust is sufficiently weak that the atom can diffuse rather easily across the surface of the dust particle. At some point, the migrating atom may encounter a second hydrogen atom on the particle's surface and combine with it to form a hydrogen molecule. Since that reaction is exothermic, it releases a small amount of heat, providing the energy needed to allow the newly formed hydrogen molecule to evaporate from the particle's surface.

Could diatomic hydrogen really be formed this way? In 1999, researchers at Syracuse University attempted to test this theory experimentally for the first time. They re-created in their laboratories the conditions under which H_2 formation would occur, according to Salpeter and Hollenbach. The Syracuse researchers confirmed that such a reaction could occur, releasing the hydrogen molecule to the surrounding atmosphere. Although the rate at which the reaction occurs is not quite fast enough to account for the amount of H_2 present in ISM, at the moment, there are no competing theories that explain the production of the species as well as the Salpeter-Hollenbach model.

Questions about the chemical origin of hydrogen molecules are very interesting, but what about the other atoms, molecules, ions, and free radicals shown in the chart on page 24? What are the chemical mechanisms by which these species are produced? An important field of research in astrochemistry is the effort to explain how structures such as NH, AlF, C_3, C_4Si, and $HC_{10}CN$ can form. As of 2007, astrochemists had examined more than 4,000 possible chemical reactions to account for the production of these substances. These reactions involve more than 400 species consisting of two to 13 atoms, primarily from the first two rows of the periodic table. Many of these reactions begin with atomic and molecular hydrogen because these species are, of course, by far the most common atoms present in the universe.

For example, consider the reaction that occurs when molecular hydrogen in the ISM is bombarded by cosmic rays. In this reaction, the H_2 molecule is converted to the H_2^+ ion:

$$H_2 + energy \rightarrow H_2^+ + e^-$$

The H_2^+ ion thus formed is highly reactive and, if it comes into contact with a second H_2 molecule, reacts to form the H_3^+ ion:

$$H_2^+ + H_2 \rightarrow H_3^+ + H$$

The formation of the H_3^+ ion marks the conclusion of this sequence of reactions since the H_3^+ ion itself does not readily react with other forms of hydrogen. It tends to accumulate in the ISM, where it appears to be rather abundant. Furthermore, the H_3^+ ion *does* react readily with other neutral atoms and molecules, providing a mechanism by which other more complex species, like those in the chart on page 24, can be produced.

For example, the H_3^+ ion may react with an oxygen atom to form the OH^+ ion and free H_2, which may then react with each other, as shown below:

$$H_3^+ + O \rightarrow OH^+ + H_2$$

followed by:

$$OH^+ + H_2 \rightarrow H_2O^+ + H$$

This pair of reaction suggests a mechanism, therefore, by which two species found in the ISM, OH^+ and H_2O^+, are produced.

In another step, the positively charged water molecule may then react with diatomic hydrogen to form a hydronium molecule:

$$H_2O^+ + H_2 \rightarrow H_3O^+ + H$$

Finally, the hydronium molecule formed in this reaction is relatively unstable, reacting with a free electron to form a variety of products, as shown in the equations below:

$$H_3O^+ + e^- \rightarrow H_2O + H$$
$$\rightarrow OH + H_2$$
$$\rightarrow OH + 2H$$
$$\rightarrow O + H + H_2$$

In a similar series of reactions, the H_3^+ ion may also react with a carbon atom and its products, as shown in the equations below:

$$H_3^+ + C \rightarrow CH^+ + H_2$$
$$CH^+ + H_2 \rightarrow CH_2^+ + H$$
$$CH_2^+ + H_2 \rightarrow CH_3^+ + H$$

This series of reactions may explain the formation of still other chemical species shown in the chart on page 24, such as CH^+, CH_3^+, and other simple hydrocarbons.

Another sequence of possible reactions begins with the reaction between the CH_3^+ ion and a hydrogen molecule to produce the CH_5^+ ion:

$$CH_3^+ + H_2 \rightarrow CH_5^+$$

Like the hydronium ion, the CH_5^+ ion may react with an electron, as shown below:

$$CH_5^+ + e^- \rightarrow CH_3 + H_2,$$

or it may react with one of the carbon monoxide molecules abundant in the ISM to form methane:

$$CH_5^+ + CO \rightarrow CH_4 + HCO^+$$

This reaction is itself involved in the formation of carbon monoxide, when the HCO^+ ion thus formed reacts with a free electron:

$$HCO^+ + e^- \rightarrow CO + H$$

A common theme in the hypothesized reactions described here is that they are likely to occur because they involve a positively charged ion and a neutral molecule. Energetically, such reactions are far more likely to occur than reactions between two neutral molecules. Another series of such reactions depends on the existence of the positively charged carbon ion (C^+), which is actually about as abundant in the ISM as is the neutral carbon atom itself. The first step in this series of reactions occurs when the C^+ ion reacts with a neutral molecule, such as diatomic hydrogen or methane:

$$C^+ + H_2 \rightarrow CH_2^+$$
$$C^+ + CH_4 \rightarrow C_2H_3^+ + H$$

The result of such reactions, of course, is the creation of a hydrocarbon molecule or an increase in the length of the carbon chain in such a molecule by one. Similar increases in chain length can occur when a positively charged hydrogen carbon ion reacts with a neutral hydrocarbon molecule, as in this example:

$$C_2H_2^+ + C_2H_2 \rightarrow C_4H_3^+ + H$$

A number of cases in which two neutral molecules react to form a larger molecule have also been studied. For example, the reaction between neutral carbon atoms and hydrocarbon molecules and between neutral hydrocarbons has been found to produce both linear and cyclic forms of higher hydrocarbons, both of which have been found in the ISM (see chart, page 24):

$$C + C_2H_2 \rightarrow C_3H + H$$
$$C_2H_2 + C_2H \rightarrow C_4H_2 + H$$

Similar reactions have been observed with nitrogen-containing molecules, leading to the formation of some of the more complex molecules shown in the chart. For example, the reaction between acetylene and the radical CN to produce cyanoacetylene (HCCCN), commonly found in the ISM:

$$CN + C_2H_2 \rightarrow HCCCN + H$$

The reactions discussed here illustrate the progress made by astrochemists in finding explanations for the presence of so many unusual chemical species found in the ISM. Low temperature and low density in the ISM mean that conditions favoring chemical reactions on Earth tend to be absent or rare, and that novel explanations must be developed for the formation of compounds, ions, and free radicals like those shown in the chart. The search for such explanations is likely to constitute an important line of research in astrochemistry for the foreseeable future.

Tools for Studying the Chemical Characteristics of the ISM

The preceding sections show how much astrochemists have learned about the composition of the interstellar medium, but how was all this information obtained? It is clear that no one has actually gone into space, collected a sample of the ISM, and subjected it to traditional chemical analysis in the laboratory. Instead, most of what we know about the ISM—and much of the rest of the universe—comes in the

◄ HENDRIK CHRISTOFFEL VAN DE HULST (1918–2000) ►

The modern science of radio astronomy was born in the early 1930s when the American engineer Karl Guthe Jansky (1905–45) detected radio waves apparently emanating from all parts of the universe. Jansky's discovery provided astronomers with an entirely new tool to use in their exploration of space. Radio waves are able to penetrate clouds of dust that are impenetrable to visible light. Before long, a few pioneer astronomers were building telescopes that were able to collect radio waves rather than light waves.

One of the first astronomers to appreciate the significance of Jansky's discovery was the great Dutch astronomer Jan Oort (1900–92). In the mid-1940s, Oort suggested to one of his younger colleagues, Hendrik van de Hulst, that he should try to calculate the spectral lines that might exist in the radio region of the electromagnetic spectrum. Van de Hulst began this project with an analysis of hydrogen, since it is by far the most common element in the interstellar medium. In 1945, van de Hulst announced that the most likely spectral line to be observed is the 21-centimeter line emitted by cool hydrogen atoms. Nearly five years later, two American astronomers, Harold Irving Ewen (1922–) and Edward Mills Purcell (1912–97), announced that, using a simple radio telescope of their own design, they had detected the presence of the 21-centimeter line.

Hendrik van de Hulst was born in Utrecht, the Netherlands, on November 19, 1918. He was one of six children born to W. G. van de Hulst, a very popu-

form of radiation produced by atoms, molecules, ions, and free radicals in the ISM, radiation that can be detected and analyzed on Earth.

Unlike the light produced by stars and other bright objects in the sky, none of the radiation from the ISM arrives in the form of spectral lines in the visible portion of the electromagnetic spectrum. Temperatures in the ISM are much too low to allow the electron transitions by which such spectral lines are produced. Particles in the ISM undergo other kinds of transitions that release radiation in other portions of the electromagnetic spectrum, radiation that *can* be collected and analyzed on Earth.

lar writer of religious books for children, and his wife Jeanette Maan. After completing his high school education, van de Hulst entered the University of Utrecht, where he majored in theoretical astronomy. World War II interrupted his education in 1939, when he was drafted for service in the Dutch army. Van de Hulst was discharged two years later but was unable to return to the university because it had essentially been shut down because of the war. Henk (as he was informally called) attempted to continue his studies on his own and, in the process, came into contact with Oort, who posed the spectral line problem to him. At a meeting of the Nederlandse Astronomen Club held at the Leiden Observatory on April 15, 1944, van de Hulst gave a talk in which he announced the results of his research, the probability of a 21-centimeter hydrogen line. Interestingly enough, van de Hulst himself was somewhat doubtful that such a line could ever be observed experimentally until the work of Purcell and Ewen proved otherwise.

After receiving his doctoral degree from Utrecht in 1946, van de Hulst spent two years as a postdoctoral fellow at the Yerkes Observatory at the University of Chicago. He then returned to the Netherlands, where he became professor of astronomy at the University of Leiden. He remained at Leiden for the rest of his academic career, retiring with the title of professor emeritus in 1984. He also visited the United States on a number of occasions, during which he studied at Harvard University, the California Institute of Technology, and the Institute for Space Studies in New York. He was also actively involved in the founding and research agenda of the European Space Research Organization and its successor, the European Space Agency. Van de Hulst died in Leiden on July 31, 2000.

Two kinds of transitions that molecules undergo result from their vibrational and rotational motions. For example, the two atoms that make up a carbon monoxide molecule vibrate back and forth, with the bond between them stretching and relaxing. When energy from some external source is added to this system, this pattern of vibrational motion changes. When the molecule returns to its original vibrational pattern, it releases energy in the infrared region of the electromagnetic spectrum. These processes are similar to what happens when the electron in an atom absorbs energy from an external source and jumps to a higher energy level, and when an excited electron in an atom returns to its original ground state, releasing energy in the process. The energy required to bring about vibrational changes is in the temperature range of about 10^2 to 10^4 K. Such changes can occur, therefore, only in warmer parts of the ISM.

Molecules also tumble end-over-end around a central axis, producing a rotational motion. Again, the input of energy to a molecule may cause it to increase or decrease its rotational motion. This rotational motion, like the changes an electron makes within an atom, is quantized. That is, it can take only certain discrete values. When a molecule changes from one rotational state to a lower rotational state, it releases a photon of energy with a wavelength in the radio wave region of the electromagnetic spectrum.

Astrochemists identify molecules in the ISM, then, by detecting the spectral lines produced by changes in one or another type of their molecular motion. They then compare those spectral lines with those of known molecules, allowing them to make an identification. In some cases, this process of identification is relatively easy. The

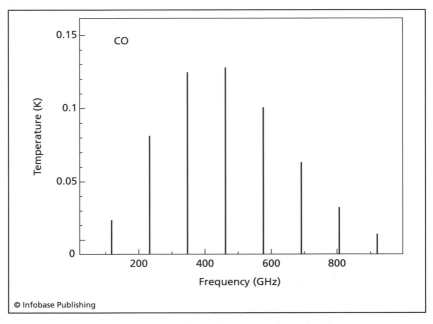

© Infobase Publishing

Spectral lines produced by rotation of a carbon monoxide molecule

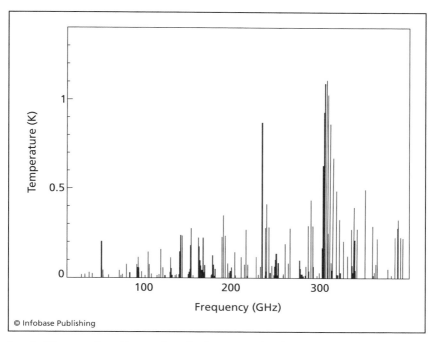

Spectral lines produced by rotation of a six-atom molecule

carbon monoxide molecule, for example, is a simple molecule that is able to vibrate and rotate in a relatively few ways. The spectrum it produces is, therefore, fairly uncomplicated, containing only a small number of easily identifiable lines. The diagram on page 42 shows an idealized version of the spectral lines produced by rotational changes in a carbon monoxide molecule.

The addition of more atoms to a molecule rapidly increases the number of vibrational and rotational options it has. The spectra produced by such molecules, therefore, are considerably more complicated than that of the carbon monoxide molecule (and other binary molecules). The diagram above shows such a spectrum for a hypothetical molecule with six atoms. Identifying the molecule that produced this spectrum is obviously more difficult than identifying that of the carbon monoxide molecule.

In practice, the spectra obtained from a survey of the ISM is likely to be extremely complex, similar to the idealized example shown

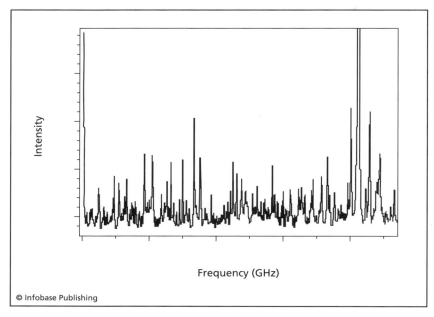

Spectral lines produced by rotation of a mixture of molecules

above. In such cases, a chemist's challenge is to locate and identify lines in the spectrum that correspond to particular molecules whose spectral patterns are already known. It is not unusual for chemists to determine the nature of some of the spectral lines in a complex spectrum such as this one, but not others.

How do scientists obtain the "raw material," the actual spectra from which they analyze the composition of the ISM? A number of possibilities are now available. First, many colleges and universities now have small telescopes that observers can use to study a portion of the sky. An example is the 1.2 meter "Mini" telescope at Harvard University's Harvard-Smithsonian Center for Astrophysics. The telescope was first built on the roof of the Pupin Physics Laboratory at Columbia University in New York City in the 1970s to survey the galaxy for carbon monoxide in the ISM. In 1986, it was moved to its current location, where it is still used for similar projects.

Much larger telescopes owned and operated by groups of universities are also used to scan the sky. Probably the most famous of these telescopes are the two that make up the Gemini system, one of which (Gemini North) is located on top of Mauna Kea in Hawaii and the other (Gemini South) at Cerro Pachón in central Chile. Gemini North was dedicated in June 2000 and Gemini South in January 2002. Both have the capability to search the skies for radiation from ISM molecules.

Finally, telescopes on orbiting satellites have become an invaluable tool in studies of the interstellar medium. Such telescopes orbit far above the Earth's atmosphere and are able to detect radiation that is otherwise absorbed by the atmosphere, which makes it largely "invisible" to human eyes. One of the "workhorses" of these satellites has been the Submillimeter Wave Astronomy Satellite (SWAS) launched by NASA in December 1998. Its primary objective was to survey water, molecular oxygen, carbon, and carbon monoxide in certain portions of the ISM. A more recent tool became available in early 2003 when NASA launched the Cosmic Hot Interstellar Spectrometer (CHIPS) satellite. During its planned one-year voyage in space, CHIPS surveyed a region in space known as the "Local Bubble," looking for evidence to explain the process by which molecules in the ISM begin to collapse upon each other during the process of star formation.

Another approach to the study of the interstellar medium includes experiments carried out here on the Earth's surface. In such experiments, researchers attempt to simulate the conditions found in various regions of the ISM and to determine if chemical reactions hypothesized for those regions actually do occur. The study by scientists at SETI and NASA on amino acids, reported earlier in this chapter, is an example of such experiments. Researchers' general approach in such experiments is to enclose certain fundamental substances (such as hydrogen, oxygen, and carbon monoxide) within a sealed container at the low temperatures and pressures common to the ISM and then expose those substances to the type of radiation that may be found in some particular region of the ISM, such as ultraviolet radiation or cosmic-ray-like radiation. The substances formed in such experiments can then be compared with those actually observed in the ISM.

Finally, computing modeling has become a powerful tool in conducting "thought experiments" similar to the actual experiments already described. In such modeling experiments, the basic properties of molecules found in the ISM along with the physical conditions encountered there are fed into computer programs, which then analyze these data and predict the types of reactions that are likely or unlikely to occur.

Research on the interstellar medium has grown dramatically in importance since the last half of the 20th century. Scientists realize that the vast regions between stars are not really "empty space" but are composed of gases, dust, and many forms of energy in which a host of unusual and fascinating chemical reactions are occurring. These reactions result in the production of more than 100 different chemical species, some identical to compounds, atoms, ions, and free radicals found on Earth, and some completely different from those particles. As the next chapter will show, the interstellar medium is also crucial because it is the breeding ground from which stars are born and the repository of atoms and compounds released when stars explode and die.

3

FORMATION OF THE
HEAVY ELEMENTS

The big bang theory provides a satisfactory explanation of the way in which a small number of light elements—hydrogen, helium, lithium, and, to a lesser extent, beryllium—were originally formed. If the universe contained *only* these elements, perhaps our story could stop here, but that notion is, of course, absurd. Earth itself consists of more than 90 additional elements, such as silicon, oxygen, carbon, iron, nitrogen, magnesium, sulfur, nickel, phosphorus, sodium, and chlorine. A few of these elements—carbon, nitrogen, and sulfur, for example—are to be found in the interstellar medium. So a fundamental puzzle has nagged astrochemists for decades: What is the mechanism by which the "heavy" elements are formed in the universe? "Heavy elements," in this case, means those with atomic numbers greater than about 4.

The big bang theory itself does not provide a very promising start to answering that question. The primary effect of the big bang was to scatter matter outward through space: Protons, neutrons, hydrogen ions and atoms, and helium ions and atoms that formed early life of the universe were propelled away from each other with enormous force, and more than 99 percent of the mass of the universe is still drifting outward in an expansion that appears as if it might go on forever. Under these circumstances, how is it possible that these fundamental particles would be able to assemble themselves into the more complex particles that we know of as the atoms of heavy elements?

Stellar Evolution

The birth of stars depends on two essential characteristics of the universe. First, the universe has apparently never been completely homogeneous. As the discovery of the cosmic microwave background anisotropy has confirmed, there are very small differences in the concentration of matter in various parts of the universe. In some regions of space, the density of matter is slightly greater than it is in other regions. Second, the force of gravity acts to attract any two particles anywhere in the universe.

Particles are thus exposed to two opposite forces: the dispersive force provided by the original energy of the big bang and an attractive force of gravity. Although the dispersive forces were far greater than the gravitational forces at first, over time particles projected outward by the big bang began to slow down, and dispersive and attractive forces became more balanced. Eventually dispersive forces were sufficiently reduced in some regions of the universe to allow gravitational forces to operate efficiently. At that point, particles began to come together, coalesce, and form larger particles. The formation of stars could then begin.

The evolution of stars is a complex process, but a simplified overview of the process is as follows:

As the average temperature of the universe cooled, at least in some regions, gravitational forces of attraction become greater than kinetic forces of dispersion. In these regions, hydrogen molecules are capable of existence at these cool temperatures, and they become attracted to each other. They begin moving toward each other with increasingly higher speeds. As they do so, gravitational energy is released, raising the temperature of the hydrogen. Eventually the temperature of the hydrogen cloud becomes great enough to permit the onset of fusion reactions. A fusion reaction is a nuclear reaction in which two nuclei join together (fuse) to form one larger nucleus. At this point, a young star forms.

These fusion reactions result in the conversion of hydrogen to helium. In this process, four hydrogen atoms combine to form one helium atom: $4H \rightarrow He$. The "burning" of hydrogen to produce helium releases very large amounts of energy, which permits the escape (dispersion) of some matter from the young star. Gravitational and dispersive forces remain balanced in the star for an extended period of time—thousands or millions of years. At some point, the amount of energy being released as a result of fusion reactions becomes so great that it exceeds the gravitational attraction of particles within the star. The star then tends to release huge amounts of matter in a short period of time. That is, the star blows itself apart, releasing much of the matter of which it is composed back into the interstellar medium. The liberated matter now consists not only of the hydrogen out of which the star was originally created but also helium and perhaps other elements, which were created in the star.

Stars in the universe today represent most of these life stages. At each stage of its evolution, a star is capable of transforming its existing matter into energy and new elements.

Classifying Stars

Stars have two, and only two, fundamental observable properties: brightness and color. Astronomers usually prefer the term *luminosity* rather than the term *brightness*. An even more precise term is *absolute luminosity*, which is defined as the brightness a star would have if it were placed at a distance of 10 *parsecs* from the Sun. The parsec is a unit of measure used in astronomy equal to 3.26 light-years.

Astronomers have been attempting to estimate the luminosity of stars for centuries. The first person to assemble a table of star luminosities was the Greek natural philosopher Hipparchus (ca.190 B.C.E.–ca. 120 B.C.E.). Hipparchus invented a system consisting of six classes of stars, ranging from Class 1 (the brightest stars) to Class 6 (the dimmest stars). Stars in Class 1 were said to be "first magnitude stars"; those in Class 2 were "second magnitude stars"; and so on. Hipparchus simply used his own eyesight and judgment to decide which stars go into which class. By the 19th century scientists had

◄ ANNIE JUMP CANNON (1863–1941) ►

Scientific work can be classified into two general categories: collecting and collating data, and drawing conclusions and building theories based on those data. Neither activity can be conducted without the other, and either, in and of itself, is incomplete. One of the great data collectors and collators in the history of astronomy was Annie Jump Cannon, who came to astronomy somewhat late in life, at the age of 31.

Annie Cannon was born on December 11, 1863, in Dover, Delaware, to a prosperous shipbuilder and state senator, Wilson Cannon, and his second wife, Mary Jump. Cannon started her educational career with a serious handicap: She was very hard of hearing. Still, she enrolled at Wellesley College in 1880 and earned her degree in physics four years later. She was primarily interested in astronomy, rather than physics, but a degree in that field was not then available.

After graduation, Cannon returned to her home in Dover. At times she expressed unhappiness and dissatisfaction with her life in Dover, however. When her mother died in 1894, she took a job at Wellesley as instructor in the physics department. At the same time, she was accepted as a "special student" in astronomy at Radcliffe College, which was then the women's arm of Harvard College. Two years later she accepted a position on the staff at the Harvard Observatory, a post she held for the rest of her life.

invented methods for measuring the amount of light produced by stars and were able to classify stars into one of the six classes by precise measurements.

Early astronomers also knew that stars seemed to have different colors, but a system for classifying stars on the basis of color was not proposed until about 1872. That system was proposed by the American astronomer Henry Draper (1836–82). Draper's system of classification was very important because a star's color is an indication of its second major property, its temperature. The hotter a star, the more likely its color is to be in the blue to white range. The cooler the star, the more likely it is to emit an orangish or reddish color. Draper died before he could complete his system of star classification. The project was completed between 1918 and 1924 by the American astronomer Annie Jump Cannon (1863–1941).

One of her first assignments at Harvard was to pick up the work of Henry Draper, which had been largely abandoned since his death in 1882. Cannon was apparently the perfect choice for that assignment. She is said to have been able to process star data at a prodigious speed. On average, she classified 5,000 stars a month between 1911 and 1915. At peak speed, she was able to study and classify up to three stars per minute. Overall, Cannon classified 225,300 stars, cataloging them in a nine-volume work entitled *The Henry Draper Catalogue.*

Like most other women of the time, Cannon found that career advancement in the field of science did not come as easily as it did for her male counterparts. For example, she did not receive a permanent appointment at Harvard until 1938, after 42 years of service with the university, at which time she was made William C. Boyd professor of astronomy. She did make a number of important gender breakthroughs, however: She was the first woman to be elected an officer of the American Astronomical Society, the first woman to receive an honorary doctorate from Oxford University (1925), the first woman to be awarded the Draper Gold Medal of the National Academy of Sciences (1931), and the first woman to receive a doctorate in astronomy from Grönigen University (1921).

Annie Jump Cannon died on April 13, 1941, in Cambridge, just a year after her retirement from Harvard.

Draper originally devised a classification system in which stars were placed into lettered groups: A, B, C, D, and so on. Over time, that system was changed and refined. Today, only seven color groups, or *spectral classes,* remain (from hottest to coolest): O, B, A, F, G, K, and M. While the variety of stars is such that more complex classification schemes have been developed to accurately describe them all, the chart on page 52 provides basic information on each of the seven spectral types.

With only two fundamental physical properties available for the study of stars, astronomers have often been tempted to search for ways in which these two variables might be related to each other. One of the first—and by far the most famous—such attempts was that of the Danish astronomer Ejnar Hertzsprung (1873–1967) in the early 1900s. Hertzsprung plotted the temperatures and luminosities of a large number of stars on a graph, like the one shown on page 53. He

◀ SPECTRAL CLASSES OF STARS ▶		
TYPE	**COLOR**	**APPROXIMATE SURFACE TEMPERATURES (K)**
O	Blue	28,000–40,000
B	Blue	11,000–28,000
A	Blue to white	7,500–11,000
F	White	6,000–7,500
G	Yellow	5,000–6,000
K	Orange to red	3,500–5,000
M	Red	Less than 3,500

made the rather unusual decision to publish his research in 1907 in a journal on photography, *Zeitschrft für wissenschafliche Photographie*. Professional astronomers were unlikely to read this journal, so it is hardly surprising that Hertzsprung's results were largely ignored for more than five years. Then the American astronomer Henry Norris Russell (1877–1957) published an almost identical analysis of the relationship of star temperatures and luminosities. Because of the equal efforts of these two men, diagrams like the one shown on page 53 are now known as *Hertzsprung-Russell diagrams* or H-R diagrams.

The graph on page 54 shows an idealized form of the H-R diagram that omits individual data points (data for individual star data) and shows, instead, the major groupings found in such diagrams. The major feature of the diagram is a long band that runs from the upper

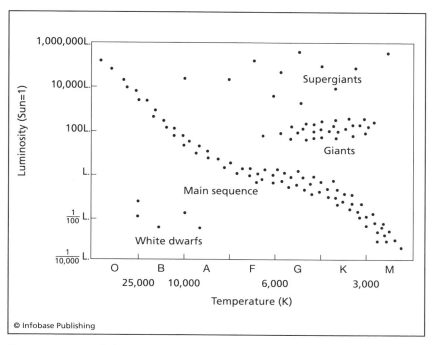

Hertzsprung-Russell diagram for stars in the solar neighborhood

left-hand corner of the graph (stars with high temperature and high luminosity) to the lower right-hand corner of the graph (stars with low temperature and low luminosity). This band is known as the *Main Sequence* because it contains the majority of stars for which data are available. The Sun lies roughly in the middle of the Main Sequence.

Other groups of stars that can be identified on the H-R diagram are supergiants, giants, and *white dwarfs*. About 90 percent of all stars studied fall on the Main Sequence; another 9 percent are classified as white dwarfs; and the remaining 1 percent are giants or supergiants. As their position shows, giants and supergiants are more luminous than Main Sequence stars of the same temperature (below them on the graph). Since they have the same surface temperature, but produce more light, they must be larger than Main Sequence stars, hence their names. Giants have a radius about 10 to 100 times that of our own Sun and a luminosity of about 100 to 1,000 times that of the Sun. Supergiants have a radius of 20 to 4,000 times that of the Sun and a luminosity of 100,000 to 1,000,000 times that of the Sun.

White dwarfs are less luminous than Main Sequence stars with the same surface temperature, so they must be smaller than those stars. White dwarfs vary considerably in size, but they tend to have a radius of about 0.01 that of the Sun and luminosities of 0.01 to 0.0001 that of the Sun.

The Hertzsprung-Russell diagram is a snapshot of a group of stars at some given moment in time. It shows what the luminosities and temperatures of those stars were at the moment that snapshot (set of observations) was taken. What the H-R diagram does *not* tell is anything about the evolution of those stars, the way their temperatures and luminosities have changed over time. For example, the Sun was not born with the temperature and luminosity shown by its current position on the Main Sequence.

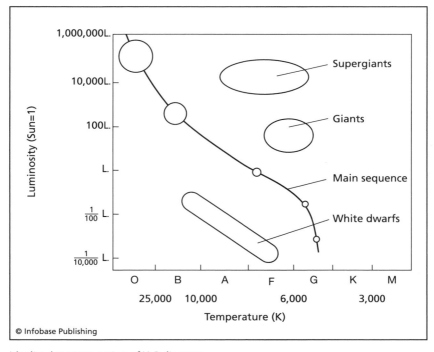

© Infobase Publishing

Idealized representation of H-R diagram

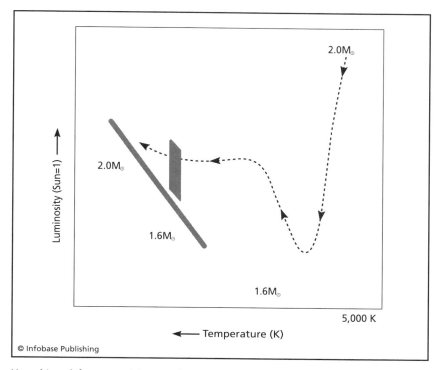

Hayashi track for a star with mass about twice that of the Sun

The graph above shows how the luminosity and temperature of some specific star changes over time, in relation to its current position on the H-R diagram. The star's evolutionary pattern (the dotted line, sometimes known as a *Hayashi track*) is superimposed on a typical H-R diagram. As the diagram shows, both the temperature and luminosity of the star change as it grows older, changing from a giant or supergiant to a Main Sequence star and then back again to a giant or supergiant phase.

A Star Is Born

Star formation begins in molecular clouds. Recall from chapter 2 that a molecular cloud is a large mass of hydrogen gas that is cool enough for the hydrogen to exist in the form of molecules (H_2). The details of star formation differ somewhat depending on the size of the star that is formed. The general pattern is, however, largely the same for stars of all sizes. The discussion that follows is based on the formation of stars about the size of our own Sun. A molecular cloud from which such stars form tends to have a mass about 100,000 times that of our own Sun with a radius of about 50 parsecs.

Two properties of molecular clouds make them ideal locations for star formation. First, the density of hydrogen molecules within a molecular cloud is relatively high. Second, the temperature of a molecular cloud (about 10–20 K) is very low. These two properties mean that the hydrogen molecules that make up a cloud are more likely to be strongly attracted to each other than they are to be dispersed into space.

In some cases, the gravitational attraction between molecules in a cloud is strong enough in and of itself to cause the cloud to begin collapsing onto itself. In other cases, some external event may initiate or accelerate that collapse. For example, the explosion of a neighboring star can produce a shock wave of sufficient intensity to force a molecular cloud to collapse suddenly. Also, two clouds may collide with each other, causing contraction of them both.

The collapse of a molecular cloud is usually not a simple, straightforward process. Two forces resist the contraction of the cloud toward a central core. First, as the cloud begins to collapse, it releases gravitational energy, causing the temperature of the cloud to rise. As the cloud temperature rises, so does the kinetic energy of the molecules of which it is composed. As a result, some hydrogen molecules attain sufficient energy to escape from the collapsing cloud.

Second, as the cloud begins to contract, it also begins to rotate. During rotation, some of the gas contained in the cloud is thrown outward, away from the center, where it forms a thin disk of material around the central core of the cloud. The more the cloud collapses, the faster it rotates and the more material it ejects into the surrounding disk. The disk that surrounds the cloud contains particles that may themselves coalesce to form small bodies (planets) that revolve around the young star.

A contracting molecular cloud is not equally dense throughout. As in the interstellar medium, some regions of a cloud are more dense than others. Thus, when the cloud contracts, it does not

◀ STAGES IN FORMATION OF SUN-LIKE STARS ▷

STAGE	OBJECT	AGE[1]	TEMPERATURE (K)		DENSITY OF CORE (PARTICLES/M³)	RADIUS (KM)
			CORE	SURFACE		
1	Interstellar cloud	0	10	10	10^9	10^{14}
2	Cloud fragment	2×10^6	100	10	10^{12}	10^{12}
3	Cloud fragment	3×10^4	10^4	100	10^{18}	10^{10}
4	Protostar	10^5	10^6	3×10^3	10^{24}	10^8
5	Protostar	10^6	5×10^6	4×10^3	10^{28}	10^7
6	Star	10^6	10^7	4.5×10^3	10^{31}	2×10^6
7	Star	3×10^7	1.5×10^7	6×10^3	10^{32}	1.5×10^6

[1] from beginning of event, in years

form a single dense core; instead it forms multiple dense cores. Anywhere from 10 to 1,000 such cores may break off from any given molecular cloud, each of which may then evolve into a new star.

During the earliest stages of core formation (stages 1 through 4 in the table on page 57; the first few thousand years) contraction occurs relatively slowly and temperatures in the cloud are still less than 100K. Once contraction begins, however, the central core begins to grow by pulling in gas and dust around it. After a few tens or hundreds of thousand years, the central core has reached temperatures of about 10,000K, although the surface may still be no more than a few hundred kelvin. At this point, contraction of a portion of the molecular cloud has resulted in the formation of an object with an identifiable surface that is called a *protostar* or *young stellar object* (*YSO*). The table on page 57 summarizes this process.

The protostar then moves through the *Kelvin-Helmholtz Contraction Phase,* during which it can first be plotted on the H-R diagram. At this point in its evolution, a protostar has a core temperature of about 1,000,000K and a surface temperature of about 3,000K. Its luminosity is about 1,000 times that of the Sun. The process an evolving star undergoes during its lifetime, as shown in the Hertzsprung-Russell diagram on page 53 is known as its *evolutionary track.* The evolutionary track is the sequence of changes that occur in a star's luminosity and temperature during its lifetime—events that provide clues to the kinds of changes that are taking place within it.

The Kelvin-Helmholtz Contraction Phase was named after two physicists, the Englishman Lord Kelvin (1824–1907) and the German Hermann von Helmholtz (1821–94). In attempting to explain how stars produced energy, Kelvin and Helmholtz hypothesized that the large mass of a star's outer layers should cause it to contract, releasing gravitational energy in the process. That gravitational energy would cause the star's overall temperature to increase. Excess energy generated in the process would be radiated away into space, producing the visible light of stars. Although the Kelvin-Helmholtz explanation is a satisfactory description of how stars produce energy, it does not apply to the short period of time after protostars are formed.

Stage 5 of a star's life begins when the star continues to contract, with an increase in the temperature of its core. Its surface temperature remains relatively constant, but its luminosity decreases significantly since the total surface area from which it radiates energy continues to decrease. During this period of its life, the star's position on the H-R diagram moves downward, along a pathway known as the Hayashi track, as shown in the diagram below. Notice that the direction of the Hayashi track differs significantly depending on the mass of the star. The larger the star, the less the change in the luminosity because the star's surface area is less of a factor.

As the star approaches the Main Sequence, it enters one of the most dramatic periods of its lifetime, the *T-Tauri* stage. The name T-Tauri comes from the first star observed that exhibited the events associated with this stage of stellar evolution. T-Tauri stars eject large proportions of their mass in violent bursts.

The spectacular events associated with the T-Tauri phase are probably the result of nuclear reactions beginning in the star's core.

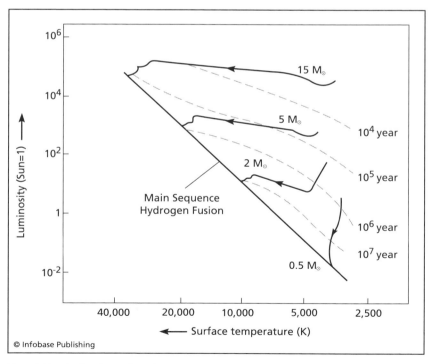

Hayashi tracks for stars of varying masses

These reactions start when the core temperature reaches about 10^7K and are the mechanisms by which hydrogen is converted (fuses) into helium. Fusion releases huge amounts of energy that produces violent activity on the T-Tauri star's surface in the form of eruptions, stellar winds, and flares, and the star loses significant amounts of matter to the surrounding environment. Typically, such a star ejects an amount of mass up to 10^{-7} that of the Sun's mass in a single year, 10^7 the rate at which the Sun itself radiates mass away. During the T-Tauri phase, a star may lose up to 50 percent of its original mass.

Eventually a balance develops between the force of gravity (which tends to pull matter inward, toward its core) and kinetic forces of dispersion (which tend to drive matter outward). At this point, the star has reached the Main Sequence, where it "settles down" to spend most of the rest of its life in a relatively balanced state. If it is a typical star, it will stay in essentially the same position on the Main Sequence for more than 90 percent of its life.

Recall that the pattern just described applies to stars of about the same mass as our own Sun. Evolutionary patterns differ for stars with greater or lesser masses. For example, more massive stars may begin their evolution in much the same way as solar-size stars, but they take less time and a somewhat different pathway during the Hayashi and T-Tauri phases of their lives. More massive stars travel more quickly across the H-R diagram, reaching the Main Sequence in a million years or less, while less massive stars may take up to a billion years before they "settle down" into the Main Sequence.

A few protostars are simply too small to "make it" as fully evolved stars. The critical point seems to be about 0.08 solar mass. Protostars with less mass than this never develop enough energy in their cores to trigger nuclear reactions. They continue to collapse and emit energy, primarily in the infrared region, but they do not "ignite" or "shine" the way stars on the Main Sequence do. These stars, known as brown dwarfs, may live up to 15 million years, after which they are unable to contract any further: They emit no energy of any kind; and they spend the rest of their lives as cold *black dwarfs.*

The existence of "failed stars" with masses of less than 0.08 solar masses, somewhere between that of a large planet like Jupiter and a star, was first hypothesized in 1963 by Shiv Kumar (1939–   ),

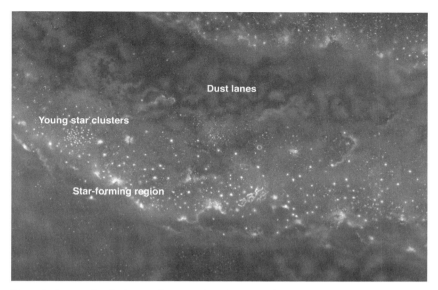

The spiral arms of galaxies, as shown in this photograph, are thought to be regions rich in dust and gas where stars are born. (Jon Lomberg/Photo Researchers, Inc.)

then an astronomer at the University of Virginia. Kumar called such objects "*black stars*," although they were given their present name in 1975 by astrophysicist Jill Tarter. Both names are somewhat misleading since brown dwarfs (or black stars) actually appear as red objects in sky.

For many years, astronomers thought that brown dwarfs were very rare, and it was not until 1995 that one was actually observed. Since that discovery, dozens of brown dwarfs have been discovered, and astronomers have come to the conclusion that brown dwarfs may be very common astronomical objects, perhaps as common as fully evolved stars.

Turning Hydrogen into Helium

Until a protostar has reached the Main Sequence, its chemical composition remains unchanged. It consists, as it has since it began life as a part of a molecular cloud, almost entirely of hydrogen gas. Once core temperatures have reached critical temperatures of more than

10^7 K, however, that situation changes. Hydrogen nuclei (protons) can begin to fuse and form helium nuclei. This process is sometimes known as *"hydrogen burning."* The term is technically incorrect because there is no combustion involved in the process. It is widely used, however, as a shorthand description of the nuclear changes that take place.

That fusion process occurs in three steps that can be summarized by three relatively simple nuclear equations. In the following equations, hydrogen is represented by its chemical symbol, H. Remember, however, that at the very high temperatures of a star's core, hydrogen is completely ionized and exists only as protons.

Step 1: $^1_1H + ^1_1H \rightarrow ^2_1H + e^+ + v$

Step 2: $^1_1H + ^2_1H \rightarrow ^3_2He + \gamma$

Step 3: $^3_2He + ^3_2He \rightarrow ^4_2He + ^1_1H + ^1_1H + \gamma$

(Where the meaning of each symbol in these equations is given in the chart on page 63.)

Note that it is possible to obtain the net reaction that occurs during fusion by deleting species that occur on both sides of the above three equations. Before doing so, however, notice that the last step (Step 3) can occur only after steps 1 and 2 have first occurred twice. That is, two helium-3 nuclei are required in order for Step 3 to occur. Therefore, it is necessary for Step 2 (and, of course, Step 1) to have taken place twice to produce that many helium-3 nuclei. The net reaction for the fusion of hydrogen into helium, then, can be calculated as follows:

$$2 \times \text{Step } 1 + 2 \times \text{Step } 2 + \text{Step } 3 = \text{Net Reaction}$$

Or:

$$4^1_1H \rightarrow ^4_2He$$

The above reactions might appear to be relatively simple and straightforward, but the nuclear equations given here do not reveal all of the details as to *how* hydrogen fuses into helium in these reactions. One of the most difficult problems is explaining how two positively charged particles—the two protons in Step 1—can get close

◀ SYMBOLS USED IN NUCLEAR EQUATIONS ▶			
SYMBOL	NAME	CHARGE	MASS (KG)
p	proton	+1	1.6726×10^{-27}
n	neutron	0	1.6749×10^{-27}
d	deuteron	+1	3.3436×10^{-27}
v	neutrino	0	0 (probably)
γ	gamma ray	0	0
e⁺	positron	+1	9.1094×10^{-31}
e⁻	electron	−1	9.1094×10^{-31}
α	alpha article; helium nucleus	+2	6.6456×10^{-27}

enough to each other to combine into a single new particle, a deuteron. According to the classical laws of physics, the mutual repulsion between these two particles should be so great that they could never actually come into contact long enough for fusion to occur.

The solution to that problem presented itself as scientists developed a more complete understanding of quantum mechanics, the mathematical system that explains the behavior of particles at the atomic level. According to quantum mechanics, there is some finite possibility that the two protons can "tunnel under" the electrostatic barrier that would normally keep them separate from each other, permitting fusion to occur. The probability that such a reaction will occur is very low indeed. It takes place, on average, about once every

10 billion years for any pair of protons. The reaction is efficient at all only because of the huge number of protons found in the core of a protostar or star. Once Step 1 has occurred, the remaining two reactions occur relatively quickly: Step 2 in about six seconds, and Step 3 in about a million years.

A second problem arises because of the structure of a deuteron, formed in Step 1 of the series already described. Notice that a deuteron is a particle consisting of one proton and one neutron. Where does the neutron come from to permit the formation of a deuteron?

One can write a nuclear equation to answer that question:

$$_1^1H \rightarrow {}_0^1n + e^+$$

The only problem with that equation is that it describes a process that cannot (or almost certainly will not) ever occur. One other possibility exists, however. Once two protons have fused with each other (Step 1 above), the particle formed *can* decay, and when it does it emits a positron, leaving behind a proton and newly formed neutron . . . a deuteron.

The proton-proton cycle thus explains the process by which helium is made from hydrogen in the core of stars. It can also be used to explain the amount of energy released during this process. Look at the net reaction resulting from the proton-proton cycle involving particles with mass only:

$$4_1^1H \rightarrow {}_2^4He$$

Then, using the information in the chart on page 63, compare the mass at the beginning of the reaction (the mass of four protons) and the mass at the end of the reaction (the mass of one helium nucleus).

$$
\begin{aligned}
4 \text{ protons} = 4 \times 1.6726^{-27}\text{kg} \quad &= \quad 6.6904 \times 10^{-27}\text{kg} \\
- \quad 1 \text{ helium nucleus} \quad &= \quad 6.6456 \times 10^{-27}\text{kg} \\
\hline
\text{Difference (loss of mass)} \quad &= \quad 0.0448 \times 10^{-27}\text{kg}
\end{aligned}
$$

The difference in the mass of four protons and one helium nucleus, 0.0448×10^{-27}kg, is called the *mass defect*. Where did that mass go?

As every chemistry student knows, matter cannot simply disappear. It can, however, be converted into another form. The equation needed to determine the amount of energy that is equivalent to a given amount of mass is one of the most famous scientific expressions in the world, $E = mc^2$, where m is the mass that apparently "disappears" during the nuclear change, c is the speed of light, and E is the energy equivalent of the mass "lost" in the reaction. When this equation is used to determine the amount of energy that can be produced when a star (our Sun, as an example) loses some known amount of mass (4.4×10^9kg per second), the result (3.9 joules per second) is very close to that actually observed.

The proton-proton cycle is not the only mechanism by which hydrogen is converted into helium in the core of stars. In stars larger than the Sun, a second cycle, known as the *CNO cycle,* also occurs. The graph below shows the relative extent to which each cycle operates in stars of various temperatures. Notice that cooler stars make use almost exclusively of the proton-proton cycle, while the CNO cycle becomes much more important in stars with hotter cores.

The term *CNO cycle* comes from the fact that three elements—carbon, nitrogen, and oxygen—play roles in the conversion of hydrogen

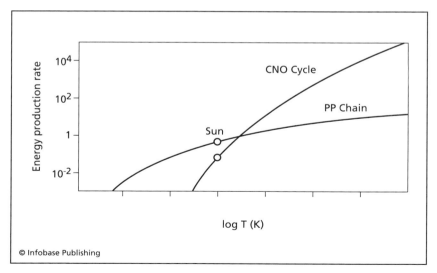

Relative importance of CNO and pp processes in energy generation

to helium. The cycle is more complex than the proton-proton cycle, requiring a total of six steps, as follows:

Step 1: $^{12}_{6}C + ^{1}_{1}H \rightarrow ^{13}_{7}N + \gamma$

Step 2: $^{13}_{7}N \rightarrow ^{13}_{6}C + e^{+} + \nu$

Step 3: $^{13}_{6}C + ^{1}_{1}H \rightarrow ^{14}_{7}N + \gamma$

Step 4: $^{14}_{7}N + ^{1}_{1}H \rightarrow ^{15}_{8}O + \gamma$

Step 5: $^{15}_{8}O \rightarrow ^{15}_{7}N + e^{+} + \nu$

Step 6: $^{15}_{7}N + ^{1}_{1}H \rightarrow ^{12}_{6}C + ^{4}_{2}He$

As with the proton-proton cycle, it is possible to determine a net nuclear reaction by deleting all species that appear on *both* left- and right-hand sides of all equations. As in the proton-proton cycle, the result of that action is the conversion of four hydrogen nuclei (protons) into one helium nucleus, with the release of many neutrinos and large amounts of energy which is carried away in the form of gamma rays:

$$4^{1}_{1}H \rightarrow ^{4}_{2}He$$

Notice that some carbon, nitrogen, and oxygen must be present for the CNO cycle to occur, but the amounts need not be very great because they act strictly as catalysts in the reaction and are not used up.

Helium Burning . . . and Beyond

The long description of the proton-proton and CNO cycles seems not to have gotten us very far in our solution to the fundamental question of this chapter: Where did the heavy elements come from? Thus far, we have been able to show only that hydrogen nuclei can fuse in the core of stars to form helium nuclei, but there is a lot more to the story of what happens in the center of stars, a story that will eventually answer the question of the origin of the heavy elements.

The next step in that story begins when nearly all of the hydrogen at a star's core has been exhausted, that is, has been converted to helium. What happens to the star next depends on the mass of the star. To keep the description simple, this discussion will continue to use a star with a mass about equal to that of the Sun.

With no more hydrogen available, fusion reactions come to an end in the star's core. That event results in a rapid decrease in the amount of energy produced in the core and, consequently, the core's temperature. The helium that now makes up the core begins to collapse in upon itself, releasing gravitational energy in the process. Under most circumstances that release of energy would cause the core to expand again, just as a balloon expands in size when the air inside it is heated up, but the helium core no longer behaves as a gas at this point. Instead, it has reached a *degenerate state,* that is, a state in which positive helium ions and negative electrons are regularly distributed throughout the core. In this state, the helium acts more like a solid than a gas, making it possible for heat to be carried away from the core to the star's outer envelope. One consequence of this heat transfer out of the core is that a thin shell of hydrogen gas remaining from the original protostar is reignited. Heat produced in fusion reactions in this inner gas is carried to the star's outer shell and dissipated into space.

As the helium core continues to contract, it continues to release gravitational energy. Eventually, the core becomes hot enough (10^8 K) to permit the next stage of stellar evolution: *helium burning.* (Again, recall that the term *burning* here does not refer to combustion but to a set of nuclear reactions that liberates very large amounts of energy.) Once helium fusion reactions begin, enormous amounts of energy are released and carried away to the star's surface. For a short time, the star's outer envelope expands and becomes much hotter in a process that is called a *helium flash.*

In the primary reaction helium burning, three alpha particles (helium nuclei) are converted to a carbon nucleus, a process sometimes referred to as the *triple helium process,* or *triple alpha particle process:*

$$3\,{}^{4}_{2}\text{He} \rightarrow {}^{12}_{6}\text{C}$$

An alert chemistry student may question the legitimacy of this equation because it suggests that three bodies (the three alpha particles) come into contact with each other at precisely the same time in order for this reaction to occur. And three-body reactions are, in Earth-based chemistry, highly unlikely.

The reason the reaction can occur at all is that it actually consists of two steps. In the first step, two alpha particles combine to form a single beryllium-8 nucleus:

$$_2^4He + _2^4He \rightarrow _4^8Be$$

The Be nucleus is very unstable, decaying in 0.968×10^{-16} s. Although that period of time seems very short, it turns out to be long enough to permit reaction of the Be nucleus with a third alpha particle:

$$_4^8Be + _2^4He \rightarrow _6^{12}C + \gamma$$

Again, the reason that such an apparently unlikely reaction can occur is that the density of alpha particles in the core is so high that the chance of collision between a Be nucleus and an alpha particle is very high indeed.

One additional stage of element formation may also occur during helium burning, the reaction between an alpha particle and a carbon nucleus to produce an oxygen nucleus:

$$_2^4He + _6^{12}C \rightarrow _8^{16}O + \gamma$$

At one time, astrochemists considered the possibility that such reactions would continue to produce even heavier elements such as neon, for example:

$$_2^4He + _8^{16}O \rightarrow _{10}^{20}Ne + \gamma$$

In stars the size of our own Sun, however, such reactions are unlikely to occur, and the production of carbon and oxygen mark the final stage of heavy element synthesis in such stars.

The onset of helium burning signals a change in the star's outward appearance and moves it away from the Main Sequence. Heat produced during helium burning causes the star to expand significantly. A star with the mass of the Sun may increase its radius a hundredfold. At the same time, because the outer surface has become so distant from the core, its temperature is relatively modest, in the range of 3,500 K. In terms of the H-R diagram, the star has migrated upward and away from the Main Sequence. It has become a red giant.

As helium is depleted from a star's interior, the star reaches the last stages of its life. As helium is converted into carbon and oxygen, these heavier elements migrate to the center of the star and the helium-burning skin moves outward. Over time, the star's outer layer, exposed to the chill of outer space, begins to cool down. Electrons and positively charged nuclei slow down sufficiently to allow the formation of neutral atoms, which then drift off into space. As the star's outer envelope blows away, it forms a cloudlike structure known as a *planetary nebula.* All that is left behind is the very hot, very dense core of the star. That core, now known as a *white dwarf,* no longer has any nuclear mechanism by which it can generate energy, and it slowly radiates heat into space and becomes more and more cool. Gravitational forces are so strong in the star that its density at the core is about 10^9 kg/m^3, about a million times the density of the Earth. After cooling for about a billion years, the white dwarf has lost essentially all of its internal energy; it no longer radiates heat or light; and it has settled down in the graveyard of stars as a black dwarf.

Bigger Stars = More Elements

Stars larger than the Sun follow a somewhat different path than do Sun-sized stars, primarily because they are more massive. In such stars, nuclear reactions that are not possible in solar-size stars can occur, and, as a result of those reactions, a larger array of elements can be formed.

For example, in a star with a mass more than 25 times that of our own Sun, carbon, oxygen, and neon can continue to "burn," that is, continue to react with alpha particles to form larger and more complex nuclei:

$$^4_2He + {}^{12}_6C \rightarrow {}^{16}_8O + \gamma$$
$$^4_2He + {}^{16}_8O \rightarrow {}^{20}_{10}Ne + \gamma$$
$$^4_2He + {}^{20}_{10}Ne \rightarrow {}^{24}_{12}Mg + \gamma$$

These reactions can continue through the production of iron:

$$^{4}_{2}He + {}^{24}_{12}Mg \rightarrow {}^{28}_{14}Si + \gamma$$
$$^{4}_{2}He + {}^{28}_{14}Si \rightarrow {}^{32}_{16}S + \gamma$$

. . . and so on, to

$$^{4}_{2}He + {}^{52}_{24}Cr \rightarrow {}^{56}_{26}Fe + \gamma$$

Beyond this point, the production of heavier elements by means of fusion is no longer possible because sufficient amounts of energy are not available.

Other fusion reactions involving large nuclei are also possible, such as the "burning" of carbon and oxygen to produce heavier nuclei:

$$^{12}_{6}C + {}^{12}_{6}C \rightarrow {}^{20}_{10}Ne + {}^{4}_{2}He$$

and

$$^{16}_{8}O + {}^{16}_{8}O \rightarrow {}^{28}_{14}Si + {}^{4}_{2}He$$

The temperatures, rates, and other conditions at which these reactions take place are very different and are summarized in the chart on page 71.

Carbon, neon, and oxygen burning can also proceed along other pathways, resulting in the formation of other isotopes. For example:

$$^{12}_{6}C + {}^{12}_{6}C \rightarrow {}^{23}_{11}Na + {}^{1}_{1}H + \gamma$$
$$^{12}_{6}C + {}^{12}_{6}C \rightarrow {}^{23}_{12}Mg + {}^{1}_{0}n + \gamma$$
$$^{16}_{8}O + {}^{16}_{8}O \rightarrow {}^{31}_{15}P + {}^{1}_{1}H + \gamma$$
$$^{16}_{8}O + {}^{16}_{8}O \rightarrow {}^{31}_{16}S + {}^{1}_{0}n + \gamma$$

The fusion reactions described thus far can account for the formation of most elements with an atomic number of less than 26 (iron). Heavier elements cannot be formed by such processes, however, because the products of fusion reactions are thermodynamically unstable; that is, they tend to break down into their component parts rather than remain as stable particles. The most common mechanism by which elements with an atomic number greater than 26 is formed is known as *neutron capture*. In a neutron capture reaction,

◄ CONDITIONS FOR VARIOUS TYPES OF FUSION REACTIONS ▷

STAGE	TEMP (K)	DENSITY OF STAR (KG/M³)	DURATION OF STAGE
Hydrogen burning	4×10^7	5	7×10^6 years
Helium burning	2×10^8	700	5×10^5 years
Carbon burning	6×10^8	2×10^5	600 years
Neon burning	1.2×10^9	4×10^6	1 year
Oxygen burning	1.5×10^9	10^7	6 months
Silicon burning	2.7×10^9	3×10^7	1 day

a neutron strikes a target nucleus. Since a neutron has a mass of 1 and an atomic number of 0, the nucleus formed in this reaction is an isotope of the original nucleus with an atomic mass one greater than that of the target:

$$\,^1_0 n + \,^A_Z M \rightarrow \,^{A+1}_Z M$$

where A is the mass number (total number of protons and neutrons), and Z is the atomic number (number of protons) in the nucleus M.

Neutron capture reactions are common in massive stars because of the abundance of neutrons available there. Look back at the equations for carbon-, oxygen-, and neon-burning (page 70). Notice that alpha particles are common products of such reactions. Astrochemists have determined that the three most common sources of neutrons in such reactions are the following reactions:

$$^{13}_{6}C + ^{4}_{2}He \rightarrow ^{16}_{8}O + ^{1}_{0}n$$

$$^{22}_{10}Ne + ^{4}_{2}He \rightarrow ^{25}_{12}Mg + ^{1}_{0}n$$

$$^{25}_{12}Mg + ^{4}_{2}He \rightarrow ^{28}_{14}Si + ^{1}_{0}n$$

In most cases, a stable nucleus (such as iron-56) can absorb an additional neutron (or two or three) and remain stable. For example, when iron-56 absorbs a neutron, it is converted to iron-57, which is stable:

$$^{56}_{26}Fe + ^{1}_{0}n \rightarrow ^{57}_{26}Fe + \gamma$$

The iron-57 formed in this reaction can absorb a second neutron, resulting in the formation of iron-58, which is also stable:

$$^{57}_{26}Fe + ^{1}_{0}n \rightarrow ^{58}_{26}Fe + \gamma$$

Finally, iron-58 can absorb yet another neutron, forming iron-59:

$$^{58}_{26}Fe + ^{1}_{0}n \rightarrow ^{59}_{26}Fe + \gamma$$

The product of this reaction, $^{59}_{26}Fe$, however, is *not* stable. It decays by beta emission with a half-life of about 44.5 days.

This pattern is common for neutron decay reactions. A target nucleus captures one, two, or more neutrons and remains stable, but as the ratio between mass number and atomic number (A:Z) becomes larger, the nucleus becomes more unstable. At some point, it reaches a size at which that it becomes unstable (radioactive) and decays with the emission of a beta particle or an alpha particle, or by some other mechanism.

When an unstable isotope decays, it forms a new isotope and a new element. In the case of iron-59, for example, the loss of a beta particle results in the formation of cobalt-59, an element not otherwise formed by fusion reactions described thus far:

$$^{59}_{26}Fe \rightarrow ^{59}_{27}Co + ^{0}_{-1}e$$

Once cobalt is formed by neutron capture, it can itself become the target for neutron capture, a process by which it is converted to radioactive cobalt-60:

$$^{59}_{27}Co + ^{1}_{0}n \rightarrow ^{60}_{27}Co + \gamma$$

Cobalt-60, in turn, decays by beta emission to form the next-heavier element, nickel:

$$^{60}_{27}Co \rightarrow ^{60}_{28}Ni + ^{0}_{-1}e$$

As this process continues, any given nucleus gradually adds protons, becomes heavier, and works its way up the periodic table, as shown in the diagram on page 76.

This pathway cannot continue indefinitely, however. What limits the process is the relationship between neutron capture time and the half-life of isotopes produced by neutron capture. The reactions just described, for example, which successively change iron to cobalt and nickel, take place very slowly and are, therefore, known as *slow neutron capture* reactions or, more simply, as *s reactions.* They are called "slow" because, on average, hundreds to thousands of years may pass before any given nucleus absorbs a neutron. These reactions can occur because they all involve the presence of a stable isotope at some point, for instance, iron-57, iron-58, or cobalt-59. As long as these isotopes are present—or as long as isotopes with half-lives greater than a few hundreds or thousands of years are present—there is enough time for neutron capture to occur.

In fact, that is the situation in many old, highly evolved stars with cores in which oxygen- and carbon-burning are taking place, such as those shown in preceding text (page 71). In such circumstances, large numbers of neutrons are being produced by fusion reactions, but large numbers of stable isotopes, such as iron-58, are still readily available.

In conditions that produce stable isotopes with very high atomic numbers, however, such as lead-208 and bismuth-209, slow processes are no longer efficient. Neutron capture reactions involving these isotopes produce isotopes with very short half-lives. For example, n, γ reactions with lead (Z = 82) as the target all result in the formation

◁ MARGARET BURBIDGE (1919–) AND GEOFFREY BURBIDGE (1925–) ▷

Scientific research consists of many different kinds of activities: building equipment, gathering data, drawing hypotheses, and developing grand theories, for example. One activity that is seldom mentioned could be called "setting the agenda." "Setting the agenda" refers to an effort by some person (or persons) to step back from the day-to-day work in a particular field of science, assess the progress that has been made in that field, and outline a program of research for future years. One of the great examples of that kind of work in astronomy is a famous paper written in 1957 by the husband-and-wife team of E. Margaret Burbidge and Geoffrey Burbidge and their colleagues, William A. Fowler and Fred Hoyle.

Margaret Burbidge was born Eleanor Margaret Peachey in Davenport, England, on August 12, 1919. Her father was an instructor at the Manchester School of Technology and her mother a student of chemistry there. The family moved to London in 1921, when her father established his own research laboratory. Margaret earned her bachelor of science degree from University College in London in 1939 and a Ph.D. from the University of London Observatory in 1943. In 1947, Margaret Peachey met fellow astronomer Geoffrey Burbidge, and a year later, the couple were married.

Geoffrey Burbidge was born in Chipping Norton, England, on September 24, 1925. He received his bachelor's degree in physics from Bristol University in 1946 and then enrolled at University College, London, for graduate work in astronomy. He completed his Ph.D. in astrophysics in 1951, in the same year that his wife was offered a position as interim assistant director of the Yerkes Observatory in Chicago. Geoffrey Burbidge spent 1951 to 1953 working at the University of Chicago, at Harvard University, and at Cambridge University's famous Cavendish Laboratories.

At the end of her two-year stint with the Yerkes Observatory, Margaret accepted an appointment as Research Fellow at the California Institute of Technology. She and Geoffrey had embarked on a career that would keep

of isotopes of polonium (Z = 83), but polonium has no stable isotope and no isotope with a half-life greater than 102 years. There is no isotope of polonium that can "wait around" for a few hundred or thousand years, therefore, for the slow process to occur. Because them in the United States for the rest of their lives. It was during this period that the Burbidges, Fowler, and Hoyle wrote their classic paper. That paper, entitled "Synthesis of the Elements in Stars," collected and summarized all of the information then known about the production of elements in the stars and suggested topics on which additional research was needed in the field. The paper eventually became widely known by the initials of the four authors, B^{2}FH. Acknowledgment of the enormous value of that paper was made in another major publication, "Synthesis of the Elements in Stars: Forty Years of Progress," written by 15 authors in 1997.

John Maddox, editor of the journal *Nature,* later explained the importance of B^{2}FH. First, he said, it provided the best explanation then available for the way elements are produced in stars. Second, it settled the ongoing dispute as to the changes that take place in stars as they move across the Hertzsprung-Russell diagram. Finally, it provided a basis for calculating the composition of stars and predicting their ultimate fate.

Margaret went on to become associate professor of astronomy at the University of Chicago (1959–62) and then associate professor and professor at the University of California at San Diego (UCSD; 1962–90). In 1990, Margaret was named professor emeritus at UCSD. Geoffrey joined her at UCSD in 1963. He later served as director of the Kitt Peak National Observatory, southwest of Tucson, Arizona, from 1978 to 1984, after which he returned to UCSD, where he continues to work as professor in the Department of Physics.

Both Burbidges received many honors. They were awarded the Bruce Medal, one of astronomy's highest prizes (Margaret in 1982 and Geoffrey in 1999). They also were elected to the Royal Society, she in 1964 and he in 1968. In 1959, the husband-and-wife team were jointly awarded the Warner Prize of the American Astronomical Society. Margaret Burbidge received more than a dozen honorary doctorates and was awarded a National Medal of Science in 1984. One of her highest honors was election to the post of president of the American Association for the Advancement of Science (AAAS) in 1976.

there are elements with atomic numbers greater than 83, however, some other nuclear mechanism must exist by which isotopes of elements with Z greater than 83 can form. That mechanism is known as the *rapid process* or *r process.*

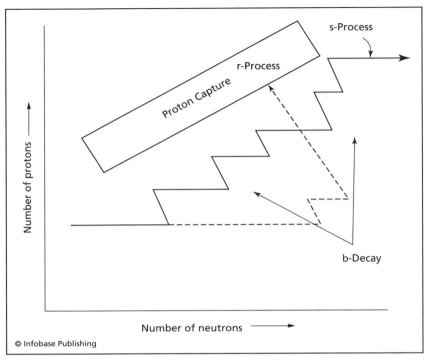

Proton capture, r-process, and s-process for various nuclides

The r process is truly rapid. It occurs at the very end of a star's lifetime, when very large amounts of iron (^{56}Fe) have accumulated in its nucleus. At this point, the ongoing battle between gravitational attraction and thermal expansion that takes place in all stars reaches a turning point. So much iron is present in the star's core that gravitational forces become very strong, and the star's mass is strongly attracted to its core. Matter moves so rapidly toward the center of the star that very high temperatures and pressures are created. They are so great, in fact, that free electrons that have been floating around within the core are driven into the atomic nuclei that occur there, and protons are converted to neutrons:

$$p^+ + e^- \rightarrow n^0$$

The "mad rush" of matter to the center of the core, however, very quickly generates sufficient heat to reverse this process. The core blows itself apart, scattering matter outward into space at incredible speeds. This event is a supernova, one of the most dramatic to be seen in the sky: A star essentially blows up and scatters its contents into space. In this event, the work of millions or billions of years—the conversion of hydrogen from a star cloud to helium, carbon, oxygen, neon, iron, and other elements—is undone in less than a second. Many of the hard-won iron nuclei in the star's core totally disintegrate, reverting into helium nuclei and, in most cases, into protons and neutrons.

The release of so many neutrons all at once provides another mechanism for the production of new elements. Now the density of neutrons is so great that n,γ reactions of the type seen for the s process can occur with isotopes having very short half-lives. Suppose, for example, that a nucleus of the only stable isotope of bismuth, bismuth-209, is projected from the center of a star during a supernova explosion. Then, an s-like n,γ reaction can occur, as follows:

$$^{209}_{83}Bi + {}^{1}_{0}n \rightarrow {}^{210}_{83}Bi + \gamma$$

The isotope ^{210}Bi is not an especially good candidate for an s process reaction, because its half-life is only about five days. It is not likely to "wait around" until an s-process neutron shows up. (Recall that such neutrons are available only about once every hundred years or more.) In the high-neutron-density environment of a supernova, however, the ^{210}Bi nucleus will encounter millions of neutrons every second. Thus, the next stage in this reaction, the addition of a neutron to the ^{210}Bi nucleus to form the next-heaviest isotope in the family, ^{210}Bi, can occur much more readily:

$$^{210}_{83}Bi + {}^{1}_{0}n \rightarrow {}^{211}_{83}Bi + \gamma$$

Under these circumstances—when the density of matter vastly increases the odds that the appropriate particles can meet in time to undergo the s process—it is possible to explain the production of any isotope with an atomic number greater than 83. Those isotopes that are not produced directly by the s process are produced by other mechanisms from isotopes that *are* products of an s reaction. For example, the next isotope formed after the reaction shown above, ^{2}Bi, decays with a half-life of about 60 minutes, but it can decay by either of two mechanisms, alpha decay or beta decay. Alpha decay results in the formation of the isotope ^{2}Tl, while beta decay option produces the isotope $^{211}_{82}$Pb:

$$^{212}_{83}Bi \rightarrow {}^4_2He + {}^{288}_{81}Tl$$

and

$$^{212}_{83}Bi \rightarrow {}^0_{-1}e + {}^{211}_{82}Pb$$

In combination, these nuclear reactions prove satisfactory for explaining the origin of the vast majority of the more abundant known isotopes in the universe. Some exceptions exist, however. The most important of these are a group of proton-rich isotopes such as those in the chart on page 79. None of these isotopes can be produced either through hydrogen, helium, carbon, or some other form of burning or by means of neutron capture reactions.

Two mechanisms have been proposed for the creation of the proton-rich isotopes. The first, which involves the capture of a proton by a nucleus, appears to be most effective in producing the lighter proton-rich isotopes. The reaction is a p, γ reaction whose net effect is simply to add one proton to a nucleus, increasing its atomic number and mass number by 1. A possible mechanism for the synthesis of vanadium-50 might be:

$$^1_1H + {}^{49}_{22}Ti \rightarrow {}^{50}_{23}V + \gamma$$

The problem with this mechanism, of course, is that a proton experiences very strong electrostatic forces of repulsion as it approaches a positively charged nucleus, like that of the Ti nucleus. How likely is it that the proton can overcome that force of repulsion and enter the nucleus? Calculations show that, given sufficient kinetic energy, the proton can overcome this barrier and add to an isotope, especially one that is smaller with fewer protons. The temperature required to bring about such a reaction is estimated at about 2 to 3 $\times$ 10^9 K, very high, but within the range some large stars reach toward the end of their lives.

A second, hypothetically more efficient possible mechanism, hypothesized for the production of larger proton-rich nuclei, is a γ, n reaction. In this type of reaction, high-energy photons collide with

◁ SOME "PROTON-RICH" ISOTOPES ▷

ISOTOPE	ATOMIC NUMBER	MASS NUMBER	PROTON TO NEUTRON RATIO
^{50}V	23	50	27:23
^{92}Mo	42	92	50:42
^{94}Mo	42	94	52:42
^{96}Ag	47	96	49:47
^{98}Ag	47	98	51:47
^{196}Hg	80	196	116:80

a nucleus and cause a nuclear rearrangement in which a single neutron is expelled. For instance, mercury-196 could be produced by this mechanism from one of its isotopes:

$$^{197}_{80}Hg + \gamma \rightarrow \, ^{196}_{80}Hg + \, ^{1}_{0}n$$

Again, very high temperatures (in the range of 2 to 3×10^9 K) are required for such γ, n reactions to occur. One of the likely locations for such events, then, are during the final stages of a heavy star's life, when it explodes as a supernova and disperses much of its material into the interstellar medium.

With these reactions explained, the story of heavy element formation is relatively complete. Once solar-size stars have formed, they begin to convert hydrogen into helium. As they reach the end of their lives, helium burning gives way to carbon burning and oxygen burning, which result in the formation of elements up to iron. While elements in that range are about all that medium-size stars can contribute to nucleosynthesis of heavy elements, heavier stars have other processes for the production of elements, such as s, r, and p reactions and high-energy photon changes. As a result of these mechanisms, virtually all of the known isotopes can be produced.

Which is not to say that the question of nucleosynthesis of the elements is closed. Much of the story of element formation related here rests on theoretical calculations that still need to be compared to observations of elemental abundances and star properties, and a few nagging questions remain about the origin of specific isotopes.

The overall picture is now clear. As a result of the variety of nuclear processes available to stars, the creation of nearly all of the known isotopes can be accounted for. Once these isotopes are formed in stars, they are released to the interstellar medium upon the star's demise. When they have become part of the ISM, these isotopes are available for capture by other young stars in the early stages of molecular cloud collapse and protostar formation. Surely stars are the ideal example of how recycling can benefit the environment!

4

THE INNER PLANETS

Chemists have long been fascinated by the composition of the planets, *asteroids,* comets, meteors, and other objects that make up the solar system. Are these bodies made of the same elements and compounds, in the same proportions, as the Earth itself? How do their surfaces and atmospheres differ, if at all, from those of Earth? If chemical differences among solar system bodies do exist, how can they be explained? What does the chemical composition of solar system bodies tell scientists about their possible origins?

Prior to 1960, chemists had few tools with which to answer these questions. In some cases, it was possible to make reasonably good estimates of a planet's density, for example, based on its mass and volume. Both characteristics can be determined relatively easily from the planet's orbital path. Once a planet's density had been estimated, scientists could develop models that would fit the estimated density.

For example, planets with densities similar to those of Earth (about 5.5 g/cm^3) were thought to contain some combination of lightweight minerals such as silicates (densities of about 3.5 g/cm^3) and more dense materials such as iron and nickel (densities of about 8.5 g/cm^3). Those with lower densities, such as Mars (density = 3.93 g/cm^3), were thought to consist primarily of rocky, silicate-like materials with little heavy metals. Those with much lower densities, such as Jupiter (density = 1.36 g/cm^3), were assumed to consist almost entirely of gaseous elements and compounds.

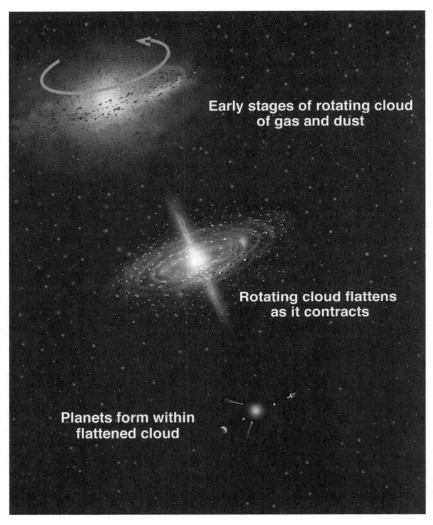

Early stages of rotating cloud
of gas and dust

Rotating cloud flattens
as it contracts

Planets form within
flattened cloud

Scientists believe that the planets were born out of a mass of gas and dust rotating around the Sun. (Jon Lomberg/Photo Researchers, Inc.)

Studying the Chemical Composition of a Planet

Probably the most important single instrument available for determining the chemical composition of a planet has long been the spectroscope, invented in 1814 by the German physicist Joseph von Fraunhofer (1787—1826). Spectroscopy is the technique by which some form of electromagnetic (EM) radiation, such as light, is dispersed, or broken up, into its constituent parts. When sunlight itself is passed through a spectrometer, it is dispersed into a continuous spectrum, a spectrum that contains every possible wavelength of energy in the visible region. A continuous spectrum in the visible region of the EM spectrum looks like a rainbow, with every possible visible color being represented.

The spectrum produced when light is given off by the heating of a pure element, compound, free radical, ion, or other chemical species, on the other hand, is not continuous, but discrete. That is, the spectrum consists of a set of narrow lines corresponding to certain specific wavelengths only. The diagram below provides an example of the line spectrum in the visible region produced when the element hydrogen is heated.

Each element and compound produces a unique, characteristic line spectrum when it is heated. Hence an element can be identified by its line spectrum. Scientists can analyze electromagnetic radiation emitted by or reflected from a planet's surface or its atmosphere with a spectrometer to identify the line spectra present. By analyzing those line spectra, a scientist can determine which elements, compounds, and other chemical species are present on the planet's surface or in its atmosphere.

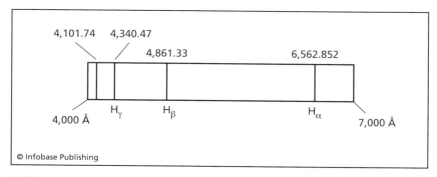

Visible spectrum of hydrogen

One of the earliest and most famous examples of the use of spectrometry to study the solar system occurred in 1868. While observing a solar eclipse in India, the French astronomer Pierre Janssen (1824–1907) found a new spectral line in sunlight very close to one found in the spectrum of sodium. Janssen was able to show, however, that the new yellow light was different from the sodium line. Indeed, it was a spectral line that had never before been observed on Earth. Janssen hypothesized that the presence of the line could be explained only if the Sun's atmosphere contained an element that had not yet been discovered on Earth. The British astronomer Sir Norman Lockyer (1836–1920) later suggested the name *helium* for the element, a name based on the Greek word for "sun," *helios.* It was almost 30 years later that Janssen's bold hypothesis was confirmed. In 1895, the British chemist and physicist Sir William Ramsay (1852–1916) first detected helium on Earth, during a series of experiments on an ore of uranium called clevite.

Today astronomers routinely study the chemical composition of a planet by analyzing sunlight reflected off its surface and atmosphere. The same method is used to analyze the chemical composition of other bodies in the solar system, such as comets, meteors, and planetary satellites. This process is challenging since, in some cases, relatively modest amounts of light are reflected from a planet or other body. Also, the spectrum observed is likely to be very complex, with the lines of many elements and compounds present in the pattern.

In the earliest spectroscopic studies of solar system bodies, only the visible light that those bodies reflected was available for study, but sunlight consists of a much broader range of radiation than that found in the visible region of the electromagnetic spectrum. As the diagram on page 85 shows, radiation in the visible region makes up only a modest portion of the complete electromagnetic spectrum. In addition to visible light, solar radiation reflected off a planet contains ultraviolet and infrared radiation. Astronomers have now developed instruments and techniques that allow them to analyze radiation from solar system bodies across a much wider range of wavelengths.

One of the great breakthroughs for astrochemists in the past half century has been the development of rockets and space vehicles that can carry spectrometers into space, far above the Earth's at-

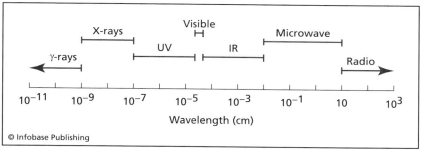

Electromagnetic spectrum

mosphere, which otherwise blocks many forms of radiation from reaching Earth's surface. One of the most famous of these spacecraft was the *International Ultraviolet Explorer* (*IUE*), a joint project of the U.S. National Aeronautics and Space Administration (NASA), the European Space Agency (ESA), and the United Kingdom, launched on January 26, 1978. *IUE* was expected to remain in orbit for only three years. It performed so successfully, however, that it continued operations for more than 18 years, finally shutting down on September 26, 1996. As its name suggests, the *IUE* collected and analyzed radiation in the ultraviolet region of the EM spectrum, in the range between 115 and 320 nm (nanometers). During its lifetime, *IUE* produced more than 100,000 spectra of planets, comets, stars, galaxies, and other astronomical bodies and objects.

Other space-based observatories have been designed and built to study radiation at the opposite end of the EM spectrum, the infrared region. The first infrared spectrometer sent into space to study the chemical properties of another planet was the Mars Infrared Spectrometer (IRS), carried by the *Mariner Mars 7* spacecraft into orbit in 1969. The IRS instrument swept the surface of Mars, collecting and analyzing radiation in the 1,800–14,400 nm range. More than 30 years after that initial flight, space scientists are still examining the IRS data to see what information it can provide about the chemical composition of the Red Planet's surface.

Overall, NASA has launched more than a dozen missions to study the planets. The chart on pages 86–89 summarizes these missions, their targets, and their launch dates. The table also includes planetary

◄ PLANETARY OBSERVATORIES TO THE TERRESTRIAL PLANETS* ►

SPACECRAFT	LAUNCH COUNTRY	TARGET	LAUNCH DATE
Venera 1	USSR	Venus	February 12, 1961
Mariner 2	USA	Venus	August 27, 1962
Mariner 4	USA	Mars	November 28, 1964
Zond 3	USSR	Mars	June 18, 1965
Mariner 5	USA	Venus	June 4, 1967
Venera 4	USSR	Venus	June 12, 1967
Venera 5	USSR	Venus	January 5, 1969
Venera 6	USSR	Venus	January 10, 1969
Mariner 6	USA	Mars	February 24, 1969
Mariner 7	USA	Mars	March 27, 1969
Venera 7	USSR	Venus	July 22, 1970
Mars 2	USSR	Mars	May 19, 1971
Mars 3	USSR	Mars	May 28, 1971

SPACECRAFT	LAUNCH COUNTRY	TARGET	LAUNCH DATE
Venera 8	USSR	Venus	March 27, 1972
Mars 5	USSR	Mars	July 25, 1973
Mars 6	USSR	Mars	August 5, 1973
Mars 7	USSR	Mars	August 9, 1973
Mariner 10	USA	Venus & Mercury	November 3, 1973
Venera 9	USSR	Venus	June 8, 1975
Venera 10	USSR	Venus	June 14, 1975
Viking 1	USA	Mars	August 20, 1975
Viking 2	USA	Mars	September 9, 1975
Pioneer Venus (orbiter)	USA	Venus	May 20, 1978
Pioneer Venus (landers)	USA	Venus	August 8, 1978
Venera 11	USSR	Venus	September 9, 1978
Venera 12	USSR	Venus	September 14, 1978

(continues)

◀ PLANETARY OBSERVATORIES TO THE TERRESTRIAL PLANETS* *(continued)* ➤

SPACECRAFT	LAUNCH COUNTRY	TARGET	LAUNCH DATE
Venera 13	USSR	Venus	October 30, 1981
Venera 14	USSR	Venus	November 4, 1981
Venera 15	USSR	Venus	June 2, 1983
Venera 16	USSR	Venus	June 7, 1983
Vega 1	USSR	Venus	December 15, 1984
Vega 2	USSR	Venus	December 21, 1984
Phobos 2	USSR	Mars	July 12, 1988
Magellan	USA	Venus	May 4, 1989
Galileo	USA	Jupiter	October 18, 1989
Mars Observer	USA	Mars	September 25, 1992
Mars Global Surveyor	USA	Mars	November 7, 1996
Mars Pathfinder	USA	Mars	December 4, 1996
Cassini	USA	Saturn	October 15, 1997

SPACECRAFT	LAUNCH COUNTRY	TARGET	LAUNCH DATE
Nozomi	Japan	Mars	July 4, 1998
Mars Climate Orbiter	USA	Mars	December 11, 1998
Mars Polar Lander/ Deep Space 2	USA	Mars	January 3, 1999
Mars Odyssey	USA	Mars	April 7, 2001
Mars Express	USA	Mars	June 2, 2003
Spirit	USA	Mars	June 10, 2003
Opportunity (Mars Rover)	USA	Mars	July 7, 2003
Messenger	USA	Mercury	August, 3, 2004
Mars Reconnaissance Orbiter	USA	Mars	August 12, 2005
Venus Express	ESA	Venus	November 5, 2005
New Horizons	USA	Pluto/ Charon	January 19, 2006

*Includes only those missions that achieved at least some portion of their objectives.
Source: Compiled from data available from the Planetary Sciences at the National Space Science Data Center, available online at http://nssdc.gsfc.nasa.gov/planetary/.

probes launched by the former Soviet Union, Japan, and the European Space Agency (ESA).

These space-based observatories and a number of terrestrial observatories have produced a growing body of data about five of the planets in the solar system—Mercury, Venus, Mars, Jupiter, and Saturn—as well as numerous other bodies, including comets, asteroids, and many planetary satellites, including our own Moon.

Mercury

Prior to the 1960s, scientists had relatively little concrete information on the chemical composition of Mercury. During periods of occultation, when one planet passes in front of another planet, it was possible to make measurements of Mercury's atmosphere, which revealed a very thin atmosphere consisting primarily of helium. Earth-based telescopes and spectroscopes were unable to discover much beyond the fact that the planet's surface appeared rocky, somewhat like the Moon's surface.

Based on the planet's density (5.4 g/cm^3), scientists had hypothesized that Mercury has an overall structure somewhat like that of Earth, with a rocky outer shell and mantle and a large core, probably made primarily of iron. The core was estimated to have a radius about three-quarters that of the planet itself.

The first (and only) space probe sent to Mercury, *Mariner 10*, was launched on November 3, 1973, to study the planet more closely. The spacecraft carried two narrow-angle cameras with digital tape recorders, an ultraviolet spectrometer, infrared spectrometer, magnetometer, charged particle telescope, plasma analyzer, and other devices for collecting, storing, and reporting data. After a trip of about 18 weeks, *Mariner 10* began taking pictures of the planet, while it was still about 3.3 million miles (5.3 million km) from the planet's surface. Four days later, it began taking pictures at a rate of about one every 42 seconds, resulting in a total of about 4,000 pictures of the planet. Mariner's closest approach to Mercury was at an altitude of about 3,600 miles (5,790 km).

The scientific equipment and analytical techniques available to researchers in the early 1970s were still too primitive to allow a detailed analysis of the chemical composition of the planet's surface or its atmosphere, but the pictures obtained during the flyby gave an extraordinary look at Mercury's surface features. They confirmed that the planet has a somewhat Moonlike appearance, with basins, craters, scarps, ridges, *highlands,* and plains. The largest basin on the planet, named Caloris, has a diameter of about 800 miles (1,300 km) across, making it about equal in size to the Moon's Mare Imbrium. A number of ray systems, crater chains, and other Moonlike features were also recorded.

More than 30 years have passed since the *Mariner 10* mission, but this does not mean that scientists have learned nothing new about Mercury since then. Knowledge of the planet has continued to grow because of two factors. First, ground-based telescopes and spectroscopes have greatly improved in their sensitivity, and they have provided significant new information about the chemical composition of Mercury's atmosphere and surface. For example, researchers at the Lunar and Planetary Sciences Laboratory (LPSL) of the University of Arizona have used the 1.5-meter Catalina Observatory planetary telescope to obtain new and more precise data about the planet's atmosphere. During the early 2000s, LPSL researchers reported more detailed information about the concentration of sodium in Mercury's atmosphere and published the first reports of the presence of potassium there.

Second, much of Mariner's original data has been reanalyzed, using new technology, to squeeze out additional information about the planet. Leaders in this research have been Mark S. Robinson, formerly with the U.S. Geological Survey in Flagstaff, Arizona, and now at Northwestern University, and Paul G. Lucey, at the University of Hawaii's Hawaii Institute of Geophysics and Planetology. Robinson and Lucey have used new techniques of computer analysis and image processing to convert Mariner's black-and-white photographs into color images that provide valuable new information about the structure and chemical composition of Mercury's surface. In combination, these studies have provided a moderately good understanding of the nature of the planet's atmosphere and surface composition.

Because of its closeness to the Sun, Mercury would not be able to maintain an atmosphere comparable to that of any other planet.

Atmospheric pressure is thought to be about 10^{-15} that of the Earth's atmosphere. Its primary components appear to be oxygen, helium, and sodium, although some recent studies have also found traces of potassium. The source of these elements in the atmosphere is of some interest. They are probably thrown off the planet's surface when meteorites collide with the planet, disintegrate, and release their components into the atmosphere. Thus, the planet's thin atmosphere is constantly regenerating itself: New particles are added by *meteorite* collisions while existing particles are being blown off by solar radiation. Some astronomers are suggesting, however, that the oxygen, sodium, and potassium found in the atmosphere may also be produced during the breakdown of rocky material on the planet's surface. If true, this phenomenon might provide further insight into the structure of the planetary surface and the planet's origin.

The Robinson-Lucey analysis has also provided information about the chemical composition of Mercury's surface and near-surface regions. It appears from this study that the chemical composition of the planet's surface differs from point to point, although the specific chemicals present cannot yet be determined. For example, some parts of the surface appear to be richer in compounds of iron and titanium, while others contain smaller amounts of these elements. Information about subsurface regions comes from Mariner photographs of craters that have been converted to color images. Differences in shading from the top of craters down the slope to the bottom of the craters suggest that different minerals are present at varying depths from the planet's surface.

Terrestrial studies have provided additional information about the chemical composition of the surface. LPSL researchers, for example, have analyzed the infrared spectra of light reflected from the planet's surface and identified chemical species that may be present on the planet. One report, by Ann L. Sprague, R. W. H. Kozlowski, and Fred C. Witteborn, "strongly suggests the presence of plagioclase, in particular labradorite, while the overall spectrum resembles anorthosite," based on the spectra observed. Plagioclase and anorthosite belong to a class of minerals known as silicates, which contain large percentages of silicon and oxygen. The Sprague paper reported that the silicon dioxide content of the rocks they studied appeared to be in the range of 49 to 55 percent. These results conform with most other studies of the planet's surface, indicating that it consists largely of silicate rocks with small amounts of iron oxide and lesser amounts of titanium.

Perhaps the most interesting and surprising discovery about Mercury's surface is the possible presence of ice caps at the planet's north and south poles. The first evidence for this discovery came as the result of studies conducted by researchers at NASA's Jet Propulsion Laboratory in Pasadena, California. The researchers bounced radar signals off the planet's north polar region and analyzed the reflected beams at the Very Large Array radio telescope system in New Mexico. They found that the spectra of the reflected beams were very similar to those for water ice. Since they first reported this result in 1991, further studies have been conducted to determine whether the poles really do contain water ice, although final confirmation has not yet been obtained.

The presence of water ice at the planet's poles would be quite remarkable in view of the fact that the planet's surface temperature is about 700 K at midday. Because Mercury is so close to the Sun, astronomers seldom considered the possibility that frozen materials of any kind could exist on the planet's surface. It appears, however, that the craters in which the purported water ice exists are deep enough to shield them from solar radiation, allowing them to remain in a solid state for extended periods of time.

At this point, virtually nothing is known for certain about the interior of the planet. Most scientists, however, believe that the surface and mantle are underlain by a large core made primarily of iron and nickel. The presence of a magnetic field around Mercury supports that hypothesis.

Clearly, much remains to be learned about Mercury. Both NASA and the European Space Agency have developed plans for new space missions to the planet to collect additional information. One such program is NASA's project, *MESSENGER* (for MErcury Space ENvironment, GEochemistry and Ranging), launched on August 3, 2004. It carries gamma-ray, neutron, X-ray, energetic particle, and plasma spectrometers; an altimeter; magnetometer; a dual-imaging system; and other data-collecting and reporting systems. The spacecraft is expected to make two flybys of the planet, in January and October 2008 and September 2009. Two years later, in March 2011, it will settle into an orbit around the planet. *MESSENGER* has a number of scientific objectives, including studies of the polar ice caps, the outer regions of the planet's atmosphere, the composition of the crust and mantle, the geologic evolution of the planet, and the planet's magnetic properties.

Shortly after *MESSENGER* reaches Mercury, ESA will launch its own spacecraft to the planet, *BepiColombo*. This spacecraft is named after the Italian physicist Giuseppe (Bepi) Colombo (1920–84) who made extensive studies of Mercury's orbital and rotational properties. *BepiColombo* has three major components: a planetary orbiter, a magnetospheric orbiter, and a surface lander. Launch is scheduled for August 2013.

Venus

Knowledge of Venus is far more advanced than that of Mercury. Indeed, the first reliable evidence about the chemical characteristics of the planet dates from the early 1930s. At that time, two American astronomers, Walter S. Adams (1876–1928) and Theodore Dunham, Jr. (1897–1984), were engaged in a spectroscopic analysis of the Venusian atmosphere. From light collected at the Mount Wilson Observatory, in Pasadena, California, Adams and Dunham concluded that the planet's atmosphere consisted largely of carbon dioxide. They found no evidence for the existence of water on the planet—somewhat to their surprise. The surprise was occasioned by a long-standing tradition that Venus and Earth were "sister planets" that must be similar in many respects, including chemical composition.

Three decades later, however, water was discovered in the Venusian atmosphere. At that point, spectrometers carried by high-altitude balloons detected small quantities of water on the planet. Values measured for the abundance of water ranged from 1 to 100 ppm but were, in any case, very much less than those found in Earth's atmosphere (which range anywhere from 0 to 4 percent).

Modern understanding of both atmospheric and surface chemistry of Venus has expanded considerably as the result of two dozen space voyages to the planet, carried out between 1961 and 1990. Sixteen of these voyages were part of the Soviet Union's Venera program. The first spacecraft in that series—and the first interplanetary spacecraft ever to be launched—was launched on February 12, 1961. The last mission in the series were the *Venera 15* and *16* spacecrafts, launched on June 2 and June 7, 1983. Some of these missions provided the most complete information about Venus ever obtained, while others were lost over the course of their missions or flew by the planet at such great distances as to produce no useful data.

The United States has launched nine spacecraft in the direction of Venus. Three of these were part of the Mariner series (*2, 5,* and *10*) and two were part of the Pioneer Venus program in 1978. Two more were part of the Vega series, in which balloons were dropped into the planet's atmosphere. Another was the Magellan spacecraft of 1989–90, and the last one was part of the Galileo mission of the same period.

The U.S. and Soviet missions experienced a wide range of success. The first Venera flight, for example, never got any closer than 60,000 miles (100,000 km) from the planet, obtaining little information of value. *Venera 3* landed successfully on the planet's surface, but its instruments were destroyed on impact, and no data were obtained from the trip. Most other missions produced at least some useful information, however, and many provided a host of data that is yet to be completely processed and analyzed.

One such is *Venera 4,* launched on June 12, 1967. It reached the planet on October 18 and dropped an instrument package containing two thermometers, a barometer, a radio altimeter, an atmospheric density gauge, 11 gas analyzers, and two radio transmitters. Data collected by these instruments were transmitted to the space vehicle "bus" parked in orbit around the planet and then sent on back to Earth. After completing the transmission, the bus deployed a parachute to reduce its speed. It then descended into the Venusian atmosphere to an altitude of 15.51 miles (24.96 km), at which point communications were lost.

In one of the most recent missions to Venus, NASA launched the *Magellan* spacecraft toward the planet from the space shuttle

Atlantis in May 1989. Over an eight-month period, Magellan mapped 84 percent of the planet's surface with a resolution of 984 feet (300 m). Twenty percent of the maps were obtained in stereo (three-dimensional) images. At the completion of its lifetime on October 11, 1994, *Magellan* plunged into the Venusian atmosphere, continuing to collect data on the atmosphere's composition during its descent.

The mission to Venus, by the *Galileo* spacecraft in 1989–90, produced relatively modest new data. The mission's primary objective was the planet Jupiter, and a visit to Venus was included only to provide a "gravity assist"—a way to give the spacecraft the impetus it needed to get to the outer planet. During its closest approach of about 10,000 miles (16,000 km) from the planet, however, *Galileo* was able to carry out additional spectroscopic studies of Venus's clouds, collect photographs of its middle atmosphere clouds, and analyze radioactive sources present in the clouds.

The most recent mission to Venus is the European Space Agency's *Venus Express* spacecraft, launched on November 5, 2005. The spacecraft reached the planet in April 2006 and settled into orbit on May 6. It has now transmitted some of the best images of and data about the planet's atmosphere ever obtained, including the first images ever of its south pole. Among the new data transmitted by Venus Express are the chemical composition of the lower atmosphere, temperature variations at different levels of the atmosphere, temperature measurements of the planet's surface, and reactions between oxygen and nitrogen oxides in the middle and upper atmosphere.

On the basis of both terrestrial and spacecraft studies, a relatively good understanding of the nature of the Venusian atmosphere and, to a lesser extent, the planet's surface is now available. For example, scientists have confirmed that the primary components of the atmosphere are carbon dioxide (about 96.5 percent) and nitrogen (about 3.5 percent), with much smaller amounts of many other gases. Current estimates for the composition of the Venusian atmosphere are shown in the chart on pages 98–99. The values given in this table are subject to some doubt because different missions have produced somewhat different values. Also, the concentration of some gases appears to vary with altitude. For example, some of the probes dropped by spacecraft have measured water concentrations ranging from as low as 10 ppm near the planet's surface to about 200 ppm at an altitude of about 30 miles (50 km).

As the chart shows, gases in the Venusian atmosphere come from four major sources. First, inert gases such as helium, neon, and argon are probably remnants of the planet's early formation. A second and major source for many gases is escape from fissures in the planet's surface, a process known as *outgassing*. A third source of atmospheric gases is weathering of rocks and minerals on the planet's surface. For example, when carbonates and sulfates break down, they release carbon dioxide and sulfur dioxide, respectively. Finally, a few gases are formed during chemical reactions in the atmosphere. For example, the *photolysis* (light-catalyzed reactions) of carbon dioxide results in the formation of carbon monoxide.

The total density of gases in the Venusian atmosphere is much greater than that of gases in Earth's atmosphere. Overall, they are responsible for an atmospheric pressure that is roughly 90 times that of Earth's atmosphere. Variations in temperature and pressure in the Venusian atmosphere, as measured during the 1991 Magellan mission, are shown in the graphs on pages 100 and 101.

Venus's atmosphere is predominantly a combination of clouds and haze that extends from an altitude of about 18 miles (30 km) above the planet's surface to an altitude of more than 50 miles (80 km). Its structure appears to consist of three parts. Closest to the surface is a haze of roughly constant density, extending from the bottom of the cloud to an altitude of about 18 miles (30 km). Next is the most obvious layer, a fairly dense, sharply defined cloud at an altitude of about 30 miles (50 km). This cloud consists primarily of droplets of sulfuric acid. Finally, a haze that gradually becomes thinner with altitude is located above the middle cloud to an altitude of about 50 miles (80 km). The density of the Venusian cloud structure at various altitudes is shown in the graph on page 102.

A comparison of the atmospheres of Earth and Venus can shed light on the processes of planetary evolution. Scientists tend to believe that the two planets were created with relatively similar structures. Hydrogen, helium, and other light gases present during their formation were probably blown away early in the history of both planets by solar radiation. The present-day atmospheres of both

◄ **COMPOSITION OF THE VENUSIAN ATMOSPHERE** ▷

GAS	ABUNDANCE	SOURCE(S)	SINK(S)
CO_2	96.5±0.8%	outgassing	carbonates
N_2	3.5±0.8%	outgassing	
SO_2	150±30 ppm* (22–42 km)	outgassing and reduction of H_2S and OCS	H_2SO_4 and $CaSO_4$
H_2O	30±15 ppm* (0–45 km)	outgassing	oxidation of Fe^{2+} and loss of H
Ar	31 ppm	outgassing and primordial	
CO	45±10 ppm* (50 km)	photolysis of CO_2	photooxidation to CO_2
He	0.6–12 ppm	outgassing from radioactive minerals	escape
Ne	7±3 ppm	outgassing and primordial	
Ar	5.5 ppm	outgassing and primordial	

GAS	ABUNDANCE	SOURCE(S)	SINK(S)
OCS	4.4±1 ppm* (33 km)	outgassing and weathering of sulfates	conversion to SO_2
H_2S	3±2 ppm (<20 km)	outgassing and weathering of sulfates	conversion to SO_2
HDO	1.3±0.2 ppm* (<50 km)	outgassing	escape as H
HCl	0.6±0.12 ppm* (top of clouds)	outgassing	formation of chloride minerals
Kr	25 ppb	outgassing and primordial	
SO	20±10 ppb* (top of clouds)	photochemical reactions	photo-chemical conversions
S	20 ppb (<50 km)	weathering of sulfide mineral	conversion to SO_2
HF	5 ppb	outgassing	formation of fluoride minerals

*Abundance of these species depends on altitude. Values given are maxima for altitudes noted.

Source: Adapted from Bruce Fegley, Jr., "Venus," Table 3, in A. M. Davis, ed. *Treatise on Geochemistry*. New York: Elsevier, 2004.

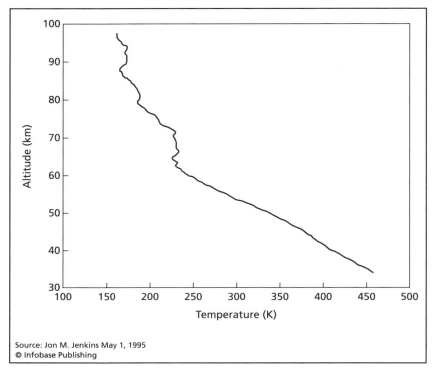

Temperature profile of the Venusian atmosphere

planets were produced by outgassing during volcanic eruptions and outflows. This outgassing probably released carbon dioxide, water vapor, and nitrogen (but little or no oxygen) to the planets' atmospheres. Scientists believe that the quantities of these gases escaping from the planets' interiors were roughly the same for both Venus and Earth.

On Earth, carbon dioxide was removed from the atmosphere over long periods of time, primarily as the result of the formation of carbonate rocks in the Earth's crust, a process catalyzed by water. As living organisms appeared and evolved on Earth's surface, they contributed to the removal of carbon dioxide—plants through the process of photosynthesis, aquatic animals by incorporating it into their shells. In addition, Earth's average annual temperature was sufficient to allow water vapor to condense into liquid water, resulting in the formation of the oceans. Consequently, Earth's atmosphere contains relatively modest amounts of carbon dioxide and water vapor. When the carbon dioxide and water that are trapped in the lithosphere and hydrosphere are taken into account, the *total amount* of these two compounds is approximately the same on Earth as on Venus.

On Venus, however, the two compounds experienced different conditions. Since Venus is closer to the Sun, temperatures are higher than on Earth, preventing the formation of liquid water and allowing the escape of outgassed water vapor into space. In the absence of water vapor, the conversion of carbon dioxide to carbonates is much more difficult, if not impossible. As a result, carbon dioxide outgassed from the planet's surface simply remained in the atmosphere, accumulating to its modern-day very high levels.

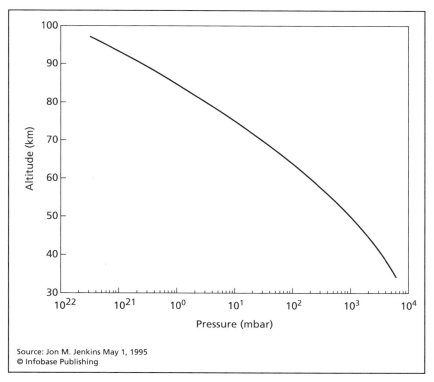

Source: Jon M. Jenkins May 1, 1995
© Infobase Publishing

Pressure profile of the Venusian atmosphere

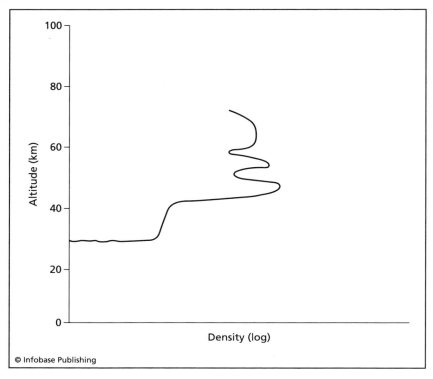

Density profile of the Venusian atmosphere

High temperatures trapped a great deal of carbon dioxide in Venus's atmosphere; the carbon dioxide, in turn, trapped heat in the atmosphere. As is well known, carbon dioxide is an important greenhouse gas, capable of trapping infrared radiation (heat) released from a planet's surface. The primary difference in atmospheric temperatures between Venus and Earth is the very large amount of heat trapped in Venus's atmosphere by the large concentrations of carbon dioxide. Earth's atmosphere, by contrast, contains relatively small amounts of heat trapped by its correspondingly small concentrations of carbon dioxide.

In fact, the conditions on Venus today are sometimes described as the result of a "runaway greenhouse effect." The planet's surface temperature of about 730 K (430°C) cannot be explained simply on the basis of the heat it receives from the Sun. Indeed, it is warmer on Venus than Mercury, even though Venus is more distant from the Sun. The additional heat retained by the planet is largely a result of the accumulation of carbon dioxide in its atmosphere.

Some of the most interesting hypotheses about the Venusian atmosphere have to do with the possible existence of life there. Given the inhospitable conditions in the atmosphere, especially the clouds of sulfuric acid and the absence of water, most scientists have viewed the likelihood of finding life there as remote, at best.

In the early 2000s, however, some scientists suggested that some types of microscopic life may, indeed, be able to survive in the Venusian atmosphere. Some of the strongest proponents of a Venusian microbe theory have been Dirk Shulze-Makuch and Louis Irwin at the University of Texas at El Paso (UTEP). The UTEP researchers have pointed to the presence of both hydrogen sulfide and sulfur dioxide in proximity to each other in the planet's upper atmosphere as evidence for the existence of microorganisms in the Venusian atmosphere. Normally, those two gases tend to react with and destroy each other. About the only condition under which they remain in equilibrium on Earth is when both are being produced by anaerobic bacteria.

Shulze-Makuch and Irwin also suggest that the presence of microbes may explain the unexpectedly low concentration of carbon monoxide in the Venusian atmosphere. One would normally expect a greater abundance of this gas, they say, because lightning and solar radiation tend to break down carbon dioxide into carbon monoxide and other products; perhaps microbes have evolved a mechanism for using carbon monoxide as a raw material in their metabolism. Shulze-Makuch and Irwin are hoping that ESA's *Venus Express* mission will provide additional data that will help resolve the question of whether even the simplest form of life can exist on Venus.

The many expeditions to Venus have also produced a good deal of information about the planet's surface and interior structure and composition. The overall structure of the planet is probably similar to that of Earth, consisting of a large central core about 2,000 miles (3,000 km) in radius, made of liquid iron and nickel. The core is probably surrounded by a molten mantle, consisting of rocky material that is, in turn, covered by a thin, solid outer surface. Many planetologists believe that the single most characteristic feature of the planet is its vulcanism. One researcher working on the Magellan project, Charles Ginenthal, has described Venus's vulcanism as even greater than that of Mars: "Everyone says Olympus Mons on Mars is the biggest volcano in the solar system," said Ginenthal. "It isn't; Venus is. The entire planet is one big volcano."

The number of volcanoes on the Venusian surface is truly astounding. NASA has estimated that there may be as many as a million volcanic centers with diameters of a kilometer or more on the planet's surface. More than 1,000 of these volcanoes are thought to have diameters of 12 miles (20 km) or more. Although many of these volcanoes are extinct, most are still active, spewing out gases that make up the current Venusian atmosphere.

One indication of the planet's active vulcanism is the relative smoothness of its surface. Although it is possible to pick out many characteristic features of a volcanic landscape, such as craters, rifts, and surface cracks, about 80 percent of the planet's surface is covered with smooth plains of frozen lava. This fact indicates relatively recent outflows of magma that have covered older features.

Another indication of vulcanism is the lack of meteoritic craters that one would expect to find on the surface of any *terrestrial planet*. Such craters are formed when meteors collide with a planet's surface. They are clearly visible on Mars and Mercury; although less clearly visible on Earth, craters are still evident in some areas of the planet's surface. On Venus, however, such craters are largely invisible because (as scientists believe) they have been filled in and otherwise covered up by constant lava flows from the planet's many volcanoes.

One of the most intriguing bits of data about vulcanism on Venus has been reported by Larry Esposito, at the University of Colorado's Laboratory for Atmospheric and Space Physics. Using data obtained from the *Hubble Space Telescope*, Esposito found that the abundance of sulfur dioxide at the top of the Venusian cloud layer in 1995 was about 20 times less than it had been when measured during the 1978 visit by the *Pioneer Venus Orbiter* spacecraft. He compared these results with some of the earliest measurements of sulfur dioxide made on the planet dating to the early 1970s. At that point, the abundance

The false-color image of Venus's 5-mile (8-km) high Maat Mons was constructed from data transmitted by the *Magellan* spacecraft. (NASA/Photo Researchers, Inc.)

of the compound in the planet's upper atmosphere was even lower than it is today.

Esposito's explanation for these changing values is that an enormous volcanic explosion occurred on Venus in the early 1970s. The explosion, he says, may have been at least as large as the massive 1883 eruption of Krakatoa, a volcano in the Indonesia islands. An explosion of that size, Esposito says, would have released huge amounts of sulfur dioxide that eventually reached the planet's upper atmosphere. Over time, however, the sulfur dioxide would have begun falling back to the surface and changing form, to sulfuric acid, for instance, resulting in the decreases in concentration observed over the two-decade period during which measurements were being made.

Data about the chemical composition of Venus's surface come from a number of sources. For example, the planet's surface is so hot that it radiates energy in the infrared range with an intensity that can be detected from Earth and from spacecraft orbiting

Venus. Reports of the chemical composition of the surface and near-surface regions of the planet, as measured by Earth-based instruments, were reported as early as the mid-1990s. The *Galileo* and *Cassini* spacecraft collected similar data in the 1 mm region of the EM spectrum during their flybys of the planet in 1990 and 1998, respectively.

The most direct information about the planet's surface comes from several Soviet Venera landers that reached the surface and conducted a number of surveys before they were destroyed by the planet's inhospitable climate. *Venera 8, 9, 10, 13,* and *14* all successfully landed on Venus and sent back at least some data on its chemical composition. All but the first of these probes also transmitted images of the planet's surface.

The most complete and reliable data about the chemical composition of the Venusian surface comes from three Soviet missions, the *Venera 13, Venera 14,* and *Vega 2* probes. These spacecraft actually reached the planet's surface and conducted studies of elements and compounds present on the planet's surface. In a typical experiment, one of the lander's tools would drill a hole into the planet's surface about 1.2 inches (3 cm) deep and extract a sample about 1 cm^3 in volume. The chart on page 110 summarizes data obtained from these three missions and gives the composition of Earth's continental crust for purposes of comparison. Notice that the major differences in crustal composition between the two planets appears to be in the relative abundance of SiO_2 (45.6 percent on Venus compared with 60.2 percent on Earth) and of MgO (about 11.5 percent on Venus compared with 3.1 percent on Earth). Otherwise, the two planets do indeed appear to be almost "sister planets," at least with regard to the composition of their outer crusts.

Scientists are particularly interested in the interactions that may be taking place on Venus between materials in the atmosphere and those contained in surface minerals. The very high temperature and pressure at the planet's surface may increase the rates of such interactions, which on Earth are relatively modest. Scientists have studied a number of reactions that would control the rate at which atmospheric or surface components—or both—are generated and removed. The so-called Urey reaction is an example. In the Urey reaction, carbon dioxide in the atmosphere reacts with calcium silicate in the planet's crust, forming calcium carbonate and silica:

$$CaSiO_3 + CO_2 \rightarrow CaCO_3 + SiO_2$$

The Urey reaction is significant on Earth because it is thought to be one way in which carbon dioxide is removed from the atmosphere; thus, it may influence climate change. It may be that a similar reaction takes place on Venus, likewise controlling the concentration of carbon dioxide in the Venusian atmosphere. As yet, however, there are no data to suggest that carbonates exist in abundance on the planet's surface.

Another reaction scientists have studied is that between carbon dioxide in the atmosphere and iron and iron oxide on the planet's surface. A key reaction would be the following:

$$CO_2 + Fe \rightarrow FeO + CO$$

This reaction can take place, however, only if the concentration of carbon monoxide is about twice that of carbon dioxide. This condition is clearly not possible in an atmosphere that is nearly pure CO_2. Thus it seems unlikely or impossible that pure iron exists on Venus's surface.

Shortly after the discovery of hydrogen chloride and hydrogen fluoride in the Venusian atmosphere in 1967, chemists begin to investigate possible atmospheric/surface interactions that would buffer (control) the amount of both gases in the atmosphere. One of the hypothesized reactions involves the interaction of HCl with the mineral nepheline ($NaAlSiO_4$), as follows:

$$9NaAlSiO_4(g) + 2HCl(g) \rightarrow Al_2O_3(g) + NaAlSi_3O_8(s) + 2Na_4(AlSiO_4)_3Cl(s) + H_2O(g)$$

At this point, it is impossible to assess the likelihood of this, or almost any other hypothesized reaction. The problem is that scientists still lack sufficient data to build models about the structure and composition of Venus's atmosphere and surface and of possible chemical interactions among the components of both. It is for this reason that Venus scholars look forward so eagerly to the results of the Venus Express mission currently under way. The results of that mission should provide much of the data needed about Venus's atmosphere

◄ THE *HUBBLE SPACE TELESCOPE* ►

Thank goodness for our atmosphere! Without the blanket of air that surrounds our planet, human life would probably be impossible on Earth. The atmosphere has its disadvantages also, especially for astronomers interested in finding out more about our solar system and space beyond. A large fraction of the light emitted by stars and reflected by planets and other bodies in the solar system is diffracted or absorbed by molecules of nitrogen, oxygen, carbon dioxide, and other gases that make up the atmosphere. Looking at the stars and the planets through Earth-based telescopes is a bit like looking through a window that has not been washed for many years. One can get a rough, general idea as to what the "outside world" (the universe) looks like, but the details are often difficult to make out.

Today, the idea of sending a telescope into orbit around the Earth, far above the interfering effects of the atmosphere, may seem obvious, but not so long ago, the concept of an orbiting telescope would have seemed absurd. To astronomers in the mid-20th century, the most basic question would simply have been: How does one get the telescope *into* space? Recall that the first space vehicles launched from Earth did not go into orbit until the mid-1950s.

So it is a bit surprising that the first suggestions for an orbiting telescope were proposed as early as 1946, a decade before the first space vehicles had left Earth's surface. In that year, the American astronomer Lyman Spitzer (1914–97) proposed the construction of a space telescope that could observe the planets, stars, and other astronomical bodies with greater clarity than any Earth-based instrument.

Although Spitzer and some of his colleagues argued strongly for an orbiting astronomical laboratory, the idea did not become a reality until the mid-1970s, when the National Aeronautics and Space Administration (NASA) and the European Space Agency (ESA) signed an agreement to design, build, and launch an orbiting telescope. The U.S. Congress allocated funds for the project two years later and chose the Lockheed Martin Aerospace Company as prime contractor for the project. Six years later, planners decided to name the telescope after the famous American astronomer Edwin Powell Hubble (1889–1953). Hubble found that galaxies are moving away from Earth at a speed that is proportional to their distance from Earth, showing that the universe is expanding. Hubble's research was a key piece of information in support of the big bang theory of cosmology.

The Hubble Space Telescope (HST) sprang to life on April 24, 1990, when it was launched into orbit from the Space Shuttle Discovery. Astronomers' great expectations for their new instrument were dashed almost immediately when the first pictures sent back by the HST were found to be defective. Scientists soon discovered that the telescope's giant mirror had been ground incorrectly. Although the flaw was minuscule (1.3 mm in the 239-cm mirror), it was enough to cause distortions of images captured by the mirror and returned to Earth.

Fearful of losing their $1.5 billion investment in the HST, astronomers set to work designing a "corrective lens" for the telescope. That lens was installed on the Hubble during the Space Shuttle Endeavour's mission of December 1993. The "corrective lens," called COSTAR (for Corrective Optics Space Telescope Axial Replacement), cost $50 million, but when tested it proved to work perfectly. With its new "contact lens" in place, the HST began to function perfectly, sending photographs of outer space, galaxies, stars, planets, and other objects far better than any Earth-based instrument had been able to achieve.

Today, the HST has accumulated a track record that far exceeds that of any other astronomical instrument and even the most optimistic hopes of its inventors and controllers. Each day, the telescope sends back 3 to 5 gigabytes of data, enough to fill the average home computer. It has made more than 330,000 separate observations of more than 25,000 astronomical targets, including stars, galaxies, planets, comets, and just about every other kind of astronomical object known to science. The HST has provided data for more than 2,700 scientific papers and produced an archive of more than 7.3 terabytes to keep astronomers busy for years into the future.

Current plans call for decommissioning of the HST in 2010, a year before it is scheduled to be replaced by NASA's new James Webb Space Telescope. In order to keep the HST in the best possible condition, anywhere from one to three maintenance trips are planned, probably to be carried out by a space shuttle. A number of astronomers are arguing for keeping the HST in orbit beyond 2010, however. They point to the instrument's numerous accomplishments and suggest that it still has much to contribute to the advancement of astronomical knowledge.

Additional information about the Hubble Space Telescope is available on Web sites maintained both by NASA (http://hubble.nasa.gov/) and by ESA (http://hubble.esa.int/).

◁ COMPOSITION OF THE VENUSIAN SURFACE (REPORTED AS ELEMENTAL OXIDE, BY MASS PERCENT) ▷

OXIDE	VENERA 13	VENERA 14	VEGA 2	EARTH
SiO_2	45.1	48.7	45.6	60.2
Al_2O_3	15.8	17.9	16	15.2
MgO	11.4	8.1	11.5	3.1
CaO	7.1	10.3	7.5	5.5
FeO	9.3	8.8	7.7	6.0
K_2O	4.0	0.2	0.1	2.9
TiO_2	1.6	1.2	0.2	0.7
MnO	0.2	0.16	0.14	0.1
Na_2O	2.0	2.4	2.0	3.2

Sources: Adapted from Bruce Fegley, Jr., "Venus," Table 6, in A. M. Davis, ed., *Treatise on Geochemistry.* New York: Elsevier, 2004, and David R. Williams, "Preliminary Mars Pathfinder APXS Results," http://nssdc.gsfc.nasa.gov/ planetary/marspath/apxs_table1.html. For more detailed information on terrestrial data, see Taylor, S. R., and S. M. McLennan, 1985: *The Continental Crust: Its Composition and Evolution.* Blackwell Scientific Publications, 1985.

to evaluate existing theories and make possible additional hypotheses about the chemical composition and reactions occurring on the planet.

Mars

Mars has intrigued humans for centuries. While Venus has long been regarded as Earth's "sister planet," Mars is the planet thought most likely to have (or to have had) some kind of life. To space enthusiasts, it is also the planet most likely to be hospitable to human colonies at some time in the future.

The first sketches of Mars that can be said to be at all scientific were made by the Dutch astronomer and physicist Christiaan Huygens (1629–95) in 1659. Huygens built a telescope about 50 times better than any used before for astronomical observations. Using it, he observed a large red spot on the planet's surface that was later given the name of the "Hourglass Sea." The object is known today as a Syrtis Major. By observing the position of the spot as the planet rotated, Huygens determined that Mars rotates on its own axis once about every 24 hours.

The first report of "white spots" at the planet's poles was announced in 1666 by the Italian astronomer Giovanni Domenico Cassini (1625–1712). Some years later, Cassini's nephew Giacomo Filippo Maraldi (1665–1729) suggested that the white spots first noted by his uncle might be interpreted as ice caps, similar to those found at Earth's North and South Poles.

The 19th century was a period when astronomers and nonscientists tried to make some sense of the surface features they were seeing on Mars. Stargazers reported often-vague observations. In many cases, the speculations that arose in response reflected an individual's desire to see objects or phenomena on the planet at least as much as they did the actual scientific observations.

Perhaps the most famous stories of the period center on the possible existence of "canals" on Mars, features that would certainly suggest to Earthlings the existence of intelligent life on the planet. The dreams of Martian canals was based on maps of the planets first drawn by Pietro Angelo Secchi (1818–78), a Jesuit monk and director of the Roman College Observatory. Secchi called the large red spot first seen by Huygens the "Atlantic 'canal'." He used the Italian word *canali* in his description, a word that means "channel," not "canal." When Giovanni Virginio Schiaparelli (1835–1910) director of the Brera Observatory in Milan, proposed a new system for naming features on the Martian surface in 1877, he also used the word *canali* extensively.

Many people who did not speak Italian assumed that Schiaparelli was talking about "canals," presumably made by intelligent beings, and with that interpretation came a flood of speculation, both scientific and literary, about the possibility that life existed on Mars, or that it had existed there at some time in the past. The debate over the possibility of life on Mars is one that continues, although in greatly reduced terms, to the present day.

The first attempts to study the Martian atmosphere by spectroscopic means were carried out in 1867, by the French astronomer by Pierre Jules Janssen (1824–1907) and the English astronomer Sir William Huggins (1824–1910). The two scientists were unable to detect the presence of any elements or compounds in their research, however. More than four decades later, the American astronomer W. W. Campbell (1862–1938) searched the Martian atmosphere for water vapor and, failing to find any, concluded that the planet had a much thinner atmosphere than that of Earth, a hypothesis that proved to be correct.

In fact, it was not until 1947 that any gas was identified in the Martian atmosphere by spectroscopic means. In that year, the Dutch astronomer Gerard Peter Kuiper (1905–73) found that the concentration of carbon dioxide in the planet's atmosphere was about twice as great as that in the Earth's atmosphere. Even then, however, astronomers did not realize the importance of carbon dioxide in the Martian atmosphere, assuming that other gases might be present in greater abundance.

An important clue to the role of water on Mars was obtained, again by spectroscopic means, in 1963 by Lewis Kaplan (1928–99) and his colleagues at the Jet Propulsion Laboratory in Pasadena. The JPL team reported that the amount of water in the Martian atmosphere could be expressed as 14 ± 7 "precipitable microns." The term *precipitable microns* (μm ppt H_2O) is a measure of the depth of water that would form on the planet's surface if all of the moisture in the atmosphere could be made to condense out. The amount of water Kaplan's team detected on Mars is less than 10^{-3} that found over the driest desert on Earth.

Kaplan and later researchers also found that the abundance of water in the Martian atmosphere is a function both of location on the planet and season. The highest concentrations of water vapor measured for the planet's atmosphere are just less than 500 μm ppt H_2O during the planet's winter and less than 10 μm ppt H_2O during its summer. Water concentrations tend to be highest over the polar caps and lowest at the planet's equator, where it may reach such low values as to be unmeasurable.

Astronomers finally had firm evidence that the Martian atmosphere was both very thin and very dry. In fact, scientists now know that the density of the Martian atmosphere (and, hence, its atmospheric pressure) is about 8 millibars, approximately 10^{-2} that on Earth. At that pressure, any water that might exist in open spaces on the planet's surface would almost certainly have escaped into the atmosphere and, from there, into outer space.

One of the surprising discoveries made by the Russian probe *Phobos 2* in 1989 was that Mars's already very thin atmosphere appears to be losing mass at a surprising rate, approximately 1–2 kg per second. A loss of that much mass from a dense atmosphere like Earth's would be insignificant. In the very thin Martian atmosphere, however, it is significant.

The availability of space-based observatories, beginning in the 1960s, provided a new and promising way of collecting further data about the composition of the Martian atmosphere. A number of the early U.S. and USSR flights confirmed earlier Earth-based discoveries and provided new values for previously calculated variables. For example, both USSR Mars and U.S. Mariner spacecraft confirmed the concentrations of carbon dioxide and water vapor in the planet's atmosphere, and Mariner confirmed the general distribution of water vapor at various locations above the planet's surface and at various seasons.

Space-based observatories were particularly useful for measuring small concentrations of gases on Mars that might not be detectable from Earth-based observatories. In 1969, Kaplan and his colleagues at the JPL discovered carbon dioxide on Mars; its presence and abundance were further confirmed by the *Mariner 6* and *Mariner 7* spacecrafts launched in the same year. In addition to carbon monoxide, the Mariner probes also found clouds made of carbon dioxide ice and water ice, ionized hydrogen, and ionized oxygen in the Martian atmosphere. Significantly, they failed to find evidence for the presence of either oxygen or nitrogen, the two primary gases in the Earth's atmosphere.

Partly because of their importance in Earth's atmosphere, the role of oxygen and nitrogen in the Martian atmosphere have long been of special interest to astronomers. Before 1969, many scholars had assumed that the planets were enough alike that their atmospheres would have relatively similar compositions. In 1950, for example, the distinguished expert on Mars Gérard de Vaucouleurs (1918–95) estimated that the Martian atmosphere, like Earth's atmosphere, consisted primarily of nitrogen (98.5 percent), with argon (1.2 percent), carbon dioxide (0.25 percent), and oxygen (less than 0.1 percent) making up the rest of the atmosphere.

The only solid evidence for the presence of nitrogen in the Martian atmosphere, however, comes from the Viking landers, which between 1976 and 1982 collected samples of Martian air just above the surface and conducted relatively imprecise studies of its composition. The results of those experiments are generally regarded as the most reliable indications of the composition of the Martian atmosphere. The chart on page 116 provides a summary of those data. Notice that, in contrast to the hopes and expectations of many generations of astronomers, nitrogen and oxygen make up only a very small proportion of the Martian atmosphere, while carbon dioxide (as on Venus) constitutes more than 95 percent of the atmosphere.

Scientists have developed models for the interior structure of Mars, based largely on its density of 3.93 g/cm^3. This density is significantly less than that of Earth (5.515 g/cm^3), suggesting the presence of a smaller core, possibly containing lesser amounts of heavy metals, such as iron and nickel. The most widely accepted model of the planet's interior is one that has a central core with a radius of about 930–1,000 miles (1,500–1,600 km), consisting of a mixture of pure iron, iron oxide, and iron sulfide. The planet's crust is thought to be no more than about 60–120 miles (100–200 km) thick, with a composition similar to that of Earth's crust, containing significant amounts of iron-bearing silicates. The mantle occupies the space between core and crust, with a thickness of about 1,100 miles (1,800 km). The chemical composition of the mantle is thought to be similar to that of the crust, which forms as a result of outflowing and cooling of mantle materials.

As is the case with the Martian atmosphere, scientists repeatedly tried to determine the chemical composition of Mars's surface long before space-based observatories were available. For example, the German-born American astronomer Rupert Wildt (1905–76) suggested as early as 1934 that the distinctive red color of Mars's surface was caused by iron oxides present in the planet's surface rocks. Spectroscopic studies of light reflected from the planet's surface did not begin, however, until the 1960s. The spectral lines then observed suggested the presence of at least two oxides of iron, goethite ($FeO[OH]$) and hematite (Fe_2O_3).

The best firsthand data about the chemical composition of Martian soils come from two space missions, the Viking Project, launched in 1975, and the Mars Pathfinder, launched in 1996. The Viking Project's two Landers carried X-ray fluorescence spectroscopes with which to analyze soil for silicon, aluminum, iron, magnesium, calcium, and other important elements thought to be present. They were not able to detect the presence of hydrogen, carbon, nitrogen, sodium, potassium, or manganese. The general results of the Viking Lander missions are summarized in the chart on page 118.

More complete and better data about the chemical composition of the Martian surface were obtained from the Mars *Pathfinder*'s *Soujourner Rover,* which landed on the planet's surface on July 4, 1997. The chart on pages 119–121 contains data on three soil samples gathered from Mars on this mission (A-2, A-4, and A-5), as well as two Martian rocks, nicknamed "Barnacle Bill" (A-3) and

◁ COMPOSITION OF THE MARTIAN ATMOSPHERE ▷

CHEMICAL SPECIES	ABUNDANCE
CO_2	95.32%
N_2	2.7%
Ar	1.6%
O_2	0.13%
CO	0.08%
H_2O	210 ppm (variable)
NO	100 ppm
Ne	2.5 ppm
HDO	0.85 ppm
Kr	0.3 ppm
Xe	0.08 ppm

Source: "Mars Fact Sheet," available online at http://nssdc.gsfc.nasa.gov/planetary/factsheet/marsfact.html.

"Yogi" (A-7), and compares the elements found in these samples with the elements contained in rocks from Earth.

As the chart shows, the percentage of oxygen and silicon tends to be similar in Mars and Earth rocks, while some elements show greater variation. In particular, the amount of iron and magnesium in Mars rocks and soil samples tends to be significantly lower than in Earth rocks.

Mars has two moons, Phobos and Deimos, discovered by the American astronomer Asaph Hall (1829–1907) in 1877. The moons orbit Mars at a

This image of the Martian rock "Humphrey" shows a hole made by a grinding tool carried on the Mars Exploration Rover *Spirit,* which landed on Mars on January 4, 2004. The grinding process revealed the inner structure of the rock and produced a sample that could be tested for chemical composition. (NASA/JPL/Photo Researchers, Inc.)

distance of 3,720 miles (5,989 km) and 12,400 miles (20,060 km) from the planet's surface. Both have irregular shapes. Phobos's shape can be described technically as a triaxial ellipsoid, a potato-like figure whose length, width, and depth are of three different dimensions, roughly 17 by 13 by 12 miles (27 by 21 by 19 km). Deimos has an irregular shape with dimensions of approximately 10 by 7 by 6 miles (16 by 12 by 10 km). Both moons are thought to be asteroids that became trapped in Mars's gravitational field and began orbiting the planet as natural satellites. Both moons are much too small to have any atmosphere.

Almost nothing can be learned about the two tiny moons from Earth-based observatories. They appear as little more than tiny dots in a telescopic image, and their spectra are contaminated by light

◁ COMPOSITION OF THE MARTIAN SURFACE (BY OXIDE; BY WEIGHT PERCENTAGE)* ▷

OXIDE	VIKING 1 DATA	EARTH (CONTINENTAL CRUST)
SiO_2	43	60.2
FeO	16.2	3.5
Al_2O_3	7.02	15.2
CaO	5.8	5.5
MgO	6.0	3.1
TiO_2	0.6	0.7

*Sources differ as to precise values for each category. These data are taken from Heinrich Wänke, *The Geochemistry of Mars,* available online at http://www.mpch-mainz.mpg.de/~kosmo/members/waenke/opus.htm.

reflected from the Marian surface. Useful information about the two moons was obtained, however, as a result of the Mariner 9 mission in 1971, from the Viking Lander missions of 1976, and from the Mars Pathfinder mission of 1997.

All of these missions confirmed the fact that the two moons are very dark, with an *albedo* of about 0.06, indicating that they reflect only about 6 percent of the light that strikes their surfaces. The moons also have a very low density, less than 2.0 g/cm³. This figure is significant because it indicates that water must almost certainly

◁ COMPOSITION OF THE MARTIAN SURFACE (BY ELEMENT; BY WEIGHT PERCENTAGE) ▷

ELEMENT	MARS SOIL SAMPLES			MARS ROCK SAMPLES		
	A-2	A-4	A-5	"BARNACLE BILL"	"YOGI"	EARTH
O	42.5	43.9	43.2	45.0	44.6	46.7
Si	21.6	20.2	20.5	25.7	23.8	27.7
Fe	15.2	11.2	13.6	9.9	10.7	5.0
Mg	5.3	5.5	5.2	1.9	3.8	2.1
Ca	4.5	3.4	3.8	3.3	4.2	3.6
Al	4.2	5.5	5.4	6.6	6.0	8.1

(continues)

▽ COMPOSITION OF THE MARTIAN SURFACE (BY ELEMENT; BY WEIGHT PERCENTAGE)
(continued) ▶

ELEMENT	MARS SOIL SAMPLES			MARS ROCK SAMPLES		
	A-2	A-4	A-5	"BARNACLE BILL"	"YOGI"	EARTH
Na	3.2	3.8	2.6	3.1	1.9	2.8
S	1.7	2.5	2.2	0.9	1.7	0.05
P	—	1.5	1.0	0.9	0.9	0.13
Cl	—	0.6	0.6	0.5	0.6	0.04
Ti	0.6	0.7	0.4	0.4	0.5	0.6
K	0.5	0.6	0.6	1.2	0.9	2.6

ELEMENT	MARS SOIL SAMPLES			MARS ROCK SAMPLES		
	A-2	A-4	A-5	"BARNACLE BILL"	"YOGI"	EARTH
Mn	0.4	0.4	0.5	0.7	0.4	0.09
Cr	0.2	0.3	0.3	0.1	0.0	0.035
Ni	—	—	0.1	—	—	0.019

Source: "Mars Pathfinder Science Results," http://mars.jpl.nasa.gov/MPF/science/mineralogy.html.

◄ ASAPH HALL (1829–1907) ►

The year 1877 promised to be an exciting time for astronomers interested in the study of Mars. The Red Planet was to be in perihelic opposition, the closest position that exists between Mars and Earth. In the two decades since the last perihelic opposition, a new 26-in (66-cm) refracting telescope had been built at the U.S. Naval Observatory in Washington, D.C. The man in charge of the telescope, Asaph Hall, had decided to focus his efforts on finding out whether Mars had any satellites.

At the time, more than a dozen planetary satellites had already been discovered for Jupiter, Saturn, Uranus, and Neptune. None had been found for Venus or Mercury, nor were they likely to be found, given the proximity of these planets to the Sun. Mars likewise had no satellites . . . or, at least, none that had yet been discovered.

In early August 1887, Hall began a nightly search for satellites of Mars. He worked systematically, starting with searches as far from the Red Planet as he thought any satellite might exist. He gradually worked his way in toward the planet's surface, searching each night for any tiny object that might be a satellite.

After a week, Hall was ready to give up. He had moved his observations so close to the planet's surface that its light was making it difficult to pick out anything that might be orbiting close to the planet. The light viewed through his telescope was "very blazing and unsteady," too difficult, he thought, for continued viewing.

His wife, Angeline Stickney Hall, convinced him not to give up. "Try it just one more night," she told him. Hall did as his wife suggested, and on the evening of August 16 he observed "a faint star near Mars." He was unable to study the object very long, however, as fog rolled in and covered the observatory. On the next night, Hall returned to his telescope to search for his new "star." Again, fog blocked his view for the early part of the evening. When it cleared enough for him to continue his research, he found not only the previous night's object, but also a second "star," the planet's inner

be present on the two moons. There is no other obvious way in which the bodies can have such low density. The presence of water in any form has not yet been confirmed directly, however, by any measurements made on the moons' surfaces.

moon. Hall later named the two moons Phobos (literally, "fear") and Deimos ("flight") after two escorts of the god Mars in Greek mythology, mentioned in the 15th book of Homer's *Iliad*: "He spake, and summoned Fear and Flight to yoke his steeds." The largest crater on Phobos was later named Stickney in honor of Hall's wife.

Asaph Hall was born in Goshen, Connecticut, on October 15, 1829. He left school at the age of 13 when his father died, and he became the sole source of support for the family. He took a job as an apprentice to a carpenter but devoted as much time as possible to self-instruction. Hall was eventually able to attend college briefly, first at Central College in McGrawville, New York, and later at the University of Michigan. It was at Central that he met his future wife, Chloe Angeline Stickney, who was his mathematics teacher. The Halls worked briefly as schoolteachers in Shalersville, Ohio, before Asaph accepted a position in 1857 as an assistant to William Cranch Bond, director of the Harvard College Observatory. His initial salary at Harvard was three dollars a week, but it was soon raised to the princely sum of eight dollars a week.

In 1863, Hall left Harvard to take a position as professor of astronomy at the United States Naval Observatory in Foggy Bottom, now part of Washington, D.C. He continued to work at the observatory until 1891. A year later his wife died, and Hall eventually moved back to his home town of Goshen, where he died on November 22, 1907.

In addition to his discovery of the Martian satellites, Hall determined the period of rotation for Saturn, the orbits of Saturn's satellites, and the properties of a number of double stars. He was awarded the Gold Medal of the Royal Astronomical Society of London for his contributions to astronomy and was awarded honorary doctoral degrees by Hamilton College in New York State, Yale University, and Harvard University. He was elected a member of the National Academy of Sciences in 1875.

The surface of both Phobos and Deimos are covered with craters. The largest of these craters on Phobos, the Stickney Crater, is about six miles (10 km) in diameter, nearly half the diameter of the moon itself. The crater is surrounded by large grooves in the moon's surface, some more than 2,300 feet (700 m) across and 300 feet (90 m) deep. The surfaces of both moons are covered with a layer of fine dust about a meter thick, similar to the dust that covers much of the Moon's surface.

The chemical composition of the surface of Phobos and Deimos is still a matter of debate. Data from the Viking Lander experiments suggested that materials present on the moons' surfaces were similar to those found in C-type asteroids. C-type asteroids are named for their similarity to carbonaceous chrondites, a type of meteorite that contains water-bearing minerals and compounds of carbon. (These and other types of meteorites are discussed in detail in chapter 6.) These results were later confirmed by studies of the moons' surfaces by the *Phobos 2* flyby of 1989, spectra captured by the *Hubble Space Telescope,* and ground-based spectroscopy. Data from the *Imager for Mars Pathfinder (IMP)* collected in 1997, however, indicated that the moons' surfaces might have a more complex chemical composition than at first realized. The new evidence suggests the presence of D-like asteroid materials in addition to the C-type materials already discovered. D-type asteroids contain little or no water and higher concentrations of carbon than C-type asteroids do.

The composition of the Phobos and Deimos surfaces are of interest to astronomers at least partly because they provide additional information about the nature of the solar system. Some individuals go further and anticipate that the information may someday have some important practical application. Those who are thinking about human travel to Mars suggest that the two moons may contain materials that can be converted into fuels for space travel and thus play an important role in future trips back and forth between Earth and Mars. The practicality of this suggestion is at question, however, since no missions to or flybys of the moons are currently scheduled.

The amount of information available to scientists about the inner planets has mushroomed in the past half century. Better ground-based telescopes, the availability of telescopes in outer space, and flights to all of the planets have produced a wealth of data about their atmospheres, surfaces, and, in some cases, interior structure and composition. Much of those data are still be analyzed, and new projects like the Mars Exploration Rover Mission promise to vastly increase the data available to researchers.

5
THE OUTER PLANETS

The solar system is sometimes divided into two parts consisting of the inner planets—Mercury, Venus, Earth, and Mars—and the outer planets—Jupiter, Saturn, Uranus, Neptune, and, until recently, Pluto. One might imagine that understanding the chemical and physical properties of the inner planets would help in understanding the chemical and physical properties of the outer planets. No such luck. The two groups of planets differ from each other in some fundamental and important ways.

One of the most obvious differences between inner planets and outer planets is size. Earth, the largest of the inner planets, has a diameter of about 7,926 miles (12,750 km). By comparison, Neptune, the smallest of the outer planets, has a diameter of about 30,800 miles (49,500 km), more than four times as far across as Earth. Jupiter, the largest of the outer planets, has a diameter of about 88,740 miles (142,800 km), 12 times that of the Earth. In fact, 1,400 spheres the size of the Earth could be fit inside Jupiter.

The composition of the outer planets is also very different from that of the inner planets. Mercury, Venus, Earth, and Mars are all made of rocky-like material with a density of about 5.5 g/cm^3. By contrast, the outer planets seem to consist largely of gases (which accounts for their sometimes being called the *gas giants*) with densities of about 0.69 g/cm^3 for Saturn to 1.54 g/cm^3 for Neptune. These densities suggest that the outer planets are made of hydrogen and helium primarily, with large amounts of other gases.

The outer planets also tend to have a number of satellites with (at last count) 56 orbiting Saturn, 63 around Jupiter, 27 around Uranus, and 13 around Neptune, compared to the virtual absence of satellites in the inner planets: Mercury with 0; Venus, 0; Earth, 1; and Mars 2.

Missions to the Outer Planets

As with the inner planets, most of what scientists first learned about the outer planets came from observation using Earth-based telescopes. The data collected from these observations was of limited value because the outer planets are so much farther away than are the inner planets. For example, Jupiter is about 430 million miles (720 million km) from Earth. By comparison, the minimum distance from Earth to Mars is only about 33 million miles (56 million km). The availability of spacecraft beginning in the 1960s provided a critical new tool for the exploration of the outer planets. Today scientists have an extensive collection of data about the chemical and physical properties of the outer planets as a result of a number of space missions to one or more of the planets.

The first such mission was *Pioneer 10,* launched on March 2, 1972. *Pioneer 10*'s mission was to fly through the asteroid belt and around Jupiter, collecting data on the planet's magnetic field, radiation belts, atmosphere, and interior. After completing this mission on March 31, 1997, the spacecraft continued in its path toward the outer limits of the solar system. It continued to send back data on the edges of the solar system and interstellar space until April 27, 2002. At that point, its power source died out and the probe was unable to send further transmissions to Earth stations.

Pioneer 10 was followed by its partner, *Pioneer 11,* launched on April 5, 1973. Like *Pioneer 10,* its primary objective was a study of the planet Jupiter, although it added other items to its list of accomplishments. After reaching the giant planet on December 2, 1974, it took pictures of the planet's Great Red Spot and collected data that allowed scientists to calculate the mass of one of the planet's moons, Callisto. The space probe also studied hydrogen and dust particles in Jupiter's atmosphere and determined other properties of the atmosphere and surface. After completing its Jupiter mission, *Pioneer 11* swung around the planet and used the gravitational boost it thereby gained to travel on to Saturn, where it became the first spacecraft to collect data from that planet. After passing beyond Saturn on September 1, 1979, it headed for the fringes of the solar system. Contact was finally lost with the spacecraft in November 1995.

Both *Pioneer 10* and *Pioneer 11* carried plaques showing what life on Earth is like, in the hope and expectation that any other life-form in the universe with which it might come into contact would know where the probe had come from and what its inventors were like.

The next mission to the outer planets consisted of two spacecraft, *Voyager 1* and *Voyager 2,* launched on September 5 and August 20, 1977, respectively. The primary goal of the Voyager mission was to fly past Jupiter and Saturn, the two largest planets in the solar system, and to collect and transmit data on their atmospheres, interiors, and satellites. *Voyager 2* was intended originally as a backup for *Voyager 1,* in case the earlier spacecraft malfunctioned or made discoveries of special interest that could be followed up with a second probe.

Voyager 2 was launched at an especially propitious moment in the history of the solar system: At the time four of the outer planets— Jupiter, Saturn, Uranus, and Neptune—were aligned in such a way as to allow the spacecraft to fly past them all, providing scientists with their first close look at the next-to-outermost planets, Uranus and Neptune, in addition to the planned targets of Jupiter and Saturn. The alignment that permitted this special tour of observation occurs only once every 175 years, so the data provided by *Voyager 2* about Uranus and Neptune has been of very special value to researchers.

The two Voyager spacecraft completed their planetary missions in late 1989, 12 years after they left Earth's surface. Even though their primary missions had ended, they did not lose their value to astronomers. They continued in flight beyond the orbit of Neptune, into the outermost reaches of the solar system. Scientists expect them to continue their flights, returning valuable data, until 2020 or later. Now called the Voyager Interstellar Mission, the two spacecraft will be collecting data on the most distant reaches of the Sun's influence. Scientists hope to learn more about the heliopause, the outermost region at which solar effects can be observed, about the solar wind and the Sun's magnetic field, and about the nature of interstellar space. As of the end of 2006, *Voyager 1* was about 9.3 billion miles (15 billion km) from the Sun, and *Voyager 2* was about 7.3 billion miles (12 billion km) from the Sun.

The fifth spacecraft to travel past Jupiter was *Ulysses,* launched on October 6, 1990. *Ulysses*'s primary goal was a study of the Sun, but in order to obtain the momentum it needed to attain solar orbit, it was launched toward Jupiter first. As the probe orbited the planet, it picked up additional energy in a slingshot-like effect that had been used with other spacecraft, sending the probe back toward the Sun, where it attained orbit in June 1994. *Ulysses* passed around Jupiter on February 8, 1992, when it collected additional data on the planet's magnetic field and the dust particles in its atmosphere that had been detected by earlier spacecraft.

The spacecraft *Galileo* was launched from the Space Shuttle *Atlantis* on October 18, 1989, with the goal of achieving orbit around the planet Jupiter. It was the first space probe to enter and remain in orbit around one of the outer planets. On its way to Jupiter, *Galileo* passed through an asteroid field and took extraordinary photographs of the asteroids Gaspra (October 29, 1991), Ida, and Dactyl (both on August 28, 1993).

The space probe neared its target in July 1995 and released a probe carrying instruments capable of measuring the temperature, pressure, and chemical composition of the atmosphere, as well as cloud characteristics, sunlight, and internal planetary energy. The probe survived for 59 minutes, during which it penetrated about 125 miles (200 km) into the Jovian atmosphere. At that point surrounding pressures caused the probe to melt and/or vaporize, and it lost contact with Earth stations.

Meanwhile, *Galileo* continued falling toward Jupiter until it was captured by the planet's gravitational field and attained orbit on

December 7, 1995. The probe remained in orbit for about two years, and during this time it discovered an intense radiation belt above the top of the planet's clouds and determined with some precision the composition of the planet's atmosphere. After completing its mission, the spacecraft disengaged itself from orbit and began falling toward the planet's surface. As it spiraled in toward the planet, *Galileo* flew past a number of Jupiter's satellites and photographed the moons Europa (December 1999) and Amalthea (November 2002). On September 22, 2003, it plunged into the planet's inner atmosphere and was destroyed. Among its many accomplishments, *Galileo* found 21 new Jovian satellites, bringing to 61 the total that orbit the huge planet. (That number has since increased to 63, as of early 2007.)

The most recent space probe sent to the outer planets is *Cassini-Huygens,* a joint project of the National Aeronautics and Space Administration (NASA) and the European Space Agency (ESA). The spacecraft was launched from Kennedy Space Center on October 15, 1997. Saturn was its primary target, but in order to gain the energy needed to make this long trip the probe was first directed toward Venus. It swung around that planet on June 24, 1999, and then around Earth on August 18, 1999. From there it headed out toward Saturn, traveling with the double slingshot-effect energy obtained from the trips around the two inner planets.

The *Cassini-Huygens* spacecraft consists of two parts. Cassini is the orbiter, designed to attain orbit around Saturn, while Huygens is a space probe, designed to be released into the atmosphere of the planet's moon, Titan. NASA was responsible for the design and construction of the Cassini orbiter, while ESA was responsible for the Huygens probe.

On its way to Saturn, *Cassini-Huygens* passed by the asteroid Masursky (on January 23, 2000) and Jupiter (December 30, 2000). In early June it passed near one of Saturn's outermost moons, Phoebe, and there took photographs and collected data that promise to reveal important new details about that moon's origin. The spacecraft arrived in the Saturnian atmosphere exactly on schedule, on June 30, and sent back some of the most astonishing astronomical photographs of any solar system object ever collected. The Huygens probe detached from Cassini on December 25, 2004, and went into an orbit around Titan for 21 days before finally crashing through the moon's atmosphere and into its surface. Meanwhile, the Cassini orbiter was expected to remain in orbit until June 30, 2008.

The last planet-like object to be explored is Pluto. Since its discovery in 1930 by American astronomer Clyde Tombaugh (1906–97), Pluto has been considered one of the nine planets in the solar system. In August 2006, however, the International Astronomical Union established a new set of criteria for planets that Pluto did not meet. It is now considered a dwarf planet. In spite of its new designation, astronomers remain very interested in the chemical composition and physical characteristics of Pluto. Astronomers do have a fair amount of information about Pluto from ground-based observatories, the *Hubble Space Telescope (HST)*, and the Infrared Astronomical Satellite. NASA's New Horizons space mission is expected to provide a great deal more detail about the strange and mysterious astronomical body. *New Horizons* was launched on January 19, 2006. It is expected to fly by Pluto and its satellite, Charon, in July 2015.

After completing its observations of the planet and its moon, New Horizons will continue outward into the *Kuiper Belt,* a region of space located beyond Neptune that includes Pluto itself. The Kuiper Belt consists of more than 70,000 bodies with diameters of 60 miles (100 km) or more. Its existence was discovered in the early 1990s, and scientists still know very little about its constitution, the physical and chemical properties of its bodies, or their orbital properties. Interest in the Kuiper Belt intensified in 2002 with the discovery of the largest nonplanet object in the outer solar system, a body that has been given the name Quaoar (pronounced "kwa-whar") in honor of a Native American creation god. Quaoar has a diameter of about 800 miles (1,250 km), making it about half the size of Pluto. It travels in a nearly perfectly circular orbit around the Sun at a distance of about 42 AU (*astronomical units*). By comparison, Neptune's orbit is located at a distance of 30.22 AU from the Sun, and Pluto's orbit is at a distance of 39.83 AU from the Sun. The diagram on page 132 shows the relative orbits of the outer planets and Quaoar.

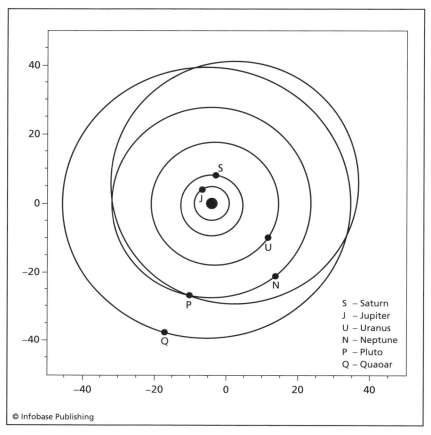

S – Saturn
J – Jupiter
U – Uranus
N – Neptune
P – Pluto
Q – Quaoar

© Infobase Publishing

Orbit of Quaoar compared to orbits of outer planets

Jupiter

Other than the Sun, Jupiter is the largest and brightest object in the solar system. It has a radius of 44,325 miles (71,492 km), 11 times that of the Earth, and an albedo of 0.51, compared with 0.4 for Earth. Jupiter's mass is about 318 times that of the Earth, and its volume is large enough to hold 1,300 planets the size of Earth. The planet's density, like that of all outer planets, is low. At 1.33, Jupiter's density is less than a quarter of Earth's.

Jupiter's chemical composition is similar to that of the Sun, consisting of about 81 percent hydrogen and 18 percent helium. In fact, if Jupiter were only 50 to 100 times larger, it would have been massive enough for thermonuclear reactions to have begun, turning the body into a star, rather than a planet.

Jupiter's general characteristics have been well known for some time. Unlike the inner planets, it has no distinct dividing line between an outer atmosphere and an inner core, mantle, and crust. Instead, Jupiter consists of elements, compounds, and other chemical species that are normally gaseous but that may occur as liquids or solids the closer they are to the planet's center. As the diagram below shows, the outermost region of the planet, the "atmosphere" that is visible from Earth, consists of clouds of ammonia, methane, and water. The pressure within the cloud layer is about one atmosphere, and the temperature, about 165 K (about −100°C).

Just beneath these clouds is a region composed primarily of molecular hydrogen and helium, whose density gradually increases with increasing depth into the layer. In the upper layers of this region, the hydrogen and helium act much like gases, while in the lower layers, they act essentially as liquids. At a depth of about 20,000 km (12,000

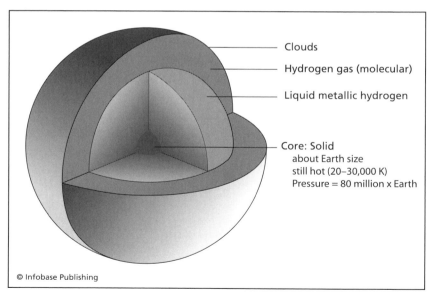

Clouds

Hydrogen gas (molecular)

Liquid metallic hydrogen

Core: Solid
about Earth size
still hot (20–30,000 K)
Pressure = 80 million x Earth

© Infobase Publishing

Cross-sectional structure of Jupiter

◁ S. ALAN STERN (1957–) ▷

The methods of astronomical research have changed. At one time researchers like Gerard Kuiper could achieve great discoveries by sitting at their telescopes, collecting data, and unraveling the meaning of those data. Today, individual accomplishments of this kind are still possible, but more and more often important discoveries are made as the result of the joint efforts of many astronomers and other scientists working together—often dozens, and sometimes hundreds. Such is the case with the New Horizons Pluto-Kuiper Belt Mission, NASA's project to launch a spacecraft to Pluto and the Kuiper Belt. The spacecraft is meant to follow a predetermined path from Earth to the outer edges of the solar system over a nine-year period with little or no margin of error, then make a host of important observations and transmit those data to Earth stations without error. The amount of effort needed to design such a spacecraft is staggering. The person responsible for organizing and overseeing such an effort takes on what must truly be one of the most demanding jobs in all of modern astronomy. That man, for the New Horizons mission, is S. Alan Stern, principal investigator of the New Horizons Mission and director of the Southwest Research Institute's Department of Space Studies in Boulder, Colorado.

S. Alan Stern was born in New Orleans, Louisiana, on November 22, 1957. He received his B.S. in physics (1978), M.S. in aerospace engineering (1980), B.A. in astronomy (1981), and M.A. in planetary atmospheres (1981) from the University of Texas, and a Ph.D. in astrophysics and planetary science in 1989 from the University of Colorado. His first professional assignment was as a summer intern at NASA's Johnson Space Center in 1979 and 1980. He then worked as a systems engineer at Martin Marietta Aerospace (1982–83) and spacecraft/instrument engineer at the University of Colorado's Laboratory for Atmospheric and Space Physics (1983–86). In 1986, he was appointed assistant director in the Office of Space Science and Technology at the University of Colorado, after which he became assistant to the vice president for research at the university.

miles), pressures and temperature are so great that hydrogen atoms become ionized and exist as separate protons and electrons in a state known as *metallic hydrogen.* The density at the upper boundary

Stern then became a research fellow at the Center for Space & Geosciences Policy (1988–91) and research associate in the Laboratory for Atmospheric and Space Physics (1989–90) at Colorado and research associate at the Center for Astrophysics and Space Astronomy (1990–91). In 1991, he joined the Southwest Research Institute, an independent, nonprofit applied research and development organization with headquarters in San Antonio, Texas. He has since served as principal scientist (1991–92), section manager (1992–97), and department director (1998–) in the Institute's Space Science Department located in Boulder, Colorado. In 2002, Stern was appointed full professor adjunct in the Department of Astrophysical and Planetary Sciences at the University of Colorado.

Stern's research has taken him to the South Pole, to a number of major astronomical observatories, and to the upper atmosphere aboard high-performance military aircraft. His areas of interest include spacecraft rendezvous theory, terrestrial polar mesospheric clouds, galactic astrophysics, and tenuous satellite atmospheres. He has been principal investigator for a number of space projects, including the European Space Agency's Rosetta/ ALICE Extreme Ultraviolet Spectrometer Experiment (a mission to study Comet 46P/Wirtanen), two Space Shuttle projects, three airborne research projects, and two research rocket projects. In 1995, Stern was selected to be a Space Shuttle Mission Specialist finalist for a forthcoming flight.

Stern has served on a number of committees responsible for the development and execution of U.S. space policy, including the Sloan Foundation Workshop on Space Policy, the 1990–93 NASA Lunar Exploration Science Working Group, the 1991–94 NASA Outer Planets Science Working Group (chair), the 1992 *Hubble Space Telescope* Planetary Telescope Allocation Committee (chair), NASA's 1994–95 New Millennium Science Working Group, and NASA's 2000 Outer Solar system Senior Survey Team. He is the author of more than 150 technical papers, 50 popular articles, and two books, *The U.S. Space Program after* Challenger (1987) and *Pluto and Charon: Ice Worlds on the Ragged Edge of the Solar System* (1997). In addition, he has edited three technical volumes and three collections of scientific essays.

of this region is about 1 g/cm^3, while the density at its lower boundary is closer to 4 g/cm^3.

The protons and electrons that make up the metallic hydrogen shell are essentially free to move without constraint, creating an electric current throughout the region. This electric current is thought to be responsible for Jupiter's magnetic field. The temperatures within the metallic hydrogen shell are thought to reach about 10,000 K and the pressures are estimated at about 3 million atmospheres.

Jupiter's core lies 24,000 miles (38,000 km) deeper into the planet's interior, a total distance of about 36,000 miles (58,000 km) from the planet's outer boundary. The core is about 15,000 miles (24,000 km) in diameter and is thought to consist of solid hydrogen and helium. Its temperature is estimated to be about 20,000 K and its pressure about 50 million to 80 million atmospheres.

The most obvious visual features of Jupiter are a number of dark and bright bands that are generally known as *belts* and *zones.* These bands are caused by ammonia clouds that blow parallel to the planet's equator. Between 15° north latitude and 15° south latitude, the clouds blow in the same direction as the planet's rotation, west to east, at speeds of about 100 meters/second (200 mph). Between latitudes 15° and 45° north and south, they tend to blow in the opposite direction, from east to west, at about half the speed of the equatorial winds. At latitudes higher than 45°, the winds appear to be largely absent, and the banded appearance on this part of the planet's face disappears.

The other prominent feature on Jupiter's face is the Great Red Spot, a nearly circular area about 24,000 miles (40,000 km) in diameter. The spot has been visible for about 300 years and is thought to be caused by very strong cyclonic (counterclockwise) winds.

The *Galileo* probe released into the Jovian atmosphere in 1995 was enormously significant because it provided the first on-site measurements of the planet's physical and chemical characteristics. Essentially all of the features just described have come from Earth-based observations, from data relayed by spacecraft flying tens of thousands of kilometers above the planet, and from theoretical models of the planet. Data relayed by the probe provided a check on the validity of these models and on the previously collected data as well as a new and extensive collection of information about the physical and chemical properties of the planet.

One of the first discoveries reported by the *Galileo* probe was the lack of clouds in the Jovian atmosphere. The probe's nephelometer (a device for measuring the amount of light scattering in the atmosphere and, hence, the amount of cloud material present) found thin wispy clouds in the regions through which it passed. It detected two such clouds at altitudes of 0.5 bar and 1.3 bar, an even thinner layer at 1.6 bar, and a few random particles at an altitude of 4 bar.

(The bar is a unit for measuring pressure, equal to the pressure exerted by Earth's atmosphere at sea level. The bar is commonly used to express positions within the atmosphere of Jupiter, Saturn, and some other planets. Low values, such as 0.1 bar, represent upper regions of the atmosphere, while high values, such as 100 bar, represent lower regions. The higher the bar value for a measurement, the deeper the level of the atmosphere represented.)

The composition of these thin clouds appears to be consistent with earlier suggestions that they consist of ammonia ice (at 0.5 bar), ammonium hydrosulfide (NH_4SH) ice (at 1.3 bar), and water ice (at 1.6 bar).

In addition, the *Galileo* probe measured temperatures in the region through which it fell, and these were generally within the range that had been expected. It also carried a device for the detection of lightning discharges (similar to a simple AM radio), which scientists had expected to observe in some abundance. The moist, windy conditions that scientists had predicted in the Jovian atmosphere would normally produce bolts of lightning in much the same way that colliding water masses produce lightning in Earth's atmosphere. The probe, however, detected no lightning in the area through which it fell, although it did pick up significant bolts of lightning at greater distances (about equal to that of Earth's diameter) from the probe's pathway.

In short, the region through which the probe fell was drier and significantly less cloudy than scientists had expected to find, although wind speeds were comparable to those that had been predicted. This result was explained in part by Earth-based observations of the probe's path after it was released from the orbiter, which indicated that the probe had fallen into a region on the planet known as a *5-micron hotspot.* Hotspots are cylinder-shaped regions from which heat generated in the planet's interior is believed to escape into the outer atmosphere. Their full name, 5-micron hotspots, refers to the primary type of radiation (5-micron wavelength) they emit.

As heat escapes·from a hotspot, masses of cool, dry gas descend into the planet's interior in a process known as *downwelling.* Scientists think downwelling might be responsible for the removal of ammonia, water, and other chemical species that would otherwise be found in the planet's outer atmosphere. This theory was confirmed to some extent in the probe's last few moments: Before it stopped functioning, the probe reported a rapid increase in the concentration of water, ammonia, hydrogen sulfide, and other chemical species. This result is what one might expect if the probe had reached the bottom of a downwelling region.

Fortunately or not, the Galileo probe had fallen through a region of the Jovian atmosphere that is not necessarily typical of its overall structure and composition. Had it descended a few thousand kilometers away, it might have found very different conditions, similar to the wet, cloudy, windy atmosphere that astronomers had always expected to find on the planet.

Besides measuring temperature, wind, and atmospheric pressure, the *Galileo* probe also recorded a precise measurement of the chemical composition of the portion of the Jovian atmosphere through which it fell. This information is important not only because it gives a picture of the planet itself, but also because it sheds light on the process by which Jupiter and the rest of the solar system may have evolved. Scientists have always believed that the chemical composition of Jupiter is very similar to that of the Sun; any differences in the abundance of elements might provide clues to what happened in the solar system after it began to form. The chart on pages 139–140 shows the best estimate of the abundances of various chemical species, as obtained from the Galileo probe and other measurements of Jupiter's atmosphere.

Collecting data about the chemical composition of the Jovian atmosphere was one of the key objectives of the Galileo mission because these data provide some of the best insights into the earliest history of the solar system. Astronomers now believe that the solar system was formed when a large cloud of dust and gas, consisting of about 75 percent hydrogen and 24 percent helium, became unstable and began to collapse in and onto itself. Dust and gas pulled together by gravitational forces formed a large sphere, which then began to

◁ ABUNDANCE OF VARIOUS CHEMICAL SPECIES IN THE UPPER JOVIAN ATMOSPHERE (BY VOLUME) ▷

SPECIES	ABUNDANCE
Hydrogen, H_2	0.86
Helium, He	0.136
Methane, CH_4	0.0018
Ammonia, NH_3	0.0007
Water, H_2O	>0.0005
Hydrogen sulfide, H_2S	77 ppm
Neon, Ne	20 ppm
Argon, Ar	16 ppm
Hydrogen deuteride, HD	15 ppm
Phosphine, PH_3	500 ppb
Deuterated methane, CH_3D	300 ppb
Krypton, Kr	7.6 ppb
Carbon monoxide, CO	0.75 ppb

(continues)

◄ **ABUNDANCE OF VARIOUS CHEMICAL SPECIES IN THE UPPER JOVIAN ATMOSPHERE (BY VOLUME)** *(continued)* ➤

SPECIES	ABUNDANCE
Xenon, Xe	0.76 ppb
Germane, GeH_4	0.6 ppb
Arsine, AsH_3	0.2 ppb

Source: F. W. Taylor, et al., "The Composition of the Atmosphere of Jupiter," in Fran Bagenal, Timothy Dowling, and William McKinnon, *Jupiter: The Planet, Satellites and Magnetosphere.* New York: Cambridge University Press, 2004, Chapter 4.

rotate. As more and more material collected into the spherical mass, its speed of rotation increased. An increasing rate of rotation, in turn, affected the shape of the mass of material. It began to change from a sphere into a flattened sphere and then into a disk, known as the *solar nebula.*

By far the greatest amount of dust and gas ended up in the central core of the rotating disk. Gravitational forces in this area were sufficient to heat the core to a temperature at which thermonuclear reactions could occur, and the core began its life as a star, our Sun. In more distant portions of the disk, much smaller quantities of material accumulated in a number of regions in a process called material accretion (the collection of dust and gas into a single body). In these regions gravitational forces were never strong enough to permit the development of a protostar. Instead, these new bodies became planetesimals, early stages of the planets that exist today. Of all the planetesimals, the one that became Jupiter had the greatest opportunity to become a star itself. Planetesimals evolved into planets not only as a result of the collapse of gas and dust from the original solar nebula but also because of the collision of smaller bodies (such as comets and meteors) with the growing planets.

The chemical composition of the growing planets was determined to a large extent by their distance from the Sun. The inner planets received enough solar energy to drive off most of the hydrogen, helium, and other light elements and compounds of which they were originally formed. Only the denser materials, such as iron and silicates, were left behind. As discussed in chapter 4, the common structure of these inner planets consists of a dense iron core surrounded by a mantle and crust made of silicate-type materials. The outer planets received far less solar energy and, in general, retained the hydrogen and helium of which they were originally formed. In fact, they were formed at distances great enough from the Sun that these elements were able to condense into liquid and, sometimes, even solid states.

Not much is left today of that early solar nebula out of which the solar system was formed. The composition of the Sun, for example, has changed as hydrogen has been converted to helium as a result of fusion reactions. In particular, essentially all of the deuterium present in the original Sun has now been depleted in such reactions. (One of the instruments on the Galileo probe measured the abundance of deuterium in the Jovian atmosphere, to permit a comparison with that found in the Sun's atmosphere.) The effects of solar radiation, interior rearrangements, volcanic action, outgassing, and other phenomena have significantly altered the appearance and composition of the inner planets, but Jupiter remains largely as it must have existed 4.6 billion years ago when the solar system was formed.

A number of the Galileo probe's instruments were designed, therefore, to detect the abundance of chemical species present in the atmospheres of both Jupiter and the Sun. One instrument, the Helium Abundance Detector, was designed specifically to measure the amount of helium in the Jovian atmosphere. It found a value for the ratio of helium to hydrogen (He:H) of 0.157, which is 0.81 that found in the Sun. Why does Jupiter have so much less helium in its atmosphere than the Sun?

Astronomers now believe that helium, with a density nearly twice that of hydrogen, tends to fall inward from the planet's outer atmosphere toward its core. If one were able to travel through the hydrogen-rich soup of the lower atmosphere, it might be possible to detect a "rainfall" of helium droplets, which are immiscible in hydrogen, falling from the "sky," the planet's outer atmosphere.

This model might also explain the observed depletion of neon in the planet's atmosphere. The *Galileo* probe's Neutral Mass Spectrometer (GPMS) observed an abundance of neon about one tenth that in the solar atmosphere. Perhaps, researchers hypothesize, neon dissolves in helium droplets as they form in the atmosphere and fall into the planet's interior. This phenomenon is possible because helium and neon, unlike helium and hydrogen, are completely miscible.

By contrast, three other inert gases—argon, krypton, and xenon—are significantly more abundant in the Jovian atmosphere than in the solar atmosphere. How could these gases have remained trapped in the planet's outer atmosphere in such high concentrations, rather than diffusing out into the interplanetary space? No satisfactory answer to this question exists. Some researchers now believe, however, that Jupiter may at one time have been much more distant from the Sun and slipped into a closer orbit only relatively recently. In that case, the three inert gases might at one time have been frozen and incapable of escaping into space.

As suggested by the cloud data reported earlier, the abundance of a number of chemical species varied unexpectedly in the regions through which the *Galileo* probe fell. The probe's mass spectrometer measured very low concentrations of hydrogen sulfide, ammonia, and water as it entered the Jovian atmosphere but found much greater abundances as it descended. As the probe reached the deepest part of the atmosphere, for example, GPMS measured an NH_3 abundance nearly four times that of the Sun; at an even deeper level it found an H_2S abundance 2.5 times that of the Sun. Although values for the abundance of water were similar, increasing from very low levels at the outermost parts of the atmosphere to significantly higher levels in deeper regions, they never reached those found in the solar atmosphere.

After the probe completed its mission, it burned and crashed in the depths of the Jovian atmosphere, having completed an extraordinarily successful mission. Although it passed through no more than 0.1 percent of the planet's atmosphere, it lasted nearly 50 percent longer and survived to twice the depth for which it had originally been designed.

The Jovian Moons

While the Galileo probe surveyed Jupiter's atmosphere, the *Galileo* orbiter continued on its mission, orbiting Jupiter a total of 35 times. Although originally planned for only 11 orbits, the mission was so successful that controllers decided to add 24 more trips around the planet. One of the most unexpected results of these orbits was the discovery of 21 new satellites of the planet, bringing the total number of known Jovian moons to 61. (Two more moons have since been discovered, making the total 63 as of the end of 2006.) In addition to the spacecraft's flights around the planet were 24 flybys of the planet's four largest satellites, Europa, Io, Callisto, and Ganymede. The four moons are sometimes called the *Galilean moons* or *Galilean satellites* because they were first observed by Galileo Galilei in 1610. The chart on pages 145–148 summarizes *Galileo*'s flybys of the Jovian moons.

The spacecraft returned spectacular photographs of the four satellites and of Jupiter itself as well as a plethora of new data about their structure and composition.

The most distant of the Galilean satellites, Callisto, orbits 1.883×10^6 km from Jupiter's surface. It is the second largest of the moons, with a radius of 1,500 miles (2,400 km). Astronomers had generally regarded Callisto as a drab, rather uninteresting place, but *Galileo* utterly disproved that view. One of the first discoveries was evidence for the existence of a liquid ocean made of salty water hidden beneath its crust. As it passed over Callisto, *Galileo* detected a pattern of electrical currents that cannot be explained by particles in the atmosphere, which is much too thin, nor by the crust, which consists largely of nonconductive materials. The simplest and probably most likely explanation is that the currents are produced by the movement of a liquid somewhere beneath the moon's surface.

A second flyby of the moon obtained further evidence for this liquid body. On an earlier flyby, *Galileo* had observed and photographed a large crater on one side of Callisto called the Valhalla basin, and scientists expected to see a matching bulge on the opposite side of the moon, caused by the same impact that produced Valhalla. When no such bulge was found, they concluded that the underground lake had absorbed the impact and prevented the expected bulge from forming.

Scientists were also quite surprised by the surface features Callisto displayed. Images taken from only 86 miles (138 km) about the moon's surface showed strong evidence of erosion. Among the most prominent features were strings of jagged hills, made of ice and rock, surrounded by dark patches of dust. Researchers hypothesize that the hills were formed when bodies from interplanetary space collided with the moon, throwing crustal material upward. Over time, ice contained within the crustal material may have evaporated away, leaving behind the solid dusty material that forms the dark patches around the hills.

Ganymede is the largest of Jupiter's satellites. Indeed, with a diameter of 3,270 miles (5,268 km), it is the largest satellite in the solar system. It is larger than both Mercury and Pluto, and if it orbited the Sun rather than Jupiter, it would undoubtedly be classified as a planet. With a density of 1.94 g/cm^3, Ganymede is thought to contain both water and rocky materials. The magnetic field that *Galileo* detected around the moon suggests that it has a metallic core that makes up about half of its volume and that may be anywhere from 250 miles (400 km) to 800 miles (1,300 km) beneath its surface. The mantle surrounding the core is thought to consist of silicate-like materials and the crust of water ice. Ganymede, like Callisto, is thought to have a layer of saltwater beneath its crust.

In its flybys of Ganymede, *Galileo*'s spectrometer detected atomic hydrogen escaping from the satellite's atmosphere into interplanetary space. Scientists hypothesize that the hydrogen forms when solar energy and/or energy from Jupiter's magnetic field strikes the moon's surface, causing water to decompose into hydrogen and oxygen. As hydrogen escapes from the moon, oxygen is probably left

◄ *GALILEO* FLYBYS OF JOVIAN MOONS ▷

ORBIT	TARGET	DATE	ALTITUDE
0	Io	Dec. 7, 1995	558 miles (897 km)
1	Ganymede	July 27, 1996	519 miles (835 km)
2	Ganymede	Sept. 6, 1996	162 miles (261 km)
3	Callisto	Nov. 4, 1996	706 miles (1,136 km)
4	Europa	Dec. 19, 1996	430 miles (692 km)
5	none		
6	Europa	Feb. 20, 1997	364 miles (586 km)
7	Ganymede	April 5, 1997	1,928 miles (3,102 km)
8	Ganymede	May 7, 1997	996 miles (1,603 km)
9	Callisto	June 25, 1997	260 miles (418 km)
10	Callisto	Sept. 17, 1997	333 miles (535 km)

(continues)

◁ *GALILEO* FLYBYS OF JOVIAN MOONS *(continued)* ▷

ORBIT	TARGET	DATE	ALTITUDE
11	Europa	Nov. 6, 1997	1,270 miles (2,043 km)
12	Europa	Dec. 16, 1997	125 miles (201 km)
13	none		
14	Europa	March 29, 1998	1,022 miles (1,644 km)
15	Europa	March 31, 1998	1,562 miles (2,515 km)
16	Europa	July 21, 1998	1,140 miles (1,834 km)
17	Europa	Sept. 26, 1998	2,226 miles (3,582 km)
18	Europa	Nov. 22, 1998	1,411 miles (2,271 km)
19	Europa	Feb. 1, 1999	894 miles (1,439 km)
20	Callisto	May 5, 1999	821 miles (1,321 km)
21	Callisto	June 30, 1999	651 miles (1,048 km)

ORBIT	TARGET	DATE	ALTITUDE
22	Callisto	Aug. 14, 1999	1,429 miles (2,299 km)
23	Callisto	Sept. 16, 1999	654 miles (1,052 km)
24	Io	Oct. 11, 1999	380 miles (611 km)
25	Io	Nov. 26, 1999	187 miles (301 km)
26	Europa	Jan. 3, 2000	218 miles (351 km)
27	Io	Feb. 22, 2000	123 miles (198 km)
28	Ganymede	May 20, 2000	502 miles (809 km)
29	Ganymede	Dec. 28, 2000	1,452 miles (2,338 km)
30	Callisto	May 25, 2001	86 miles (138 km)
31	Io	Aug. 6, 2001	120 miles (194 km)
32	Io	Oct. 16, 2001	114 miles (184 km)

(continues)

◁ **GALILEO FLYBYS OF JOVIAN**
MOONS *(continued)* ▷

ORBIT	TARGET	DATE	ALTITUDE
33	Io	Jan. 17, 2002	63 miles (102 km)
34	Amalthea*	Nov. 5, 2002	99 miles (160 km)
35	Jupiter	Sept. 21, 2003	impact

*Amalthea is one of the four small moons inside the orbit of Io. *Galileo* visited it during its last orbit before falling into the Jovian atmosphere. Source: Jet Propulsion Laboratory, "Galileo Mission to Jupiter," online at http://www.jpl.nasa.gov/news/fact_sheets/galileo.pdf

behind, either trapped in the moon's icy surface or forming a thin, low-lying atmosphere just above it.

Ganymede's surface indicates that a great deal of tectonic activity is taking place on the moon. It is covered with folds, faults, and fractures, similar to those of mountainous regions on Earth, where land movements are frequent and large. Although craters are visible on the moon's surface, Ganymede's wrinkled tectonic shapes are most characteristic.

Like Callisto and Ganymede, Jupiter's moon Europa is thought to have a saltwater ocean buried beneath its crust. Evidence for this hypothesis includes not only the changing electrical fields in the moon's atmosphere, but also the fact that its north pole changes direction every 5½ hours, a phenomenon that can best be explained by the presence of a conductive layer (such as saltwater) beneath the moon's surface. Some scientists believe that an underground salt-water ocean of this kind might be able to support primitive forms of life.

Images of Europa relayed by *Galileo* also showed features that had quite obviously been separated from each other at some time in the past, like pieces of a jigsaw puzzle. Scientists hypothesize that the features broke apart, floated about on an ocean of saltwater on the moon's surface, and then were fixed in place when that saltwater froze.

Like Ganymede, Europa is thought to have a large core that contains significant amounts of iron. The diagrams below show cross sections of the four Jovian moons as currently hypothesized by researchers. Of the four, only Callisto lacks an iron core.

Researchers have also discovered the presence of an ionosphere outside Europa's surface. They suggest that ultraviolet radiation from both the Sun and Jupiter's magnetosphere cause oxygen atoms in the Europa's atmosphere to lose electrons, leaving behind the charged oxygen atoms (O^+) that are the primary components of the moon's ionosphere.

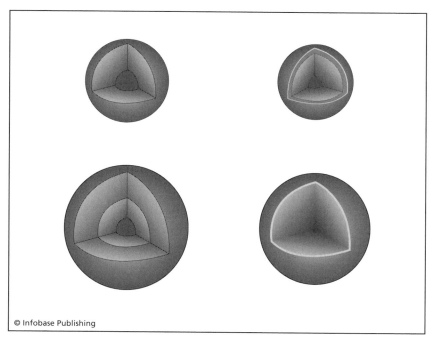

© Infobase Publishing

Cross-sectional structures of the four Jovian moons: Io (upper left corner), Europa (upper right corner), Ganymede (lower left corner), Callisto (lower right corner)

Io is the innermost of the four Galilean satellites and the most dense of the Jovian moons. Its density is estimated at 3.5 g/cm^3. In some ways, its size, structure, and chemical composition are similar to those of our Earth's Moon. As the illustration shows, Io probably has the largest core for its size of any of the four moons. Io's surface is unusually smooth, essentially lacking in any impact craters. This evidence suggests that the moon's surface is fairly new, probably no more than about a million years old.

Io is almost certainly the most volcanically active of any major body in the solar system. Its volcanic activity has been estimated at about 100 times that of Earth. *Galileo* discovered a total of 120 volcanic sources on the moon's surface and sent back images of 74. This number was far greater than had been anticipated by scientists, who expected to find no more than "a dozen or two." Especially surprising to researchers was the number of significant changes on the moon's surface, not only between the *Voyager 2* flyby and the *Galileo* trips but also among the seven flybys and numerous images *Galileo* made of the moon. For example, images of Io taken on September 19, 1997, showed a new, very large dark spot on the moon's surface about the size of the state of Arizona, which was not present in images taken just five months earlier on April 4. The dark spot surrounds Pillan Patera, a volcanic center named after the South American god of thunder, fire, and volcanoes.

The dark spot is of special interest to researchers because it represents a kind of volcanic outflow unusual on Io. Most such outflows are white, yellow, or red, due to the presence of sulfur. The new outflow is much darker than any that had been observed before, suggesting that its chemical composition differs significantly from others on the moon's surface. Scientists believe the dark spot may be a new lava flow produced during a violent eruption on the moon's surface observed by the *Hubble Space Telescope* in June 1997. That eruption released a plume of gas nearly 100 km (75 miles) high into the moon's atmosphere.

The general appearance of Io's surface also appears to have changed rather dramatically between the Voyager 2 and Galileo missions. Scientists have determined that one reason for these changes is the continuing vulcanism on Io. Typically, Io's volcanic sources release large clouds of sulfur dioxide into the atmosphere, which then condense and settle back to the surface, forming a white or yellow covering. The sulfur dioxide "frost" thus formed may then sublimate, releasing the substance to the atmosphere once more in the form of a gas.

Saturn

Saturn is the second-largest planet in the solar system, after Jupiter. Its equatorial radius is 37,448 miles (60,268 km), about nine times that of Earth, and its mass is 568.46×10^{24} kg, about 95 times that of Earth. As of early 2007, scientists had found 56 satellites of Saturn, the largest of which is Titan, with a radius of 8,448 feet (2,575 km, about 50 percent larger than that of Earth's Moon), and a mass of $1,345.5 \times 10^{20}$ kg (about twice that of the Moon). Saturn's density is 0.687 g/cm^3, less than that of water. This fact means that (if one could find a body of water large enough) Saturn would float on water. It is the only planet with a density less than that of water.

Saturn's most familiar feature is its rings, a group of concentric disks encircling its equator. The ring system consists of about 14 distinct structures with a thickness ranging from about 10 to about 200 meters. The closest of the rings, known as the *D ring,* is located about 4,300 miles (7,000 km) from the planet's outermost atmosphere, while the outermost ring, the *E outer edge,* is located about 300,000 miles (480,000 km) away.

Voyager 1 flew by Saturn on November 12, 1980, at a distance of three planet radii from the planet's atmosphere, while *Voyager 2* flew past the planet on August 26, 1981, at a distance of 2.67 planet radii. The two spacecraft carried a variety of instruments that allowed them to measure the chemical composition of the planet's atmosphere, the presence and strength of its magnetic field, any electrical properties associated with the planet, and other physical characteristics of the planet, its satellites, and ring system.

Voyager 1 and 2 collected new information about Saturn and confirmed or corrected earlier data. (Where the two spacecraft reported somewhat different data, the values considered to be most reliable are presented here.) According to the Voyager transmissions, the temperature at the 0.1 bar point of Saturn's atmosphere (the outermost fringe) is about 84 K (−189°C); at a depth of about 1 bar, it is about 134 K (−139°C). The pressure deep within the planet's atmosphere is thought to reach well over 1,000 bars, that is, more than 1,000 times atmospheric pressure on Earth at sea level. Wind speeds in the upper atmosphere vary according to latitude, reading a maximum of about 400 meters/s (900 mph) between the planet's equator and 30° latitude and a maximum of about 150 meters/s (350 mph) at higher latitudes in both northern and southern hemispheres.

The largest component of Saturn's atmosphere is hydrogen, which accounts for 96.3 percent ± 2.4 percent. The remainder consists of a much smaller amount of helium (3.25 percent ± 2.4 percent) and minor gases, such as methane (4,500 ppm), ammonia (125 ppm), hydrogen deuteride (HD; 110 ppm), and ethane (7 ppm). As on Jupiter, the primary solid constituents of the atmosphere appear to be ammonia ice, ammonium hydrosulfide ice, and water ice. Scientists were surprised that the abundance of helium is so much lower in the Saturnian atmosphere than in the Jovian and solar atmospheres. These data may suggest that helium has settled out of the upper atmosphere and is accumulating in larger concentrations in the lower atmosphere. The chart on page 153 compares the composition of Saturn's atmosphere with those of the other major planets.

Voyager 1 found three new satellites of Saturn—Atlas, Prometheus, and Pandora. They are three of the four satellites closest to the planet's surface. (The fourth is Pan.) Early analysis of the Voyager data suggested the existence of at least a dozen new satellites around Saturn. Since then, many additional satellites have also been identified, although many have not yet been named. Researchers are still uncertain as to exactly how many satellites the planet has and how distinct they are from each other. Since the newly discovered moons appear to travel together in groups of three or four, some scientists believe that they may be the remnants of a small number of larger moons that broke apart as the result of Saturn's gravitational pull.

◁ **A COMPARISON OF THE APPROXIMATE CHEMICAL COMPOSITION OF THE ATMOSPHERES OF THE OUTER PLANETS** ▷

SPECIES	JUPITER	SATURN		NEPTUNE
H_2	89.8%	96.3%	82.5%	80.0%
He	10.2%	3.25%	15.2%	19.0%
CH_4	3,000 ppm	4,500 ppm	2.3%	1.5%
H_2O	~4 ppm (varies)	*	*	*
NH_3	260 ppm	125 ppm	*	*
HD	28 ppm	110 ppm	148 ppm	192 ppm
C_2H_6	5.8 ppm	7 ppm	1.5 ppm	*

*Absent or not measured
Source: NASA Planet Fact Sheets, available online at http://nssdc.gsfc.nasa.gov/planetary/planetfact.html.

Both Voyager spacecraft detected Earthlike auroras near Saturn's poles. Nearly two decades later this discovery was confirmed when the *Hubble Space Telescope* took dramatic photographs of the planet that clearly showed the auroras. Scientists believe that the auroras occur when the solar wind interacts with Saturn's magnetic field, causing the formation of atomic hydrogen, which emits the aurora's eerie glow.

Some of the most interesting results of the Voyager flights past Saturn involve their discoveries about the planet's famous ring system.

Until the Voyager flybys, astronomers thought that the system consisted of three rings, separated by a gap known as the *Cassini division,* named in honor of the Italian astronomer Giovanni Domenico Cassini (1625–1712) who first observed it. The gaps are named, in order of their discovery, the A-ring (most distant from the planet), B-ring (between A and C), and C-ring (closest to the planet).

The Voyager images, however, show that the system is far more complex, interesting, and puzzling than had been imagined. In the first place, four additional rings were detected, which have been named the D- through G-rings. The D-ring is closest to the planet, even closer than the C-ring, while the E-, F-, and G-rings are the most distant, ranging from 87,000 miles (140,600 km) to 140,000 miles (230,000 km) away. Photographs show that each ring is itself very complex, consisting of numerous smaller rings. Overall, Saturn's ring system may contain more than a thousand smaller "ringlets" within the seven major ring systems.

The rings appear to be made of gas and dust particles, ranging in size from a millimeter or less in diameter to as large as a barn. Currently the most popular hypothesis for the origin of the rings is that they were formed when one or more asteroids (or other bodies) entered Saturn's gravitational field, shattered, and fell into orbit around the planet. Spectra of the rings suggest that they consist primarily of water ice, although impurities such as rocky materials embedded within the ice may also be present. Color images of the rings show spectacular variations, ranging from white to orange, green, and blue, suggesting that different parts of the system may have different chemical compositions.

Images of the rings returned by the Voyager spacecraft also revealed a number of interesting and unexpected features within the ring system. One of these features is a "braided" ring, located within the F-ring. This ring consists of three distinct, but intertwined, ringlets. The ringlets appear to be kept in position by two of the newly discovered moons, Prometheus and Pandora. Apparently the gravitational fields of the two moons act on the particles within the ring to keep it in this configuration. Some astronomers believe that other "shepherd moons" buried within the rings may have a similar effect on other ringlets in the system.

Another interesting discovery was the presence of "spokes" within the rings. The spokes actually are fine markings that spread from the inner rings to the outer limits of the system. They appear as dark streaks in reflected light but are bright when lighted from behind. Although the spokes may be caused by the relative absence of matter compared to the regions in which they are found, scientists have not yet developed a good explanation for their existence.

Without doubt, the most extensive and precise information about Saturn ever obtained was that collected by the *Cassini* orbiter and the *Huygens* probe beginning in 2004. As the orbiter passed through the planet's outer atmosphere and its ring structure, it sent back an amazing collection of photographs that Dr. Carolyn Porco, leader of the project's imaging team, described as "mind-boggling, just mind-boggling." The photographs showed new detail about the rings, including scalloping along their edges, that has yet to be explained. Scientists will be analyzing the data collected by *Cassini* for years following its four-year tour around the planet.

The major portion of the Cassini-Huygens mission consists of 74 orbits of Saturn and 44 close flybys of its largest moon, Titan. During one of these flybys, the orbiter released the *Huygens* probe, which then began its descent into the moon's atmosphere. A fair amount of information was available about Titan before the Cassini-Huygens mission, some obtained from Earth-based observatories and some from earlier flybys of the Voyager spacecraft. During *Voyager 1*'s contact with Titan, for example, scientists learned that the moon is not as large as had been thought. It was earlier regarded as the largest satellite in the solar system, but *Voyager 1* revealed that the moon's very thick atmosphere hides a considerably smaller solid body beneath. In fact, the solid portion of Titan is probably just a bit smaller than Ganymede. It is still a satellite of some significance, however. It is larger in diameter than either Mercury or Pluto and its mass is greater than Pluto's.

Furthermore, Titan still retains the important distinction of being the only satellite in the solar system to have an atmosphere. Its atmosphere appears to be about 50 percent denser than that Earth's, with a surface pressure of about 1.5 bar. Titan's atmosphere, like that of Earth, appears to consist primarily of molecular nitrogen with a number of minor constituents, as shown in the chart on page 157. Most astronomers believe that argon is present, with abundance ranging anywhere from 0 to 7 percent, although pre-*Huygens* data were insufficient to allow a more precise determination of that value. The organization Students for the Exploration and Development of Space (SEDS) has characterized the Titan atmosphere as a "very thick smog" in which "there appears to be a lot of chemistry going on."

Researchers currently hypothesize that Titan has a rocky center about 3,400 km (2,000 miles) in diameter, surrounded by layers of icy material. The interior may still retain heat produced during its formation, although the surface temperature is estimated to be about 94 K ($-179°C$).

Uranus

Uranus is the third of the outer planets, also known as the *"gas giants,"* because they have no solid surface. It has a radius of 15,872 miles (25,559 km), about a third that of Jupiter and less than half that of Saturn. Its mass is about 8.66×10^{25} kg and its density about 1.3 g/cm^3. Prior to *Voyager 2*'s flyby of the planet in 1981, observers recorded five moons, discovered between 1787 and 1948: Oberon, Titania, Umbriel, Ariel, and Miranda, all named after characters in plays by William Shakespeare. Voyager discovered 10 additional moons, most of which are also named for characters from Shakespearean plays: Cordelia, Ophelia, Desdemona, Portia, Juliet, Puck, Belinda, Rosalind, Cressida, and Bianca. Further analysis of Voyager data and additional observations by orbiting and Earth-based observatories has increased the number of Uranian moons to 27 (as of early 2007).

In 1977, astronomers discovered that Uranus is surrounded by a system of rings similar to those of Saturn. They lie in a concentric pattern around the planet's equator. Uranus's axis of rotation is parallel with its plane of revolution, rather than perpendicular to it, like Earth's. In other words, instead of spinning like a top on its path around the Sun, as Earth does, Uranus "rolls" along it like a barrel. Consequently, the planet's rings form a "bull's-eye" pattern pointing at the Sun.

◄ CONSTITUENTS OF THE TITAN ATMOSPHERE ►

SPECIES	ABUNDANCE
Nitrogen	90–97%
Methane	2–10%
Ethane	13 ppm
Ethene (ethylene)	10.1 ppm
Ethyne (acetylene)	2.2 ppm
Propane	0.7 ppm
Hydrogen cyanide	160 ppb
Cyanoacetylene	1.5 ppb

Source: Linda J. Spilker, ed. *Passage to a Ringed World: The Cassini-Huygens Mission to Saturn and Titan*. NASA Special Publication SP-533. Washington, D.C.: National Aeronautics and Space Administration, October 1997, Chapter 3. Also available online at http://saturn.jpl.nasa.gov/gallery/products/pdfs/chapter3.pdf.

Apart from its most general features, the physical and chemical characteristics of Uranus were largely unknown to astronomers prior to the *Voyager 2* flyby in 1981. That mission, however, provided a host of new data about the planet, its ring system, and its moons. For example, *Voyager* reported that the temperature of the planet at both poles is approximately the same, about 58 K ($-215°C$), in spite of the fact that one pole always points toward the Sun and the other pole away from the Sun. The average temperature of the planet overall is 60 K (−213°C), with a minimum of 52 K (−221°C) at the 0.1 bar level in the atmosphere.

Spectroscopic analysis of Uranus's atmosphere suggests that hydrogen is the predominant gas, with an abundance of about 84 percent, followed by helium (14 percent), methane (2 percent), and trace amounts of acetylene, hydrogen cyanide, and carbon monoxide. The planet appears blue when viewed through a telescope because methane gas in the planet's atmosphere absorbs sunlight's red wavelengths, reflecting blue light. There is reason to believe that the planet may also have colored bands, similar to those seen on Jupiter, although their presence is hidden by the overlying methane layer.

As they do with other planets, scientists base their hypotheses of the structure of Uranus's interior on observed physical properties. According to one popular model, the planet consists of a large core composed primarily of silicon and oxygen that is surrounded by first, a layer consisting of water ice and rock; then, by an envelope of liquid hydrogen; and, finally, by an outermost envelope made of gaseous hydrogen, helium, methane, ammonia, and water.

Scientists have classified Uranus's ring system into 10 distinct sets, named (from the planet's surface outward) 6, 5, 4, alpha, beta, eta, gamma, delta, lambda, and epsilon. Uranus's rings differ markedly from those surrounding Saturn in a number of ways. First, their albedos tend to be very low, about 0.03, meaning that they reflect only about 3 percent of the light that falls on them. Also, they tend to be even thinner than the Saturnian rings; epsilon is the thickest at about 10 miles (15 km), while the other nine are about 0.05 miles (0.1 km) thick. Finally, the composition of Uranus's rings seems significantly different from those of Saturn, consisting almost entirely of basketball-sized particles, with very few tiny and very few very large particles.

Spectroscopic evidence suggests that the rings are made primarily of water ice. Some scientists believe that the ice may be covered by a thin layer of carbon, accounting for their very low albedo. Interestingly enough, pairs of "shepherd moons," like those observed above Saturn, have also been observed in the Uranian ring system. After the discovery of the Saturnian shepherd moons, researchers

This *Hubble Space Telescope* image of the planet Uranus shows its ring system and six of its moons. They are, clockwise from the top, Desdemona, Belinda, Ariel, Portia, Cressida and Puck. (SPACE TELESCOPE SCIENCE INSTITUTE/NASA//Photo Researchers, Inc.)

predicted that they would find 18 such moons above Uranus, although *Voyager* was able to photograph only two. The most popular current theory about the rings' origin is that they were formed relatively recently when a larger body, such as a moon, became trapped in the planet's gravitational field and was broken apart by gravitational forces.

The two largest Uranian moons, Titania and Oberon, have diameters of about 1,000 miles (1,600 km), making them about half the size of Earth's moon. The smallest of the moons known prior to *Voyager* is Miranda, with a diameter of about 300 miles (500 km), about one-seventh the size of the Moon. The newly discovered moons are all much smaller than the five previously known moons, ranging in size from 16 miles (26 km) in diameter for Cordelia to 96 miles (154 km) for Puck.

The photographs of the Uranian moons taken by *Voyager* have provided astronomers with a challenging mass of data to interpret. The moons appear to be very different from each other in some ways, raising questions of how they may have formed and how they have evolved over the millennia. The moons appear to be made mostly of water ice (about 50 percent), rock (about 30 percent), and carbon- and nitrogen-based compounds (about 20 percent). None of the moons has an atmosphere, but they all have striking and, sometimes, quite different surfaces. For example, Titania, the largest satellite, has very large fault systems and canyons that suggest a good deal of geologic activity. Such features usually suggest crustal movements in which two portions of the surface collide, causing uplift in some places and opening deep fissures elsewhere.

Miranda is, in some ways, the most interesting of the moons. It contains fault canyons, some of which plunge 12 miles (20 km) into the moon's surface. The moon also has terraces on its surface and a strange mixture of young and old features. The presence of large geologic features, such as canyons, is especially puzzling because they suggest a hot interior for the moon, but the moon is so small and cool that this is difficult to imagine. Whatever the explanation, the face of Miranda is one of the most striking and interesting to be seen in the solar system. With no new voyages scheduled to visit Uranus in the near future, it may be some time before astronomers are able to answer some of the questions raised by the Voyager mission.

Neptune

Neptune is very nearly the same size as Uranus, with an equatorial radius of 15,378 miles (24,756 km). It is somewhat more massive, however, with a mass of 1.03×10^{26} kg and a density of about 1.76 g/cm^3. *Voyager 2* visited the planet on August 24 and 25, 1989. Like *Voyager*'s surveys of Jupiter, Saturn, and Uranus, this visit provided astronomers with by far the best images and data of the planet ever to be recorded.

The planet's atmosphere is generally similar to that of the other outer planets. The three most abundant chemical species are molecular hydrogen (84 percent), helium (14 percent), and methane (2 percent). Minor constituents of the atmosphere that have been identified include hydrogen deuteride (about 192 ppm) and ethane (about 1.5 ppm). These species appear to exist in the form of water ice, ammonia ice, ammonium hydrosulfide ice, and, possibly, methane ice. As with Uranus, Neptune's bluish color is a result of the absorption of red light from solar radiation by methane molecules.

Astronomers were surprised at the close-up view of Neptune's atmosphere provided by *Voyager 2.* Since the planet is at such a great distance from the Sun, they had expected it to be relatively dark and quiet, but images relayed by *Voyager*'s cameras indicated that this was not the case. As on Jupiter, very high winds and storms sweep through many parts of the atmosphere. One particularly violent storm called the *Great White Spot* was observed with winds of up to 1,200 mph (2,000 km/hr), the strongest winds ever recorded anywhere in the solar system. Interestingly enough, when the *Hubble Space Telescope* photographed the same area of the planet 20 years later, the spot had disappeared. *HST* did, however, find a new "Great White Spot" (which was actually a dark spot) similar to the one seen by *Voyager* but in the planet's northern hemisphere rather than its southern hemisphere.

Current theories suggest that Neptune's internal structure is similar to that of the other gas giant planets in that its density gradually increases from the outer atmosphere to the center of the planet. Deeper into the atmosphere, normally gaseous materials are exposed to greater and greater pressures until they become very dense gases and, eventually, liquids. The center of the planet is thought to consist of an Earth-size core made of molten rock and liquid water, ammonia, and methane.

Prior to the Voyager mission, Neptune was thought to have only two moons: Triton, discovered by British astronomer William Lassell (1799–1880) in 1846, and Nereid, discovered by the Dutch-American astronomer Gerard Kuiper (1905–73) in 1949. During its flyby of the planet, *Voyager* detected an additional six moons, ranging in size from about 37 miles (60 km) in diameter (Naiad) to about 240 miles (400 km) in diameter (Proteus). As of early 2007, scientists listed 13 moons for Neptune.

Triton is of special interest to scientists because of a number of unusual characteristics. In the first place, it is the only satellite in the solar system to revolve around its parent planet in a retrograde motion—that is, in a direction opposite to that of the planet's rotation. In addition, it is only one of three bodies in the solar system (Earth and Titan being the others) with an atmosphere consisting primarily of nitrogen gas. Triton's atmosphere is very thin, with a surface pressure of only 14 microbars, about 0.0014 percent that on Earth. Also, Triton is the coldest body ever measured in the solar system, with a surface temperature of 38 K ($-235°C$). At that temperature, nitrogen is frozen, so that Triton's atmosphere consists primarily of thin clouds made of nitrogen ice and the surface is covered with a thin layer of nitrogen frost.

Voyager's photographs of Triton's surface have raised a number of questions about the satellite's structure, composition, and evolution. Its surface is covered with many very large cracks that may have been formed by some sort of tectonic activity. *Voyager* actually photographed a number of eruptions in progress, in which nitrogen gas mixed with dark particles were spewed several kilometers into the atmosphere. *Voyager* also photographed a polar cap that extended over a very large portion of the planet's southern hemisphere. The pinkish color of the ice cap is thought to be caused by methane ice that has been transformed by solar radiation into other components. Dark streaks running across the pink ice cap may have been formed as the result of liquid nitrogen flows produced during volcanic eruptions. The fascinating characteristics of this moon explain why future flybys of Triton are a high priority in planned space explorations, such as NASA's Neptune Orbiter Mission, initially planned for launch in 2006 or 2007 but now on hold because of budget constraints.

One of the key questions about Neptune answered by the *Voyager* flyby was the nature of the planet's rings. Earth-based observations in the mid-1980s suggested that the planet did, indeed, have rings, but they were of a peculiar nature. Instead of complete rings, such as those observed around Jupiter, Saturn, and Uranus, observers were able to find only incomplete rings, or *arcs,* that were present on one side of the planet, but not the other. A considerable amount of effort was devoted to explaining how such incomplete rings could form and retain their shape. One explanation was that one or more shepherd satellites, such as those found on Saturn, might exert gravitational forces on the partial rings, preventing them from spreading out to produce complete rings such as those found on other planets.

Voyager provided a simple and happy answer to that difficult problem. As it turns out, Neptune *does* have rings and they are *complete* rings. Earth-based observations were unable to detect the complete rings because they are so thin in some regions that they do not reflect enough light to be seen. The presence of more dense regions in the rings (the arcs) is, indeed, correct, and the shepherd satellite theory (the moon in question being Galatea) may well explain this anomalous behavior.

Overall, *Voyager* observed four Neptunian ring systems, located at distances of 26,000 miles (41,900 km), 33,000 miles (53,200 km), and 39,000 miles (62,930 km) from the planet's center. The three rings located at these distances are very narrow, only about 10 miles (15 km) wide, while a fourth ring in close proximity to the middle ring is much larger, about 3,600 miles (5,800 km) wide. As with Saturn, one of Neptune's rings has a "braided" appearance that may result from the accumulation of material in some parts of the ring, but not in others.

Pluto

The status of Pluto as an astronomical body was changed in August 2006 when the International Astronomical Union (IAU) voted to adopt a new definition for a body's designation as a planet. The IAU decided that the only bodies that are to be considered planets are those that (1) orbit around the Sun, (2) have sufficient mass for gravity to maintain a nearly round shape, and (3) have cleared the neighborhood around its orbit. Pluto satisfies the first two of these conditions, but not the third. As a result, it was placed in the newly created category of dwarf planet, along with two other solar bodies: Ceres (formerly classified as an asteroid) and Eris (a large body located beyond the Kuiper belt).

Pluto is the only member of the solar system traditionally classified as a planet not to have been visited by a spacecraft from Earth. As a result, much of the information about this most distant member of the solar system is still incomplete and partially in doubt. It is smaller than any planet in the solar system, with a equatorial radius of 714 miles (1,501 km), about half the size of Mercury and 20 percent the size of Earth. Its mass is about 1.5×10^{22} kg, about 0.0024 that of Earth. Pluto's density is the higher than that of any of the outer planets, about 2.10 g/cm^3.

For many years Pluto was thought to have a single moon, Charon, first seen in 1978. In May 2005, however, astronomers working with data from the *Hubble Space Telescope* identified two additional moons, provisionally designated as S/2005 P 1 and S/2005 P 2. In June 2006, the IAU approved the names of Nix and Hydra for these two satellites, bringing to three the number of Pluto's moons. Charon was discovered only fairly recently because it and Pluto are so close to each other that light reflected off Pluto's bright surface (albedo = 0.5) masks its satellite. In fact, scientists now believe that Pluto and Charon may not really be dwarf planet and moon at all, but a double-dwarf-planet system, the only one in the solar system. A double system is one in which two bodies revolve around each other and around a common center of gravity. A popular hypothesis today is that Charon may have been born as the result of a collision between Pluto and another large body, in much the way that Earth's Moon is thought to have formed.

◄ JAMES E. WEBB (1906–1992) ►

Great scientific discoveries and important scientific expeditions are usually thought of, planned, and carried out by scientists, but major projects that involve the investment of billions of dollars of public money are often administered and managed by individuals who have little or no background in science and technology itself. The efforts of such individuals are often responsible for the ultimate success (or failure) of research projects. One of the best examples of this truism is James E. Webb, second administrator of the U.S. National Aeronautics and Space Administration (NASA).

James Webb was born in Tally Ho, North Carolina, on October 7, 1906. He attended the University of North Carolina, from which he received his A.B. in education in 1928. He then joined the U.S. Marine Corps and served as a pilot from 1930 to 1932. After leaving the service, he entered the George Washington University School of Law and earned his L.L.B. in 1936 and was admitted to the District of Columbia Bar.

Webb's first post-military job was as secretary to Representative Edward W. Pou, of North Carolina's 4th Congressional District, from 1932 to 1934. He then worked for the Washington law firm of O. Max Gardner, former governor of North Carolina, and for the Sperry Gyroscope Company in Brooklyn, New York. When World War II broke out, Webb returned to active duty with the Marine Corps.

At the end of the war, Webb returned to Washington, where he worked as an assistant to Gardner, who was then undersecretary of the Treasury. In 1946, Webb was appointed director of the Bureau of Budget and in that position drafted the first balanced U.S. budget since the days of the Hoover administration in 1930. Three years later, Webb was appointed undersecretary of State under Dean Acheson. His primary responsibility at the time was the reorganization of the State Department along the lines that had been recommended by the Hoover Commission report of 1949. When Dwight Eisenhower was elected president in 1952, Webb left Washington to take a position with the Kerr-McGee Oil Company in Oklahoma. He stayed with Kerr-McGee until 1961, when he returned to Washington as NASA's new administrator.

Webb began his tenure as administrator of NASA on February 14, 1961, replacing NASA's first administrator, T. Keith Glennan. He served in this role

(continues)

◁ JAMES E. WEBB (1906–1992)

(continued) ▷

for seven years, arguably the most critical period in the agency's history. Shortly after Webb's arrival at NASA, President John F. Kennedy announced (on May 25, 1961) the U.S. government's intention to place a man on the Moon before the end of the decade. With that announcement, Kennedy energized the young U.S. space program and, at the same time, opened the gates to the greatest public works program in all of human history. The man who saw that program through, from birth to conclusion, was James Webb. Webb left office in October 1968, just a few months before Neil Armstrong took humankind's first steps on the Moon.

According to NASA's official biography of Webb, he "politicked, coaxed, cajoled, and maneuvered for NASA in Washington" in an effort to ensure that Kennedy's dream would come true. Many authorities believe that Webb's finest hours came after the fire that occurred during the test of an Apollo spacecraft on January 27, 1967, a disaster in which three astronauts were killed. Webb told the nation, "We've always known that something like this was going to happen soon or later," but he promised that the tragedy would not mean the end of the U.S. space program. He eventually accepted personal responsibility for the disaster—although it is doubtful that a single individual was to blame—and went back to Congress and the public to work for the successful completion of the Apollo program.

After retiring from NASA in 1968, Webb remained in Washington, where he served on a number of advisory boards and as regent of the Smithsonian Institution. He died in Washington on March 27, 1992, and was buried in Arlington National Cemetery. In his honor, NASA has chosen to name its latest new telescope the James Webb Space Telescope (JWST). The telescope is designed to replace the *Hubble Space Telescope*, which has been in orbit around Earth since 1990. Launch date of the JWST is scheduled for August 2011. It will have a primary mirror 6 meters in diameter and a host of ancillary instruments, including a near-infrared multi-object spectrometer, a near-infrared camera, and a mid-infrared camera and spectrometer. The telescope has five major goals: investigations of cosmology and structure of the universe, the origin and evolution of galaxies, the history of the Milky Way and its neighbors, the birth and formation of stars, and the origin and evolution of planetary systems.

The Pluto-Charon system raises additional questions because it lies within the Kuiper Belt, which extends about 20 AU (astronomical units; about 3×10^9 km) beyond the orbit of Neptune. NASA's New Horizons space mission, launched in January 2006, should help provide a better understanding of the nature of Pluto and Charon, especially in relation to other Kuiper Belt Objects.

For the present, knowledge of these two bodies is still somewhat limited and speculative. Earth-based observations and data provided by orbiting telescopes indicate that Pluto's atmosphere is very thin, with a pressure on the planet's surface of between three and 50 microbars (0.3–5 percent that of Earth's atmosphere). The maximum temperature observed in the upper atmosphere is 106 K (−167°C), and the most abundant gases present are expected to be nitrogen, methane, carbon monoxide, and species produced by the photolysis of these substances.

The most abundant species on Pluto's surface appears to be nitrogen, followed by carbon monoxide, methane, and water ice, all of which occur in the solid state. Based on the planet's density, scientists predict that its interior consists of some type of hydrated silicate mixed with up to 30 percent water ice.

Almost nothing is known about the composition of Charon's atmosphere or surface. The surface appears to be covered primarily with water ice. Spectral lines for other species have been detected but not identified as belonging to specific compounds.

Kuiper Belt Objects

It just keeps going and going. The solar system, that is, or so it seems. For many decades, astronomers thought that Pluto was probably the most distant object in that group of bodies that orbit the Sun, but that idea is now obsolete. Scientists have learned that an even more distant group of objects—Kuiper Belt Objects, or KBOs—populate a vast region of space beyond the orbit of Neptune. Although predicted as early as 1951 by the Dutch-American astronomer Gerard Kuiper (1905–73), the first Kuiper Belt Object was not discovered until 1992. By early 2007, more than 800 KBOs had been discovered, with the list of such objects being updated weekly and, sometimes, daily.

◄ GERARD PETER KUIPER (1905–1973) ►

Where did the solar system come from? How was the Sun born? What are the origins of Earth and other planets in the solar system? Questions such as these have challenged philosophers and scientists for centuries. One of the earliest theories for the formation and evolution of the solar system was proposed by the French philosopher and mathematician René Descartes (1596–1650). Descartes suggested that the Sun and planets originally formed out of a swirling mass of matter that slowly condensed into one very large body (the Sun) and other smaller bodies (the planets) at various distances from the Sun. With some important refinements, that theory is one most astronomers subscribe to today.

Descartes and other theorists inspired not only their colleagues and immediate successors in the field of science but also younger generations for centuries after. One person whose life was influenced early on by the work of Descartes was Gerard Kuiper. As a young man, Kuiper read the works of Descartes and became interested in the same questions to which the great French thinker had applied himself more than three centuries earlier. Eventually, Kuiper suggested modifications in the Descartes "solar nebula" theory that have made it the current popular explanation as to how the solar system was formed.

Gerard Peter Kuiper was born in the little town of Haringcarspel (now Harenkarspel), The Netherlands, on December 7, 1905. After completing primary and high school, Kuiper decided to "leapfrog" over the traditional path that Dutch students followed in preparation for a university education. He took—and passed—a special examination that allowed him to go directly to Leiden University, which he entered in 1924. There he studied physics and astronomy and earned his B.Sc. degree in 1927. Upon graduation, he began graduate studies at Leiden immediately. In 1929, he joined the Dutch Solar Eclipse Expedition to Sumatra, where he spent eight months. Four years later, Leiden University awarded Kuiper his Ph.D. in astronomy. His doctoral thesis dealt with the subject of binary stars, pairs of stars that revolve around each other and a common center of gravity.

Kuiper's first job was in the United States, at the Lick Observatory, operated by the University of California. At Lick, Kuiper worked with one of the great double-star (binary star) astronomers of all time, Robert Grant Aitken. Although he went on to make contributions in many other fields, Kuiper always thought of himself as first and foremost a double-star astronomer.

Although he experienced considerable success in his research at Lick, Kuiper decided that he was not likely to be chosen as Aitken's successor, and in 1935 he accepted an offer to teach astronomy at Harvard University. That job lasted for only one year, and in 1936 Kuiper moved to the University of Chicago to take the post of associate professor of practical astronomy at the Yerkes Observatory. In 1943, Kuiper was appointed professor of astronomy, a position he held until 1960.

Kuiper took a leave of absence from Chicago in 1943 to work on the war effort. He was assigned to Harvard's Radio Research Laboratory, where he studied methods for counteracting enemy radar searches. He was then transferred to the Eighth Air Force Headquarters in England and, at war's end, was assigned to the Alsos mission developed to assess the state of German science. (*Alsos* is the Greek word for "grove," a play on the name of Major General Leslie M. Groves, director of the Manhattan Project for the development of the atomic bomb.) During a brief period of time in the winter of 1943–44, Kuiper continued his own research at the University of Texas's McDonald Observatory. During this research, he detected methane in the atmosphere of Saturn's moon Titan. It was the first time anyone had found a specific gas in the atmosphere of a satellite. From that time on, Kuiper had a very special interest in the atmospheres of planets and satellites. He later carried out pioneer spectroscopic studies of Mars, Jupiter, Saturn, the Galilean satellites of Jupiter, and the rings of Saturn. Much of his work is described and summarized in a book that he edited, which is now considered a classic in the field, *The Atmospheres of the Earth and Planets,* published by the University of Chicago Press in 1949.

By 1949 Kuiper had come full circle in his astronomical pursuits by publishing his own theory of the formation of the solar system. His hypothesis was, of course, considerably more developed than that of his idol, Descartes. It suggested that the flattened disk out of which the Sun was born eventually broke apart in distinct masses, called *protoplanets,* which later grew by the accretion of matter into the planets that exist today. In connection with this hypothesis, Kuiper suggested also that a large, flat belt of bodies might exist beyond the orbit of Neptune, out of which certain types of comets might develop and travel into the solar system. That belt of bodies has since been named the *Kuiper belt* in his honor.

(continues)

◁ GERARD PETER KUIPER (1905–1973)

(continued) ▷

Kuiper's list of astronomical accomplishments is impressive. In addition to his work on binary stars, the atmospheres of planets and satellites, and the formation of the solar system, he discovered the fifth moon of Uranus, Miranda, and Neptune's second moon, Nereid; he was an early advocate of the use of jet airplanes for high-altitude astronomical observations; and he accurately predicted the nature of the lunar surface before any human had walked on it. In recognition of these achievements, Kuiper was awarded the Janssen medal of the French astronomical society and the Order of Orange Nassau by the Dutch government. Kuiper died in Mexico City on December 24, 1973, while examining a number of possible sites for a new observatory.

Some astronomers estimate that there may be more than 35,000 KBOs in total.

KBOs promise to provide exciting new information about the most distant reaches of the solar system. They might finally allow us to learn, for example, the true nature of Pluto and Charon—whether they are true dwarf planets are simply two of the largest KBOs yet discovered. KBOs are also of special interest to astronomers because they may be among the most pristine examples of the materials present during the formation of the solar system and, hence, provide important clues as to how that process occurred. Small wonder, then, that researchers from many fields are looking forward with anticipation to the results of the New Horizons space mission launched in 2006.

Researchers have learned a vast amount of new information about Jupiter, Saturn, Uranus, Neptune, Pluto and the Kuiper Belt Objects in the last century. Improved terrestrial telescopes, the *Hubble Space Telescope,* and space explorations such as *Voyager 1* and *2,* Galileo, and Cassini have produced new data that will take astrochemists years to analyze and interpret, providing them with even more detailed information about the chemical composition of the atmospheres, satellites, surfaces, and other features of the outer planets and their associated bodies.

6

COMETS, METEORS, ASTEROIDS, AND THE MOON

In October 1066, a bright new star appeared in the skies above England. It was so bright that it terrified millions of people, not only in England but throughout Europe. When the Normans under Duke William of Normandy ("William the Conqueror") defeated King Harold II's Anglo-Saxon army on October 14 in the Battle of Hastings, many people were convinced that the new star had foretold that great historical event.

The "bright new star" was actually a comet, known today as Halley's comet. Halley's comet reappears on a regular basis every 76 years. Each of its appearances has caused fear and amazement among people around the world. Indeed, comets are among the most dramatic of all astronomical events.

Meteorites also inspire fascination and concern among people. These chunks of rock fall out of the sky in apparently unpredictable patterns, often causing enormous destruction in the regions where they land. The largest meteorites to strike Earth are thought to be responsible for some of the most severe climatic changes ever to occur on the planet. Scientists now believe, for example, that the primary cause for the extinction of dinosaurs and many other species about 65 million years ago was the enormous cloud of dust produced when a meteorite struck Earth's surface.

Comets and meteorites are examples of astronomical bodies whose behavior can be predicted with a high degree of reliability (comets) or with only the lowest reliability (meteorites). This chapter deals with both types of astronomical bodies, as well as other bodies about which scientists are just beginning to obtain detailed information—asteroids—and the only extraterrestrial body on which humans have set foot—the Moon.

Comets

Because of their irregular and unexpected appearances, comets and meteors have long been regarded as harbingers of dramatic events: the birth or death of kings and queens, success or failure on a battlefield, and the rise or downfall of great civilizations. The more humans came to understand and trust the regularity of planetary and stellar motions, the more they came to worry about astronomical events that were *not* regular and predictable. Adding to the wonder created by comets and meteors is the spectacular nature of their appearances in some cases. For example, a comet that appeared in 1910 was so bright that it could be seen during the day, accounting for its popular name, the Daylight Comet of 1910.

Accounts of the warnings posed by comets date back almost as far as recorded history. The ancient Chinese, for example, were convinced that the occurrence of a comet presaged the death of an emperor, the onset of war, or the spread of disease across the country. Historians reported at least 10 epidemics in China that they claimed were associated with the appearance of a comet. Such beliefs were hardly unique to the Chinese, however. Seven days after Julius Caesar was assassinated on March 15, 44 B.C.E., for example, a comet streaming across the skies convinced many Romans that their leader had gone directly to heaven, from which he was announcing his presence. At about the same time, a number of Roman writers discussed the warnings posed by comets. Both the poet Tibullus (ca. 54–19 B.C.E.) and the natural philosopher Pliny (23–79 C.E.) warned that comets foretold the outbreak of war or other civil unrest. Astronomers also believe that the star that foretold the birth of Jesus was also a comet.

A number of events in addition to the Battle of Hastings have been associated with the appearance of Halley's comet. In 1456, when the Turks were extending their power into southeastern Europe, Halley's comet suddenly appeared in the skies. Convinced that the comet was a warning of impending doom, Pope Callixtus III (1455–58) called the faithful to take part in "several days of prayer for the averting of the wrath of God, that whatever calamity impended might be turned from the Christians and against the Turks." To emphasize his concerns, the pope then excommunicated the comet, calling it an instrument of the devil. Unfortunately for his flock, the pope's actions were unsuccessful; the Turks solidified their hold on Constantinople, remaining in power there for four more centuries.

The belief in comets as harbingers of doom is not a strictly historic and "quaint" belief. In 1997, for example, 39 members of the Higher Source Group, a subset of the Heaven's Gate religious group, committed suicide in Rancho Santa Fe, California. In a statement left for the press, members of the group announced that they were returning to their original home in distant space, Level Above Human. They were encouraged to make this decision apparently because of the anticipated appearance of Comet Hale-Bopp, which they believed carried with it an unidentified flying object (UFO) that was to take them to their home in the sky.

The first attempt to determine the orbit of a comet was made by the English astronomer Sir Edmund Halley (1656–1742), a close friend of Sir Isaac Newton. In 1687 Newton published his *Principia,* one of the most important books in the history of science. In it Newton described his theory of gravitation and demonstrated how that theory could be used to explain the motion of the planets and the Moon. Halley was intrigued by the possibility that Newton's theory might also be useful in explaining the behavior of the most unpredictable of all astronomical objects, the comets.

He began his work by looking back through historical records to see if he could find one or more comets that had appeared at somewhat regular times in the past. One comet that met this criterion was one that had appeared most recently in 1682. Halley believed that the same comet had been seen in 1378, 1456, 1531, and 1607. The intervals between sightings were 75, 76, 75, and 78 years. These results suggested to Halley that the same comet had been reappearing at regular intervals, but its periodicity was too imprecise to meet the demands of Newton's new and accurate theory.

Halley finally discovered an explanation for the slight changes in the comet's orbital path. Apparently its proximity to Jupiter varied on each of its passes through the solar system and past Earth. The gravitational attraction of that giant planet had disturbed the comet's orbit enough to account for differences in its orbital period. When Halley introduced this "Jupiter" correction into his calculations of the comet's orbit, he found that Newton's laws very closely explained the body's path through the sky. He went on to predict that the comet would reappear next during the winter of 1758–59. Unfortunately, neither Halley nor Newton lived long enough to find out whether Halley's prediction was true . . . but it was. The comet returned on Christmas Day, 1758. It was named Halley's comet (or Comet Halley) in honor of the English astronomer who first calculated its orbit. Comet Halley is now known to be the comet that appeared prior to the Battle of Hastings, and it may well have been the "star" that led the three wise men to the site of Jesus' birth. It last appeared in 1986 and is scheduled to return next in 2061.

The era of space travel has provided astronomers with a valuable new tool for the study of comet structure, composition, and behavior. During the two-year period 1985–86, no fewer than six spacecraft made flybys of comets. The first of these was NASA's *ISEE-3 (International Sun-Earth Explorer 3),* which after completing its primary mission of studying the Sun was targeted to pass through the tail of Comet Giacobini-Zinner in September of 1985. At that point, it was renamed the *International Comet Explorer (ICE). ICE* also observed Comet Halley from a distance of 17 million miles (28 million km) in March 1986.

The close approach of Comet Halley in 1986 also prompted the launch of five separate spacecraft to study the comet's structure and composition: *Vega I* and *Vega II* (Soviet Union), *Giotto* (European Space Agency), and *Sakikage* and *Suisei* Institute of Space and Aeronautical Science (ISAS) of Japan. Although the five missions experienced varying degrees of success, the images and data they returned to Earth have provided an unmatched look at the nature of comets.

The first U.S. spacecraft mission dedicated exclusively to the study of comets was Stardust, launched on February 7, 1999. *Stardust* flew past asteroid AnneFrank on November 2, 2002, on its way to its primary target, Comet Wild-2. The spacecraft flew past Wild-2 at a speed of 13,650 mph (21,960 km/h) on January 2, 2004, with a number of instruments operating successfully. Its onboard camera collected some of the best photographs of comets ever made, while a particle collector in the shape of a tennis racket filled with a silicon-based foam called *aerogel* scooped up particles from the comet's *coma* (the cloud of gas and dust around the comet's core). Particles collected on the foam were transferred to a parachute, which was then dropped onto the Utah salt flats on January 15, 2006. *Stardust*'s spectrometer also recorded spectra from the comet's *nucleus,* coma, and tails. Scientists will be analyzing photographs and particle samples collected during the Stardust mission for many years.

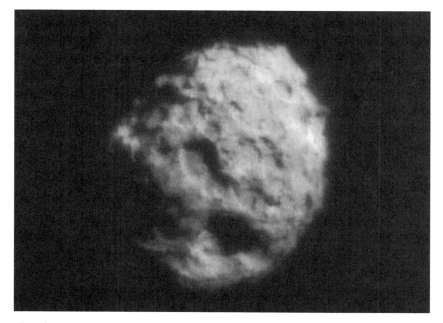

This photograph of Comet Wild-2 was taken by the *Stardust* spacecraft's navigation camera on January 2, 2004, at a distance of about 300 miles (500 km) from the comet. (NASA/Photo Researchers, Inc.)

◁ EDMUND HALLEY (1656–1742) ▷

In the early 18th century, when Edmund Halley did most of his scientific work, the world's scientific community was small and relatively close-knit. It was not unusual for the leading physicists in the world (and the leading chemists, and the leading astronomers, and so on) to know each other quite well and, in some cases, to work closely with each other.

Such was the case with Halley and Sir Isaac Newton. Halley apparently was still in his 20s when he first met Newton. The two became fast friends and encouraged each other's research. Halley seems to have been instrumental in encouraging Newton to complete his famous book, *Philosophiae Naturalis Principia Mathematica* (Mathematical Principles of Natural Philosophy). Better known simply as *Principia,* this book is one of the most important works of science ever written. In fact, Halley probably contributed financially to the cost of having the book published in 1687. In turn, Newton is thought to have been responsible for Halley's appointment as deputy controller of the Mint at Chester in 1696.

Perhaps the most important connection between the two men was Halley's use of Newton's theory of gravitation to explain the motion of comets. Within a decade of the publication of the *Principia,* the scientific world had become convinced of the value of his theories in the explanation of the motion of the planets and of the Moon around the Earth. The same theories also explained a number of well-known physical phenomena that occur here on Earth. Scientists were not so certain, however, that Newton's theories had more general application, such as to the motions of stars, comets, meteors, and other astronomical objects. When Halley undertook to study the orbital properties of the comet of 1682, he was able to show that Newton's theories had much broader applications than had previously been appreciated.

Edmund (also Edmond) Halley was born in Haggerston, near London, on November 8, 1656. He attended St. Paul's School in London and then Oxford University. Halley had developed an interest in astronomy early in life and majored in that subject at Oxford. While there, he wrote and published a book dealing with the laws of Johannes Kepler (1571–1630), a work that attracted the attention of John Flamsteed (1646–1719), then astronomer royal of England. Flamsteed suggested to Halley that he establish an observatory on the island of St. Helena in the South Atlantic which would provide him the opportunity to chart the sky from the Southern Hemisphere, a task that had not yet been attempted. Halley accepted the challenge, left Oxford in 1676 without finishing his degree, and traveled to St. Helena. When he returned to England in 1678, he had been able to plot the location of only 34 stars, but since it was the first work of its kind his catalog of stars in the Southern Hemisphere brought him some measure of fame.

Shortly after his return from St. Helena, at the age of 22, Halley was elected a fellow of the Royal Society. He then left for mainland Europe and spent much of his time over the next decade attending conferences and visiting with fellow scientists on the continent. In 1684, when Edmund was 28, his father was murdered. The elder Halley was a wealthy business-man, and upon his death, young Edmund Halley inherited a considerable fortune. The inheritance provided financial security for only a brief time, however, as he spent much of it in obtaining the publication of Newton's *Principia*. Before long, Halley was looking for employment to supplement his dwindling financial resources. He worked for the Royal Society in a va-riety of roles from 1685 to 1693, as warden at the Royal Mint from 1696 to 1698, and as commander of a warship in the Royal Navy from 1698 to 1700. In 1704, Halley was appointed Savilian professor of geometry at Oxford in 1704, a post he held until 1720, when he was appointed Astronomer Royal to replace Flamsteed, who had died. Halley remained in that post until he died in Greenwich on January 14, 1742.

Halley's research in astronomy was not limited to studies of the com-ets. One of his other major fields of interest was the history of astronomy. He read the works of early astronomers, including Ptolemy, Apollonius, Menelaus of Alexandria, and others and prepared translations of some of the original works. One of the discoveries he made while engaged in this research was that stars appeared to have shifted their positions in the skies between the time of the Greek astronomers and his own day. Astronomers had never considered such a notion possible, but Halley was able to show that stars did, in fact, move, based on star charts from the ancient Greeks. He was even able to show how three stars in particular, Arcturus, Procyon, and Sirius, had shifted position in only a century, between the time of Kepler and his own life.

A second successful U.S. comet mission was *Deep Space 1,* launched from Cape Canaveral on October 24, 1998. Its principal goal was to test a variety of new space technologies. It completed this primary mission in September 1999. The spacecraft's mission was then extended to include a flyby of Comet Borrelly, which it accomplished on September 22, 2001. *Deep Space 1* sent back black and white photographs of the comet, infrared spectrometer readings, ion and electron data, and measurements of the magnetic field and plasma waves in the vicinity of the comet.

NASA's most recent comet missions are Deep Impact and Rosetta. *Deep Impact* was launched on January 12, 2005, with Comet Tempel 1 as its target. The spacecraft encountered Tempel 1 on July 3, 2005, at which time it released a 770-pound (350 kg) copper projectile at the comet. Cameras and spectrometers on the spacecraft photographed and collected samples of materials ejected from the comet nucleus and relayed that information to scientists on Earth. *Rosetta* was launched on March 2, 2004, with Comet 67P/Churyumov-Gerasimenko as its target. The spacecraft will orbit the comet and make observations for about two years as the comet approaches the Sun. It will also release a small package of instruments that make the first-ever landing on the surface of a comet.

Not all space missions to comets have been as successful as Stardust and Deep Space 1. For example, NASA's *CONTOUR* (*Comet Nucleus Tour*), launched on July 3, 2002, was designed to rendezvous with and study Comet Encke on November 12, 2003, and Comet Schwassmann-Wachmann 3 on June 18, 2006. All contact was lost with *CONTOUR* on August 15, 2002, however, and the mission was canceled.

In a 1955 article announcing the discovery of a new comet, the *National Geographic* magazine called a comet "the nearest thing to nothing that anything can be and still be something." They are so small relative to other astronomical objects that they can be seen only when they approach the Sun, which vaporizes and illuminates the materials of which they are made. The central part of the comet, as shown in the diagram on page 179, is the *nucleus.* The nucleus is typically relatively small, no more than a few kilometers in diameter. The *Vega* and *Giotto* spacecraft found the nucleus of Comet

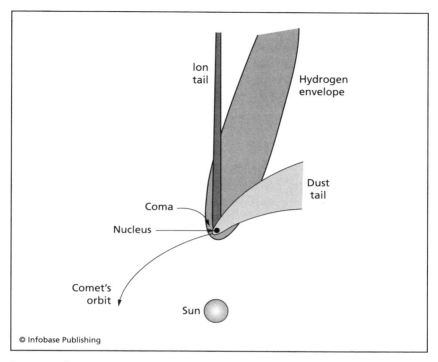

Structure of a comet

Halley to be 8.8 by 5.1 by 4.6 miles (14.2 by 8.2 by 7.5 km), about the size of a large mountain. As a comet approaches the Sun, some of the materials that make up the nucleus are vaporized, expanding to form a larger glowing coma around the nucleus. Comas tend to be about 10^5 km in size.

The most visually distinctive part of a comet is its long tail, which always extends from the nucleus and coma in a direction away from the Sun. The tail consists of two parts, one that extends outward in a straight line away from the nucleus, and one that has a curved "ballistic" shape. The first of these two tails, the ion or gas tail, is formed when solar radiation ionizes neutral atoms and molecules in the coma and nucleus. Ions found in cometary tails include CO^+, CH^+, OH^+, CN^+, CO_2^+, and N_2^+. These ions are then pushed away from the nucleus and coma by the solar wind, which consists of charged particles emitted from the Sun. The *ion tail* is visible partly because of sunlight reflected off cometary particles and partly because those particles become excited and give off their own radiation. The spectra produced by ion tails is, therefore, quite complex.

The second of the two tails, the *dust tail,* consists of tiny particles of matter expelled from the coma and nucleus by the Sun's radiative pressure. This tail is visible only because the particles of which it is composed reflect sunlight. The composition of cometary dust is thought to be similar to that of interstellar dust, but much remains to be learned about this portion of the comet's structure. In April 2003, NASA launched an experiment to obtain better data about the composition and structure of cometary dust. High-altitude research airplanes were flown through the upper atmosphere toward the tail of Comet Grigg-Skjellerup. Special collectors in the planes scooped up samples of the cometary dust. Analysis may take years.

The final major component of a comet is an elongated region filled with hydrogen gas. This hydrogen envelope surrounds the coma and extends away from the Sun a distance of millions of kilometers. The source of this hydrogen gas is not entirely clear. The rate at which hydrogen is being produced in some comets—10^{29} hydrogen atoms per second—is far too great for the hydrogen to be coming from the comet nucleus itself. The most popular hypothesis is that the hydrogen forms when sunlight decomposes OH radicals formed during the decomposition of water.

Probably the best general description of a comet ever made was by the American astronomer and comet authority Fred Whipple (1906–2004). Whipple called comets "dirty snowballs." That term is apt because cometary nuclei consist primarily of ices of water, ammonia, carbon dioxide, and methane mixed with dust particles. A comet that is distant from the Sun is essentially invisible because its nucleus is so small and dark. As the comet approaches the Sun, however, solar radiation vaporizes some of the ices that make up the nucleus. The gases thus released, along with some of the dust in the nucleus, form the familiar and spectacular features of a comet.

Comets can be classified into two major groups: short-term and long-term comets. Short-term comets are those with orbital periods of less than 200 years. They can be further subdivided into two groups: the Jupiter family, with periods of less than 20 years, and the Halley group, with periods of 20 to 200 years. The comet with the shortest known period is Comet Encke, which completes its trip around the Sun in just 3.3 years. At *perihelion* (the closest approach to the Sun) Encke comes within 0.33 AU of the Sun. The abbreviation AU stands for one astronomical unit, a distance of about 150 million km (93 million miles), or the distance from Earth to the Sun. Short-term comets travel in elliptical orbits with low eccentricity (that is, they tend to be more circular than "flattened") and low inclination to the ecliptic (that is, they tend to travel in the same plane around the Sun as do the planets).

Long-term comets are those with orbital periods greater than 200 years. According to some estimates, long-term comets may have orbital periods of a few tens or hundreds of thousands of years. Included among the long-term comets are those that pass through the solar system once and then are lost to interstellar space. Unlike short-term comets, long-term comets have orbits that lie at every possible inclination to the ecliptic. For comparison, one can picture short-term comets as traveling around the Sun on the same flat disk as the planets, while long-term comets are traveling around the Sun on the face of a sphere whose center is the Sun.

Astronomers have used the differing orbital paths of short- and long-term comets to hypothesize a possible source for each kind of comet. The first person to devise such a theory was the Dutch astronomer Jan Hendrick Oort (1900–92). Oort argued that, since long-term comets could appear from any point in the sky, their "home" must reside outside the solar system. Oort calculated that this "home" would consist of a spherical shell of debris located between 50,000 and 100,000 AU from Earth. This shell or cloud (now known as the *Oort cloud*) would be very stable, and individual pieces (comets) would be torn away only when the solar system passed close to a star, an interstellar cloud, or some other massive body. In such cases, a comet would be propelled out of the Oort cloud either toward the center of the solar system, becoming a comet visible to Earth, or away from the solar system, where it would be lost to interstellar space.

Oort's explanation for the origin of long-term comets does not apply to short-term comets. As noted earlier, short-term comets do not travel in random orbits around the Earth but move in constrained orbits that correspond to those of the planets. An explanation for the origin of these comets was provided by the Dutch-American astronomer Gerard Peter Kuiper (1905–73) in 1951. Kuiper suggested that "home" for short-term comets is a disk-shaped region extending outside the orbit of Neptune, at a distance from about 30 to 100 AU from the Sun. Again, the debris that makes up this belt is quite stable, and fragments escape from the region only when the solar system passes near some massive body, whose gravitational attraction propels them out of their "home" space.

The relatively simple explanation of orbital paths suggested here is deceptive, because comets can be affected by any number of factors as they travel around the Sun. One of the most important factors is the planets themselves, especially the most massive among them, Jupiter. Should a comet's path take it in the vicinity of Jupiter, that planet's gravitational attraction will deflect the comet's path into a new, slightly altered orbit. How Jupiter's gravitational field alters the otherwise regular orbital path of Comet Halley was discussed earlier in this chapter. Jupiter may also act on long-term comets that pass nearby, deflecting their paths sufficiently to turn them into short-term comets with orbits that can then be calculated and return visits that can be predicted. Alternatively, short-term comets may travel close enough to Jupiter to receive an extra "kick" that sends them on an elongated orbit that may take them out of the solar system and into interstellar space.

The chemical composition of short- and long-term comets tends to be somewhat different. Probably the most important factor difference is that short-term comets tend to spend more time close to the Sun than long-term comets do. Each time a comet passes around the Sun, it loses some of its mass because of outgassing caused by solar radiation. As a result, short-term comets tend to have lower amounts of "volatile" substances (those that sublime or evaporate at relatively low temperatures), such as water ice, methane ice, and ammonia ice.

Nearly all assured knowledge about the composition of comets comes from three sources: (1) data collected from Comet Halley by the Soviet Union's two Vega spacecraft and the ESA's Giotto mission,

(2) spectroscopic analysis of the coma of comets, especially very bright comets, such as Hale-Bopp and Hyakutake by Earth-based observatories, and (3) laboratory simulations of comet structures.

Based on information from these sources, scientists estimate that the nucleus of a comet consists of about 42 percent volatile compounds (about 80 percent of which is water) and 58 percent solid particles, generally described as "dust." About 45 percent of this nuclear dust is similar in chemical composition to the carbonaceous chondrites found in meteorites; that is, they are primarily silicate in composition. (Carbonaceous chondrites are discussed at greater length in the next section.) Another 40 percent of the nuclear dust is organic in nature, that is, composed of carbon compounds of varying degrees of complexity. The final 15 percent of nuclear dust is composed of very small particles with masses of only a few attograms (10^{-18}g).

At least three dozen gaseous species have been identified in the comas or nuclei of comets, including H, O, OH, NH, NH_2, and S. It is presumed that these gases form when sunlight causes the decomposition of basic compounds in the comet's nucleus, the ices of water, ammonia, methane, and hydrogen sulfide. Other compounds that have been identified in comets include acetylene (C_2H_2), acetonitrile (CH_3CN), hydrogen isocyanide ($HN=C$), hydrogen cyanide (HCN), formaldehyde (H_2CO), formic acid ($HCOOH$), isocyanic acid ($HNCO$), cyanoacetylene ($HNC=CCN$), and thioformaldehyde ($H_2C=S$). The chart on page 184–188 lists a few of the gaseous compounds identified in comets.

The carbon-based particles found in nuclear dust are of special interest to astronomers and other scientists. Such particles often contain fairly complex organic molecules, many of which are precursors of the complex biochemical molecules of which living organisms are formed. The chart on page 189 lists some of the organic molecules that may have been observed, with an indication of the confidence with which astronomers view the determination of each species.

Besides those molecules listed in the chart, an additional two dozen or so compounds are suspected of being present in comets, although evidence to support this view is still quite weak. Among the compounds that have been suggested are pentyne, hexyne, butadiene,

◀ MOLECULAR ABUNDANCES OF CERTAIN GASES IN COMETS ▷

SUBSTANCE	ABUNDANCE*	COMET
H_2O	100	Halley, Hale-Bopp, Wilson, many others
CO	2–20	Halley, Austin, several others
	2–8.5	Halley, Austin, Bradley, Levy
	<1	Hartley 2
	5	Hyakutake
	30–43	Hyakutake
	20	Hale-Bopp
CO_2	2.7	Halley
	3.5	Halley
	4–7	Halley, Austin, Bradfield, Hartley 2
	7–13	Levy
	4	Hyakutake
	6	Hale-Bopp

SUBSTANCE	ABUNDANCE*	COMET
H_2CO	0.03–1.5	several
	4	Halley
	>3.8	Halley
	0.2–1	Hyakutake
	~1	Hale-Bopp
CH_3OH	1–7	several
	1–7	Halley
	0.9–2	Hyakutake
	2	Hale-Bopp
C_2H_5OH	<0.5	Levy
HCOOH	<0.2	Austin, Levy
	0.05	Hale-Bopp
CH_4	>0.5–2	Halley, Wilson, Levy
	2	Halley
	0.7	Hyakutake
	~1	Hale-Bopp

(continues)

◁ MOLECULAR ABUNDANCES OF CERTAIN GASES IN COMETS *(continued)* ▷

SUBSTANCE	ABUNDANCE*	COMET
C_2H_2	0.4	Hyakutake
	~0.5	Hale-Bopp
NH_3	0.1–0.4	several
	0.4–1	Halley
	0.5–2	Halley
	0.55	Halley
	0.3	Hyakutake
	1.4	Hale-Bopp
HCN	0.05–0.2	several
	0.02	Halley
	0.1–0.2	Hyakutake
	0.2	Hale-Bopp
HNC	0.007	Hyakutake
	<0.004	Hale-Bopp
HNCO	0.07	Hyakutake
	0.04–0.13	Hale-Bopp

SUBSTANCE	ABUNDANCE*	COMET
CH_3CN	0.02	Hyakutake
	0.02	Hale-Bopp
HC_3N	<0.02	Halley, Levy
	0.019	Hale-Bopp
N_2	0.02–0.2	Halley, Bradfield
	<1.5	Halley
H_2S	0.1–0.3	Austin, Levy
	0.4–0.5	Halley
	0.3–0.6	Hyakutake
	1.6	Hale-Bopp
CS_2	0.1	several
	0.2	Hale-Bopp
S_2	0.005	Hyakutake
OCS	<0.3	Levy
	<0.5	Halley, Austin
	0.1	Hyakutake
	0.6	Hale-Bopp

(continues)

◄ MOLECULAR ABUNDANCES OF CERTAIN GASES IN COMETS *(continued)* ►

SUBSTANCE	ABUNDANCE*	COMET
SO_2	<0.001	Halley, Bradfield
	0.15	Hale-Bopp
SO	0.2–0.8	Hale-Bopp
He	<3	Austin
Ar	<17	Austin, Levy
Ne	<0.6	Hale-Bopp

*Abundances compared to $H_2O = 100$; different values may be reported for the same comet because of differences in measurement technique used. Where a range of values is listed, that range indicates the variations observed in observations of two or more comets.
Source: Adapted from H. Cottin, M. C. Gazeau, and F. Raulin, "Cometary organic chemistry: A review from observations, numerical and experimental simulations," *Planetary and Space Science* 47 (1999), Table 2, 1,148–1,149.

pentadiene, cyclopentene, cyclopentadiene, cyclohexane, cyclohexadiene, benzene, toluene, propanenitrile, purine, adenine, cyanic acid, and xanthine. In addition to the molecules listed in the chart, a large number of other carbonaceous species have been observed, including C^+, CH^+, CO^+, CO_2^+, C_2, C_3, CH, and CN.

Among the most interesting organic molecules recently discovered in comets are polyoxymethylene [$(-CH_2-O-)_n$], also known as POM, a polymer of formaldehyde (CH_2O); and hexamethylenetetramine (HMT; $C_6H_{12}N_4$). These two compounds are thought to be the source of simpler compounds, such as the organic species listed in

◁ ORGANIC MOLECULES IDENTIFIED IN COMETS ▷

MOLECULE	CONFIDENCE LEVEL*
hydrocyanic acid (HCN)	confirmed
acetonitrile (CH_3CN)	confirmed
formaldehyde (CH_2O)	confirmed
formic acid (HCOOH)	confirmed
acetaldehyde (CH_3CHO)	high
acetic acid (CH_3COOH)	high
polyoxymethylene [$(-CH_2-O-)_n$]	high
iminoethane [$CH_3C(=NH)NH_2$]	medium
aminoethane ($CH_3CH_2NH_2$)	medium
pyrroline (C_4H_8N)	medium
pyrrole (C_4H_5N)	medium
imidazole ($C_3H_5N_2$)	medium
pyridine (C_5H_5N)	medium
pyrimidine ($C_4H_4N_2$)	medium
cyclopropenyl (C_3H_3)	medium

*Level of astronomers' confidence as to the existence of the species in comets
Source: Adapted from H. Cottin, M. C. Gazeau, and F. Raulin, "Cometary organic chemistry: A review from observations, numerical and experimental simulations," *Planetary and Space Science* 47 (1999), Table 3, 1,150.

the preceding paragraph (from polyoxymethylene) and CN and HCN (from hexamethylenetetramine). For example, it is known that poly-oxymethylene decomposes to form not only the original *monomer*, formaldehyde, but also a variety of simpler fragments, such as CH_2 groupings and individual oxygen atoms (O).

Astrochemists recognize that the chemical species most easily observed in comets—simple molecules, ions, and free radicals such as H, O, OH, C^+, CH^+, CO^+, CO_2^+, C_2, C_3, CH, and CN—are probably formed by the photolysis of more complex molecules buried within cometary nuclei. The action of solar energy on a water molecule in a comet's nucleus is an example. When radiation energy (hv) from the Sun strikes a water molecule, it causes that molecule to dissociate into two or more parts. Among the possible reactions are the following:

$$H_2O + hv \rightarrow H + OH$$
$$H_2O + hv \rightarrow H_2 + O$$
$$H_2O + hv \rightarrow H + O + H$$

Radiation energy may also bring about the *photodissociation* of a water molecule, in which an electron is expelled, leaving behind a charged water ion:

$$H_2O + hv \rightarrow H_2O^+ + e^-$$

Photodissociation is far more likely to occur than *photoionization*, however, because the energy needed to bring about dissociation is much less than that required for photoionization. In fact, once a water molecule escapes from the comet nucleus into the coma, the average time in which it is likely to be broken apart by solar radiation is about 25 seconds. By contrast, the average amount of time during which a water molecule is ionized by solar radiation is likely to be a few hours. Such reactions are more likely to occur when water molecules have trailed off into the comet's tail at distances of about 1 AU. Consequently, the coma of a comet can be expected to consist largely of neutral remnants of the photolysis of water molecules, such as H and OH, while ionized species, such as H^+ and free electrons, are more likely to be found in the comet's tail.

Similar arguments can be put forward for compounds other than water. For example, carbon, nitrogen, sulfur, and their compounds are likely to be photodissociated within the coma, and photoionized in regions more distant from the cometary nucleus. This line of reasoning is consistent with observations that a comet's coma is likely to contain species such as C_2, C_3, CH, CO, CO_2, CN, NH, NH_2, CS, COS, and S, while its tail is more likely to contain ionized species, such as C^+, CH^+, CO^+, CO_2^+, N_2^+, CN^+.

One of the intriguing conclusions that might be drawn from the discovery of organic molecules in comets is that such molecules could have provided the seeds for the origin of life on Earth. Some scientists posit that the simple organic molecules of comets survived collision with Earth, providing the basic building blocks from which more complex molecules were formed. As these molecules continued to grow, they may eventually have evolved into the simplest form of living organisms found on the primitive Earth.

Such hypotheses are confirmed in two ways. One is the discovery of precursors to complex biochemical molecules already detected in comets, such as those listed in the chart on page 189. The other is through laboratory experiments that test (1) whether the organic molecules found in comets can survive collision with Earth and, if so, (2) whether they can then evolve into more complex molecules from which life can develop.

Over the past few years, a number of such experiments have been carried out, all with encouraging results. In 2001, for example, scientists at the Argonne National Laboratory (ANL), the University of California at Berkeley (UCB), and the Lawrence Berkeley National Laboratory (LBNL) simulated the effects of the collision of a high-velocity comet with Earth's surface. The scientists fired a bullet the size of a soda can into a metal target that contained a droplet of water mixed with amino acids. Not only did the amino acids survive the impact but they began to polymerize shortly thereafter, evolving first into dipeptides (two-amino-acid units), then into tripeptides (three-amino-acid units), and finally into more complex peptides. When this type of polymerization continues for an extended period of time, even more complex molecules, known as *polypeptides,* could be formed. Polypeptides are proteins, one of the basic types of biochemical molecules of which all living organisms are formed. Although the notion that life could have originated from materials found in comets is still very controversial, this experiment suggests it is possible. "Our results suggest," Jennifer Blank at UCB said, "that the notion of organic compounds coming from outer space can't be ruled out because of the severity of the impact event."

Meteors, Meteoroids, and Meteorites

When asked to describe our solar system, most people are likely to name the Sun, the eight planets, and their satellites. Some people may also mention asteroids (the topic of the next section) and comets. An even smaller number of individuals may know that *meteoroids* are also a part of the solar system. Meteoroids are small chunks of matter, ranging in size from a few grams to more than 10 metric tons, that travel around the Sun in orbits close to that of Earth. From time to time, meteoroids come close enough to Earth to enter its atmosphere, where they flash through the sky in brilliant streaks of light sometimes called *"shooting stars."* That name goes back many centuries to when some observers believed that the streaks of light were actually produced by stars traveling through Earth's atmosphere. Meteoroids that enter Earth's atmosphere are correctly known as *meteors.* When many meteors are seen at about the same time in the sky, the event is known as a *"shower."*

Friction heats most meteors to such high temperatures during their transit through the atmosphere that they burn up, leaving only fine dust to fall to Earth's surface. A few are able to survive contact with the atmosphere, however, and fall to Earth. These meteors are called *meteorites.*

Any careful study of the skies reveals the existence of meteors. It is no surprise, then, that records of meteors are among the earliest astronomical records. Apparently the oldest written account of a meteor shower is a Chinese document dating to 654 B.C.E. Some of the more spectacular meteor showers, those that reappear on a regular basis, have also been recorded and commented on for centuries. The first record of the famous Perseid meteor shower, which now occurs annually in early August, dates to a Chinese document written in 36 C.E., while Chinese astronomers made the first report of the Leonid meteor shower (now occurring each year in mid-November) in 902 C.E.

Similar accounts of meteor sightings and meteor showers can be found in the historical records of every civilization. Along with these accounts are a great variety of explanations as to what meteors are made of, where they come from, and what, if any, meaning they have. Some scholars argued that meteors were rocks expelled from volcanoes on the Moon or from volcanoes here on Earth, pieces of rock tossed off the Moon's surface, aggregates of smaller particles floating about in the atmosphere, or rocky materials fallen to Earth from some source beyond the solar system. Like comets, meteors were considered portents. In some cultures, they were thought to be gifts showered on Earth by gods, goddesses, angels, or other supernatural beings. In other cultures, they were regarded as a form of punishment, signs of anger by deities and their agents.

An important turning point in the study of meteorites occurred on April 26, 1803, when a shower of about 2,000 meteorites fell near the town of L'Aigle in France. The event was documented and reported by the French physicist Jean Baptiste Biot (1774–1862). Biot's careful description of the meteorite event convinced scientists that meteorites were not of terrestrial origin but truly did originate from interplanetary space. Scientists soon appreciated the enormous significance of this fact, because it provided the first direct evidence that humans had of the nature of materials contained in the solar system outside our own planet.

Still, it was not until three decades later that the study of meteors gained full scientific status. The event that brought about the birth of *meteoritics,* the scientific study of meteors, was the great Leonid meteor shower of November 12 and 13, 1833. While analyzing their observations of this shower, astronomers Dennison Olmsted and A. C. Twining concluded that the meteors that made up the shower all appeared to have come from a single point in the sky and were, therefore, components of a single mass of bodies in the interplanetary space. Some time later, in 1863, Yale astronomer and mathematician Hubert Anson Newton (1830–96) calculated the orbit of the Leonid meteors, finding that their orbital period was 33 years. He confirmed the appearances of the shower as far back as its first recorded sighting in 902 C.E. and predicted its reappearance in 1866—a prediction that was confirmed.

Meteorites are generally classified into two categories: falls and finds. A *meteoritic fall* occurs when an observer actually sees a meteorite fall to Earth and is able to track and recover the meteorite. The term *meteoritic find* is used to describe a meteorite that has been found on Earth's surface, although there is no evidence as to when it fell to Earth. In one summary of meteorites, reported in *The Handbook of Iron Meteorites,* 55 percent of all discoveries were falls and 45 percent finds.

Over the years, scientists have developed a very detailed and somewhat complex system for the classification of meteorites. It is based on the chemical composition and (to a somewhat lesser degree) the physical characteristics of meteorites. The chart below summarizes the main elements of the system.

◄ CLASSIFICATION OF METEORITES ►

STONY		IRON	STONY-IRON
Chondrites	Achondrites	Hexahedrites	Pallasites
Enstatite (E)		Octahedrites	Mesosiderites
Ordinary Chondrites: H Chondrites L Chondrites LL Chondrites	Howardites: Eucrites Diogenites Shergottites:	Ataxites	
Carbonaceous Chondrites	Nakhlites		
Kakangari-type	Ureilites		
Rumurutiites	Aubrites		

Notice that meteorites are classified first of all into three large categories: stony, iron, and stony-iron. As their name suggests, stony meteorites are similar in appearance and chemical composition to rocks found on the Earth's surface. Stony meteorites are divided into two major categories: chondrites and achondrites. Chondrites are stony meteorites that contain small spheres, called *chondrules,* with diameters of about 1 mm, consisting of minerals that were once melted and that have now aggregated to form the meteorite. Stony meteorites lacking chondrules are called achondrites.

Chondrites are, in turn, divided into five major categories according to their chemical composition. Enstatite chondrites are those rich in the mineral of the same name, a form of magnesium silicate, $Mg_2Si_2O_6$. Enstatite chondrites are further classified into 13 subgroups according to the amount of iron present and the appearance of chondrules. An EH3 meteorite, for example, is an enstatite (E) chondrite with a high (H) iron concentration and an abundance (3) of chondrules.

Ordinary chondrites are also classified according to the amount of iron present and the characteristics of the chondrules present. For example, an LL7 chondrite is one with very low iron content (about 2 percent) whose chondrules have largely melted to form a solid mass.

Carbonaceous chondrites are so named because they contain the element carbon in one form or another. Their names include symbols to indicate the presence of carbon (C), what type they are (Ivuna, Ornans, Vigarano, or Mighei, for example), and sometimes the degree to which they have been altered. A CV2 meteorite, for example, is a carbonaceous chondrite of the Vigarano general type that has undergone moderate alteration.

In some regards, carbonaceous chondrites are among the most interesting kinds of meteorites to scientists. Such meteorites often contain relatively large amounts of water (as much as 20 percent by weight of the meteorite) and light hydrocarbons. This point is significant because water and light hydrocarbons are very volatile and tend to evaporate easily even at low temperatures. Any meteorite that falls to Earth with water and hydrocarbon embedded in it must have avoided most of the changes that other bodies in the solar system have undergone as a result of heating by the Sun. Such meteorites might, therefore, serve as very good models of what the early solar system was like.

Carbonaceous chondrites are also of interest because of the fascinating mix of relatively complex organic molecules they contain. Scientists have now discovered both amino acids and nitrogen bases in meteorites. Amino acids are the compounds of which proteins are made, and nitrogen bases are one of the building blocks of nucleic acids such as DNA and RNA. Researchers have found 92 amino acids in just one meteorite, the Murchison meteorite that fell about 60 miles (100 km) north of Melbourne, Australia, in 1969. Of these 92 amino acids, only 19 are found on Earth. Studies of other meteorites have shown that the Murchison results are not unique. In fact, amino acids occur in a number of carbonaceous chondrites.

The potential significance of such findings is profound. If amino acids and nitrogen bases are present in meteors, are meteors candidates for one of the earliest sources of life on Earth? While much research still needs to be done on this question, it is apparent that this possibility cannot now be ruled out.

Kakangari (K meteorites) and rumurutiite (R meteorites) are the least common types of chondrites found on Earth.

As mentioned earlier, achondrites are stony meteorites that are lacking in chondrules. They are very different in physical structure and chemical composition from chondrites because they have generally undergone extensive heating, resulting in at least partial melting. In many cases, this melting has produced a layered structure, with a stony outer crust rich in sodium, potassium, calcium, and rare earth metal silicates and a iron-nickel sulfide core. Achondrites are subdivided into about two dozen groups, based on their chemical composition. For example, the diogenites consist almost entirely of the mineral orthopyroxenite, while the eucrites are composed of about 60 percent pyroxenes and 30 percent plagioclase, with smaller amounts of ilmenite, chromite, apatite, and quartz. Scientists suspect that some types of achondrites originated on the Moon or Mars and these are classified as *Moonmeteorites* (the LUN group) and Marsmeteorites (SNC group).

Iron meteorites, the second large category of meteorites, are so designated because they consist almost entirely of iron, alloyed with nickel and, sometimes, other metals. The two iron-nickel alloys most commonly found in iron meteors are kamacite, which is low in nickel, and taenite, which is high in nickel. The iron meteorites are classified according to either their physical structure or their chemical composition. Physically, iron meteorites are classified as hexahedrites, octahedrites, and ataxites. Hexahedrites contain kamacite, but not taenite, and have a nickel content of less than 6 percent. Octahedrites contain both kamacite and taenite and have a nickel content of up to 17 percent. Ataxites have nickel concentrations of more than about 17 percent.

Although iron and nickel are by far the most common elements in iron meteorites, other elements are often present in small amounts. These additional elements make possible the second, chemical, method of classifying meteorites, which consists of about 13 groups. The IAB group of iron meteorites, for example, contains silicates, iron sulfite, and nodules of black graphite. The IID group can be identified by the presence of gallium and germanium, and the IC group by the presence of gold and arsenic.

The third large category of meteorites, the stony-iron meteorites, has traditionally been divided into two major groups, the pallasites and the mesosiderites, again based on their chemical composition. The pallasites consist of olivine crystals embedded in matrix of iron-nickel alloy, while the mesosiderites have a complex structure that includes pyroxene, plagioclase, olivine, and other minerals interspersed with an iron-nickel base. Some authorities now recognize a number of other classes of stony-iron meteorites that are different from the pallasites and mesosiderites in the kinds and amounts of minerals present.

Today, about a hundred discrete minerals have been identified in various types of meteorites. The chart on pages 198–200 provides a partial list of those minerals. In many cases, only trace amounts of some minerals have been reported, although many others occur in significant abundances.

One of the great questions in the science of meteoritics is the source of meteorites. Once it was ascertained that these bodies do not originate in the Earth or its atmosphere, the problem became one of finding a likely source of meteorites.

◄ MINERALS THAT HAVE BEEN FOUND IN METEORITES ►

TYPE	EXAMPLE(S)	FORMULA
Metals	Copper	Cu
	Kamacite	alloy of Fe and Ni (<6% Ni)
	Taenite	alloy of Fe and Ni (>6% Ni)
	Tetrataenite	alloy of Fe and Ni
	Awaruite	Ni_3Fe
Nonmetals	Sulfur	S_8
	Carbon (as graphite, diamond, and lonsdalite)	C
Oxides	Corundum	Al_2O_3
	Perovskite	$CaTiO_3$
	Scheelite	$CaWO_4$
	Hematite	Fe_2O_3
	Magnetite	Fe_3O_4
	Spinel	$MgAl_2O_4$
	Quartz, tridymite, cristobalite	SiO_2
	Baddeleyite	$FeTiO_3$

TYPE	EXAMPLE(S)	FORMULA
Sulfides	Troilite	FeS
	Marcasite, pyrite	FeS_2
	Chalcopyrite	$CuFeS_2$
	Cubanite	$CuFe_2S_3$
	Heazlewoodite	Ni_3S_2
	Oldhamite	CaS
	Sphalerite	$(Mg,Fe)S$
Carbides	Haxonite	$Fe_{23}S_6$
	Carlsbergite	CrN
	Osbornite	TiN
	Sinoite	Si_2N_2O
Silicates	Olivine	$(Mg,Fe)_2SiO_4$
	Enstatite	$MgSiO_3$
	Ferrosilite	$FeSiO_3$
	Wollastonite	$CaSiO_3$
	Orthoclase	$KAlSi_3O_8$
	Ureyite	$NaCrSi_2O_6$
	Zircon	ZrSiO

(continues)

◁ **MINERALS THAT HAVE BEEN FOUND IN METEORITES** *(continued)* ▷

TYPE	EXAMPLE(S)	FORMULA
Halides	Lawrencite	$FeCl_2$
Oxysalts	Calcite, aragonite, vaterite	$CaCO_3$
	Apatite	$Ca_5(PO_4)_3(OH,F)$
	Gypsum	$CaSO_4 \cdot 2H_2O$
	Bloedite	$Na_2Mg(SO_4)_2 \cdot 4H_2O$

Source: Adapted from John S. Lewis. *Physics and Chemistry of the Solar System*, revised edition. San Diego: Academic Press, 1997, Table VIII.3, page 333.

That source almost certainly has to be some portion of the solar system that is physically close to Earth's orbit. For an object to collide with our atmosphere and reach the ground, it must begin its path in the near-Earth region of space. Four obvious possibilities exist. First is the Moon. Some observers have long suspected that pieces of the Moon could be ejected from its surface by impact with an asteroid, a comet, or some other body. Those pieces might then fall into orbit around Earth and eventually reach the atmosphere as meteors or meteorites. About 50 lunar meteorites are now known or suspected to exist. Chemists have identified these meteorites as lunar objects by comparing their chemical composition with that of lunar rocks collected during the Apollo voyages to the Moon. (A list of lunar meteorites is available online at http://epsc.wustl.edu/admin/resources/meteorites/moon_meteorites_list.html.)

A second possible source of meteorites is the planet Mars. Although much more distant from Earth than the Moon, Mars could be the source of rocky pieces ejected during collision with another body. About 50 meteorites have now been identified as having come from Mars. (A list of these meteorites is available online at http://www. jpl.nasa.gov/snc/nwa1068.html.)

A third possible source of meteorites is comets. Certainly some comets pass close enough to Earth's orbit for Earth's gravitational field to pull pieces of their comas and tails into the atmosphere, where they could become meteors and, eventually, meteorites. There are some convincing arguments against this explanation. Cometary materials are more fragile and are traveling too rapidly to be likely to survive impact with Earth's atmosphere. Although they could be responsible for some of the meteor trails we see, they appear to be unlikely candidates for the meteorites that actually reach the Earth's surface.

Nonetheless, some scientists continue to argue that at least some meteorites originated from comets. In 1998, for example, two astronomers at the University of Florida and the Lunar and Planetary Laboratory at the University of Arizona concluded in their paper "Are there cometary meteorites?" that there is strong theoretical support for the existence of such meteorites; we have just not found any of them yet. "Based on studies of cometary fireballs," they wrote, "we should have collected approximately the same number of cometary meteorites as CI [carbonaceous] chondrites. In other words, we should be on the verge of collecting or identifying a cometary meteorite."

The vast majority of meteorites that have been identified thus far, however, appear to have originated from the fourth possible near-Earth source, the asteroids. Located in a heliocentric band between Mars and Jupiter, the asteroids are close enough to Earth's orbit to be a source of meteorites; it is reasonable to expect that some of these bodies might periodically pass close enough to Earth to fall into its gravitational field and to enter a geocentric orbit, from which they could eventually fall into the atmosphere. Many scientists now believe that meteorites are produced in this way and/or when a larger body in the asteroid belt is broken apart by impact with another body and the fragments are pulled into Earth's orbit. The latter explanation would help to account for why there are three major types of meteorites: stony, iron, and stony-iron. If a large body in the asteroid belt were demolished in an impact, pieces from the outer shell of the body (consisting of rocky material) could become the raw material of stony meteorites; pieces from the body's interior (consisting of iron and nickel) could become the raw material of iron meteorites; and pieces from the boundary between crust and core (consisting of a mixture of rocky and iron/nickel materials) could become the raw material of stony-iron meteorites.

Asteroids

In 1772, the German astronomer Johann Elert Bode (1747–1826) published a paper that described the locations of the known planets around the Sun by a simple mathematical formula, a formula that became known as Bode's Law. Unfortunately, Bode neglected to mention that the law had actually been discovered about six years earlier by a colleague, Johann Daniel Titius (1729–96). In any case, the Titius-Bode Law, as it is more properly known, can be derived from the formula:

$$a = \frac{n+4}{10}.$$

Bode and Titius then substituted a series of values for n chosen from the following series:

$$n = 0, 3, 6, 12, 24, 48 \ldots$$

Neither the formula nor the series selected for the values of n was based on any stroke of observational genius or theoretical insight . . . they were chosen simply because they produced an interesting practical result. When these values of n area applied to the formula, it yields the following values for a: 0.4, 0.7, 1.0, 1.6, 2.8, 5.2, and so on. As shown in the chart on page 203, these values correspond very closely to the semimajor axes of the planets that were known at the time that Titius and Bode announced their law, that is Mercury through Saturn. The law also agreed with the orbit of Uranus, discovered in 1781, less than a decade after the Titius-Bode Law was announced.

The problem for the Titius-Bode Law is that no planet exists for the position corresponding to $n = 24$, at a distance of 2.8 AU from the Sun. The discovery of Uranus, in another position predicted by the Titius-Bode Law, encouraged astronomers to begin a serious search

◀ TITIUS-BODE LAW AND OBSERVED ORBITS OF THE PLANETS ▶

PLANET	N	A (AU)	
		TITIUS-BODE LAW	OBSERVED
Mercury	0	0.4	0.39
Venus	3	0.7	0.72
Earth	6	1.0	1.0
Mars	12	1.6	1.52
(no planet)	24	2.8	
Jupiter	48	5.2	5.20
Saturn	96	10.0	9.54
Uranus	192	19.6	19.2
Neptune	384	38.8	30.1
Pluto	768	80.0	39.4

for the "missing" planet at a position corresponding to $n = 24$. They formed an international committee to search carefully in the region between Mars and Jupiter for a body whose orbit would correspond to that predicted by Titius-Bode.

A computer simulation of the appearance of the asteroid Ceres, based on data collected from telescopic and spacecraft data (Mark Garlick/Photo Researchers, Inc.)

On January 1, 1801, the Italian astronomer Guiseppe Piazzi (1746–1826) found an object in the constellation Taurus that changed position over a period of 24 days during which he was able to see it. He called the object *Ceres Ferdinandea* after Ceres, the Roman goddess of plants and motherly love, and Ferdinand III, King of Sicily. That name was later shortened simply to *Ceres.* Piazzi found that the object's orbit lay between those of Mars and Jupiter and wrote to Bode to tell him of his discovery. Unfortunately, Piazzi fell ill on February 13 and was unable to follow up on his observations. Instead, Piazzi's data were turned over to the great German mathematician Johann Gauss (1777–1855), who calculated Ceres' orbit and decided that it lay at a distance of 2.767 AU from the Sun, very close to that predicted by the Titius-Bode formula. When informed of Gauss's calculations, Piazzi was ecstatic, believing that he had actually found the missing planet for which so many of his colleagues had been searching. Those on the search team, Piazzi later wrote, "were instantly of the opinion that it was a new planet."

This optimistic assessment was soon dashed, however, as other astronomers began to calculate the size and mass of the newly discovered object. It turned out to be much smaller than any of the established planets. The English astronomer William Herschel (1738–1822) reported an estimated diameter of only 162 miles (261 km), about one-fiftieth that of Earth. Was it possible, astronomers asked, that such a tiny object could really be classified as a planet?

As it happens, that question never had to be answered. In less than a decade three additional objects, similar in size to Ceres and at comparable distances from the Sun, were also discovered. They were Pallas, discovered by the German astronomer Wilhelm Olbers (1758–1840) in 1802; Juno, discovered by another German astronomer Carl Ludwig Harding in 1804; and Vesta, also discovered by Olbers in 1807. Astronomers looking for the new planet predicted by Titius and Bode had turned out to be more successful than they had ever anticipated. They had found not one but four "baby planets." Herschel suggested that these new discoveries be called *asteroids,* a term from the Greek meaning "starlike." Although that term continues to be used widely today, these bodies are also known as *minor planets* or *planetoids.* In 2006, the International Astronomical Union (IAU) reclassified Ceres as a member of the new category of dwarf planets, along with Pluto and the distant body Eris.

Since the early 18th century, thousands of additional asteroids have been discovered. There is no official count of such bodies, although astronomers have found about 220 asteroids with diameters of 60 miles (100 km) or more. They estimate that there must be hundreds of thousands or even millions of asteroids with diameters of 70 feet (20 m) or more. The chart on pages 207–209 summarizes some properties of the major asteroids. The numbers given in column 1 of the table represent the sequence in which the asteroids were discovered.

The asteroids are hardly a homogeneous group of bodies. Some of them, for example, appear to have satellites or to be members of a double asteroid. The first asteroid satellite was discovered by the space probe *Galileo* on August 23, 1993; the asteroid was Ida, and its satellite was given the name Dactyl. Astronomers now believe that at least 24 asteroids either have satellites or are, themselves, members of double-asteroid systems. In addition to Ida, these asteroids include Diotima (423), Herculina (532), Crocus (1220), Ophelia (171), Lucina (146), Sylvia (87), Pales (40), Kalliope (22), Pulcova (762), Antiope (90), Kleopatra (216), and Eugenia (45).

Asteroids also have a variety of shapes. As the chart on pages 207–209 shows, some are essentially spherical (with a single diameter in all dimensions), while others have dimensions that differ in each direction. Pallas, for example, has a shape somewhat like a distorted potato. The radio telescope at Arecibo, Puerto Rico, found that Kleopatra has one of the most unusual shapes of all asteroids, best described as similar to a dog biscuit.

The orbital properties of asteroids also differ significantly. While the semimajor axes of many fall within the "magic zone" predicted by Titius and Bode (about 2.8 AU from the Sun), others have orbits that carry them much closer to the Sun (Icarus and Geographos are examples), and others have orbits that carry them much farther from the Sun (Chiron is an example).

Data about the chemical composition of asteroids comes primarily from three sources: (1) the spectrographic analysis of light reflected off an asteroid by Earth-based observatories and the *Hubble Space Telescope;* (2) the laboratory analysis of meteorites, which in most cases are known or presumed to have originated in the asteroid belt; and (3) observations made by the spacecraft *Galileo* on its

◄ INFORMATION ON SELECTED ASTEROIDS ▶

NUMBER	NAME	DIAMETER (KM)	MASS (10^{15} KG)	PERIOD OF ROTATION (HRS)	ORBITAL PERIOD (YRS)	SEMI-MAJOR AXIS (AU)
1	Ceres	960 × 932	870,000	9.075	4.60	2.767
2	Pallas	570 × 525 × 482	318,000	7.811	4.61	2.774
3	Juno	240	20,000	7.210	4.36	2.669
4	Vesta	530	300,000	5.342	3.63	2.362
45	Eugenia	226	6,100	5.699	4.49	2.721
140	Siwa	103	1,500	18.5	4.51	2.734

(continues)

◁ INFORMATION ON SELECTED ASTEROIDS *(continued)* ▷

NUMBER	NAME	DIAMETER (KM)	MASS (10^{15} KG)	PERIOD OF ROTATION (HRS)	ORBITAL PERIOD (YRS)	SEMI-MAJOR AXIS (AU)
216	Kleopatra	217×94	?	5.385	4.67	2.793
243	Ida	58×23	100	4.633	4.84	2.861
253	Mathilde	$66 \times 48 \times 46$	103.3	417.7	4.31	2.646
433	Eros	$33 \times 13 \times 13$	6.69	5.270	1.76	1.458
951	Gaspra	$19 \times 12 \times 11$	10	7.042	3.29	2.209
1566	Icarus	1.4	0.001	2.273	1.12	1.078

NUMBER	NAME	DIAMETER (KM)	MASS (10^{15} KG)	PERIOD OF ROTATION (HRS)	ORBITAL PERIOD (YRS)	SEMI-MAJOR AXIS (AU)
1620	Geo-graphos	2.0	0.004	5.222	1.39	1.245
1862	Apollo	1.6	0.002	3.063	1.81	1.471
2060	Chiron	180	4,000	5.9	50.7	13.633

Source: "Asteroid Fact Sheet," http://nssdc.gsfc.nasa.gov/planetary/factsheet/asteroidfact.html.

way to Jupiter. *Galileo* flew within 1,000 miles (1,600 km) of Gaspra and within 1,500 miles (2,400 km) of Ida and produced the best photographs of asteroids ever made, along with abundant data on the chemical composition of Gaspra and Ida.

Using data from these sources, astronomers usually classify asteroids into about a dozen categories based on two major characteristics: its albedo and its apparent mineral composition.

The choice of class names (A, B, C, and so on) was originally based on the primary constituent of the asteroid: C for carbonaceous, M for metallic, S for silicaceous, E for enstatite, and R for red, for example. Classes created later were given letter names based on alphabetical criteria, not chemical composition. The vast majority of asteroids fall into one of the three classes marked with an asterisk in the chart on pages 211–213. The system of classification given in this chart is not universally accepted, however. Some experts use an even larger number of spectral classes, some of which are created by subdividing classes with larger numbers of examples. For example, class C asteroids are sometimes further divided into subclasses CI, CK, CM, CV, CO, and CR, corresponding to a similar classification for carbonaceous chondrites.

Almost since the moment that the first asteroids were discovered, scientists have been intrigued by an obvious question: How were these bodies first created? One possible answer is that the asteroids are the fragments left of a large planet that exploded. Such an explosion, caused by internal forces, by gravitational forces exerted by a passing comet or other body, or by some other force, could have blown such a planet into millions of small pieces that eventually became the components of the asteroid belt observed today.

That idea was finally put to rest in the 1960s, however, as astronomers developed the ability to estimate the mass of asteroids. They found that the total mass of all bodies in the asteroid belt is probably not much more than twice the mass of Ceres, the largest asteroid. If all that mass were collected into a single body, it would be about 5 percent the mass of the Moon, or 0.0006 the mass of Earth. It is difficult to imagine a "real" planet of this size.

Since the "exploding planet" theory has been discarded, another hypothesis has been suggested for the formation of the asteroids.

(continues)

◁ **CHEMICAL COMPOSITION OF ASTEROIDS** ▷

CLASS	ALBEDO	FRACTION OF ALL KNOWN ASTEROIDS	PREDOMINANT MINERAL(S)	METEORITE ANALOGUES
A	high	~0%	olivine	achondrite, pallasite, brachinite
B	low	~0%	hydroxy silicates, carbon, organics	altered CI or CM chondrites
C*	very low	~75%	hydroxy silicates, carbon, organics	CI or CM chondrites
D	very low	~0%	carbon, organics	similar to carbonaceous chondrites
E	very high	~0%	enstatite, forsterite	enstatite achondrites
F	very low	~0%	hydroxy silicates, carbon, organics	altered CI or CM chondrites

◁ **CHEMICAL COMPOSITION OF ASTEROIDS** *(continued)* ▷

CLASS	ALBEDO	FRACTION OF ALL KNOWN ASTEROIDS	PREDOMINANT MINERAL(S)	METEORITE ANALOGUES
G	very low	~0%	hydroxy silicates, carbon, organics	altered CI or CM chondrites
M*	moderate	~8%	metals	irons
P	very low	~0%	carbon, organics	dry carbonaceous chondrites
Q	high	~0%	olivine, pyroxene, metals	ordinary chondrites
R	high	~0%	pyroxene, olivine	pyroxene- and olivine-containing achondrites
S*	moderate	~17%	pyroxene, olivine, metals	pallasites

CLASS	ALBEDO	FRACTION OF ALL KNOWN ASTEROIDS	PREDOMINANT MINERAL(S)	METEORITE ANALOGUES
T	very low	~0%	hydroxy silicates, carbon, organics	very altered CI or CM chondrites
V	high	~0%	pyroxene, feldspar	basaltic achondrites

Source: Adapted from John S. Lewis. *Physics and Chemistry of the Solar System*, Revised Edition. San Diego: Academic Press, 1997, Table VIII.4, page 361. This taxonomy was originally suggested by Edward Tedesco and his colleagues at the Jet Propulsion Laboratory, based on data collected from the IRAS [Infrared Astronomical Satellite] Minor Planet Survey ("A Three-Parameter Asteroid Taxonomy," *The Astronomical Journal 97*, 580).

Most astronomers now believe that the asteroids were formed when two bodies, both about the size of the state of Rhode Island, collided in space, breaking both objects into millions of pieces, ranging in size from dust particles to the largest asteroid. The remnants of that collision continue to orbit the Sun in a relatively cohesive band because they are still held together by mutual gravitational attraction.

Confirmation of this hypothesis was offered in 2002 when researchers at the Southwest Research Institute (SwRI) announced that they had found a group of asteroids that are similar enough to each other that they can be said to have been formed in a collision between two larger bodies about 5.8 million years ago. The SwRI scientists believe that an asteroid about two miles (3 km) in diameter collided with a second asteroid about 16 miles (25 km) in diameter with a mass about 600 times that of the smaller body. They calculated that the smaller asteroid was traveling at a speed of about 11,000 mph (5 km/s) when it hit its larger cousin. As a result of the collision, both bodies shattered into thousands of pieces ranging in size from 0.5 miles (1 km) rocks to dust particles. The group of related asteroids has now been given the name the *Karin group,* after the largest member of the group, 832 Karin.

So what is the relationship, if any, among comets, asteroids, and meteorites? Part of the answer to that question is fairly clear: It appears nearly certain that the vast majority of meteorites are remnants of bodies that originated in the asteroid belt. There is now enough evidence to say with some certainty that carbonaceous chondrites came from C chondritic asteroids, iron meteorites came from M asteroids, enstatite achondrites came from E asteroids, and so on. It can also be said with some assurance that no known meteorites came from a comet. Many astronomers are willing to agree that comets *may* be the source of meteorites and that a cometary meteorite may someday be found, but that day has not yet arrived.

The intriguing puzzle that remains is what connection there is, if any, between comets and asteroids. Some members of both families follow very similar orbits around the Sun and could conceivably be related to each other. One of the most fascinating clues to this puzzle was discovered in 1992 when an asteroid then known as 1979 VA was rediscovered. The asteroid had been discovered in 1979 and then shortly afterward lost. That is, astronomers were not able to find the asteroid in the position at which it had been expected. Upon the rediscovery of 1979 VA in 1992, astronomers were able to plot the asteroid's orbit with good accuracy. They were amazed to find that that orbit matched the orbit of Comet Wilson-Harrington 1949 III. Photographs taken of the comet showed that it looked just like an asteroid. The conclusion researchers drew was that Comet Wilson-Harrington 1949 III had changed its basic nature and turned into an asteroid.

Another tantalizing clue about the relationship between comets and asteroids is provided by asteroid 2060 Chiron, which has a very unusual orbit that takes it through the orbit of Saturn and almost to the orbit of Uranus, as shown in the diagram below. When it reaches perihelion, Chiron has a clearly detectable coma characteristic of comets. Yet its volume is about 50,000 times that of a typical comet, large enough for astronomers to have designated it as an asteroid when it was first discovered. Its true nature is now in question, particularly since three similar bodies with unusual

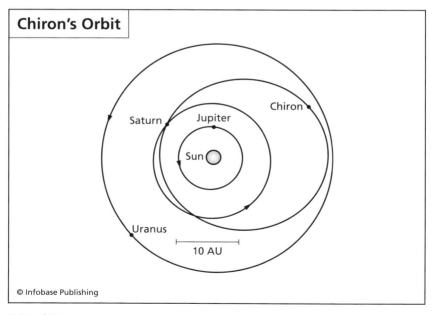

Orbit of Chiron

orbits were discovered. Some astronomers now believe that Chiron and its cousins (collectively known as the *Centaurs,* after the half-man, half-horse creatures of Greek mythology) are comets that have escaped from the Kuiper belt but that have not yet achieved their ultimate orbits.

Thus, questions remain as to the true relationship of comets and asteroids. As a recent paper by M. Di Martino and others put it, "it is becoming more and more difficult to distinguish comets from asteroids and indeed there are some examples of small bodies first designated as comets which had, later, to be reclassified as asteroids and vice versa."

The Moon

As the closest extraterrestrial body to Earth, the Moon has long been the subject of scholarly study. A number of Greek astronomers, for example, attempted to measure the size of the Moon and its distance from Earth. Two of the greatest of these scholars, Aristarchus (ca. 310–230 B.C.E.) and Hipparchus (ca. 190–120 B.C.E.), obtained values for the size of the Moon that are remarkably close to those accepted today. Both used geometric means to make their calculations, and given the lack of precision of the instruments with which they had to work, the results are quite impressive. Aristarchus obtained a value for the Moon's diameter of 0.35 times that of the Earth, while Hipparchus gave a value of 0.29, both of which are close to the accepted value today of 0.27 times Earth's diameter. The best value for the Moon's diameter today is 2,158 miles (3,476 km). Its mass is 7.349×10^{22} kg, its average distance from the Earth is 238,754 miles (384,467 km), and its density is about 3.350 g/cm^3.

Massive amounts of data about the physical characteristics and chemical composition of the Moon have been collected from Earth-based observatories, orbiting telescopes (such as the *Hubble Space Telescope*), and orbiting spacecraft and lunar landers. Knowledge of the Moon was advanced immeasurably, however, during the six missions to the Moon conducted under the auspices of the U.S. Apollo Space Program. The graphs on page 217 compare the extent of research conducted during each of these six missions and record the amount of lunar material returned by each. So much material was returned, in fact, that even 30 years after the completion of the Apollo program, only a small fraction of it has been completely analyzed.

Scientists have long known that the Moon has a very little, if any, atmosphere. That fact can be determined rather easily by observational techniques. When a star passes behind the Moon, its light blinks on and off very quickly—almost instantaneously—which it would not do if the Moon had an atmosphere.

A number of Apollo experiments were designed to find out if the Moon has any atmosphere at all and, if so, what its chemical composition is. These experiments proved to be difficult to carry out and

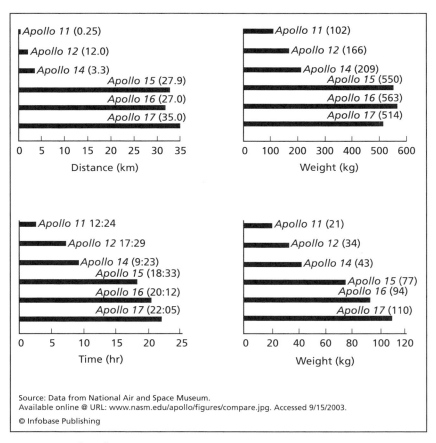

Source: Data from National Air and Space Museum.
Available online @ URL: www.nasm.edu/apollo/figures/compare.jpg. Accessed 9/15/2003.
© Infobase Publishing

Comparison of Apollo missions

interpret for two reasons. First, the Moon's atmosphere is, in fact, very thin, and the amount of any one gas in it is very low. Second, gases associated with the Apollo orbiters and landing craft were of sufficient concentration to mask values obtained from lunar sources.

Nonetheless, some approximate values for the nature and composition of the lunar atmosphere have been obtained. Temperatures in the atmosphere vary widely, from a low of about 100 K ($-173\,^\circ$C) during the lunar night to a high of about 400 K ($127\,^\circ$C) during the lunar day. Surface pressure at night on the Moon is about 3×10^{-15} bar, or about one quadrillionth that on Earth. There are about 2×10^5 particles per cubic centimeter at the Moon's surface.

The chart on page 219 summarizes the gases found in the lunar atmosphere and the abundance of each. The values given here reflect measurements made by Apollo experiments during the lunar night, when interference by heating of the lunar surface and the presence of Apollo experiments was at a minimum.

Species listed in this chart appear to originate from three different sources. Some gases, such as helium-4 and argon-40, are probably released from the Moon's interior. Other gases, such as hydrogen and helium, are probably captured by the Moon's weak gravitational attraction from the solar wind, although they remain in the lunar atmosphere only briefly (a few hours or a few days). Other gases are probably added to the lunar atmosphere when a comet, small asteroid, or other body collides with the Moon's surface, breaking apart and releasing trapped gases from its interior.

The Moon's general features have been known for centuries. Its surface reflects a long history of bombardment by comets, asteroids, and other planetary bodies. A topographic map of the Moon shows many individual craters created by such bombardments, often surrounded by plains covered by materials ejected by the blasts (*regolith*); *maria* (singular: mare, which means "sea"), which are large, flat regions that seem to have been formed by outflows of lava that cooled millennia ago; highlands, consisting of large numbers of craters overlying each other; and rills and rays, apparently formed by movement of the Moon's crust.

Knowledge of the chemical nature of the lunar surface, like that of the lunar atmosphere, was significantly advanced by the six Apollo

◁ ESTIMATED COMPOSITION OF THE LUNAR ATMOSPHERE ▷

CHEMICAL SPECIES	ABUNDANCE (PARTICLES PER CM³)
^4He	40,000
^{20}Ne	40,000
H_2	35,000
^{40}Ar	30,000
^{22}Ne	5,000
^{36}Ar	2,000
CH_4	1,000
NH_4	1,000
CO_2	1,000
O^+	trace
Al^+	trace
Si^+	trace
P^+	possible constituent
Na^+	possible constituent
Mg^+	possible constituent

Source: "Moon Fact Sheet," http://nssdc.gsfc.nasa.gov/planetary/factsheet/moonfact.html.

◁ SUCCESSFUL MISSIONS FOR THE STUDY OF THE LUNAR SURFACE ▷

MISSION	DATE OF LUNAR ARRIVAL	ACCOMPLISHMENT(S)
Luna 10 (USSR)	Achieved orbit: April 3, 1966	Gamma-ray spectrometer analysis of surface materials
Surveyor 6 (USA)	Landed in Sinus Medii: November 10, 1967	Studied surface composition with alpha-scattering equipment
Surveyor 7 (USA)	Landed at crater Tycho: January 10, 1968	Studied surface composition with alpha-scattering equipment; studied soil characteristics with Soil Mechanics Surface Sampler
Apollo 11 (USA)	Landed at Mare Tranquillitatis: July 20, 1969	44 pounds (20 kg) of rocky material collected
Apollo 12 (USA)	Landed at Oceanus Procellarum: November 19, 1969	75 pounds (34 kg) of rocky material collected
Apollo 14 (USA)	Landed at Fra Mauro: February 5, 1971	98 pounds (44 kg) of rocky material collected

MISSION	DATE OF LUNAR ARRIVAL	ACCOMPLISHMENT(S)
Apollo 15 (USA)	Landed at Hadley Rille: July 30, 1971	173 pounds (78 kg) of rocky material collected
Apollo 16 (USA)	Landed at Descartes: April 20, 1972	213 pounds (96 kg) of rocky material collected
Apollo 17 (USA)	Landed at Taurus-Littrow: December 11, 1972	240 pounds (109 kg) of rocky material collected

landings between July 1969 (*Apollo 11*) and December 1972 (*Apollo 17*). In addition, a great deal of data were collected by various unmanned missions to the Moon, including successful landings of the Soviet Union's Luna program and the U.S. Surveyor program. The chart on pages 220–221 summarizes the data collected by the successful missions in these programs.

Lunar rocks fall into two general categories: igneous and metamorphic. Igneous rocks are formed when molten material, such as that extruded from a volcano or other opening in the surface of a body, solidifies. Metamorphic rocks are formed when existing rocks or rocky materials are exposed to high temperatures and/or pressures, converting them into another form. The third class of rocks found on Earth, sedimentary rocks, is essentially absent from the lunar surface. Sedimentary rocks are usually formed by the consolidation of particles created by water or wind erosion, or by some other destructive process. Since the Moon lacks both water and air, similar processes cannot occur there. Instead, the most sedimentary-like material on the Moon's surface is regolith, a complex mixture of particles ranging in size from tiny dust particles to large boulders. Regolith is produced when meteorites, comets, and other bodies collide with the Moon's surface. Regolith can form a rock only as the result of the impact of some extralunar body on the Moon's surface. In such cases, the temperatures and pressures produced by the impact may be sufficient to convert the regolith to a metamorphic rock.

The vast majority of lunar rocks collected during the Apollo missions fall into one of three categories: (1) basalts, (2) breccias, and (3) KREEP rocks, a somewhat unusual form of igneous rock rich in potassium (K), rare earth elements (REE), and phosphorus (P). Basalts are a type of igneous rock, formed when molten material, such as lava, cools. It is a dark rock composed largely of the minerals pyroxene and plagioclase feldspar, with varying amounts of olivine. Basalts are found most commonly on the lower, flat regions of the Moon's surface known as maria. Scientists believe that the maria were formed by lava pouring out from beneath the Moon's surface.

Breccias and KREEP are more likely to be found in the higher elevations of the Moon's surface known as the lunar highlands. Breccias are metamorphic rocks formed when the heat and pressure caused by the impact of a meteorite, comet, or other body on the Moon's surface fuses a section of regolith, converting it into a rock. KREEP is similar to the basalts found in lunar maria except for its higher concentrations of potassium, phosphorus, and rare earth elements.

Analysis of lunar rocks returned by Apollo astronauts reveals the presence of three major minerals, which occur in concentrations of more than 10 percent in some rocks; an equal number of minor minerals, which occur in concentrations of 1 and 10 percent; and a somewhat larger number of minerals that occur in only very small quantities, always less than 1 percent. The chart on pages 223–224 lists these minerals. Many of these minerals occur in more than one form. For example, the various forms of pyroxene differ in what cation is present (iron, magnesium, and/or calcium). Enstatite, one form of pyroxene, has the formula $MgSiO_3$; wollastonite is $CaSiO_3$; and hedenbergite is $CaFeSi_2O_6$.

Analysis of lunar rocks returned by the Apollo missions and of data reported by the *Surveyor* lander now provides a large amount

◄ SOME MINERALS FOUND IN LUNAR ROCKS ►

MINERAL	CHEMICAL FORMULA
MAJOR MINERALS	
Ilmenite	$FeTiO_3$
Pyroxene	$(Mg,Fe,Ca)SiO_3$
Feldspar	$(Ca,Na,K,Al)Si_3O_8$
MINOR MINERALS	
Cristobalite	SiO_2
Tridymite	SiO_2
Olivine	$(Mg,Fe)_2 SiO_4$
Pyroxferroite	$CaFe_6(SiO_3)_7$
ACCESSORY MINERALS	
Kamacite	alloy of Fe and Ni with <6% Ni
Taenite	alloy of Fe and Ni with >6% Ni
Troilite	FeS
Chalcopyrite	$CuFeS_2$
Perovskite	$CaTiO_3$

(continues)

◁ **SOME MINERALS FOUND IN LUNAR ROCKS** *(continued)* ▷

MINERAL	CHEMICAL FORMULA
ACCESSORY MINERALS	
Chromite	$FeCr_2O_4$
Quartz	SiO_2
Rutile	TiO_2
Whitlockite	$Ca_3(PO_4)_2$
Orthoclase	$KAlSi_3O_8$

of information about the composition of rocks and regolith on the lunar surface. As the chart on pages 225–226 shows, the abundance of various chemical compounds differs widely from rock to rock and from rock to regolith.

Surveyor and the Apollo missions have provided an unmatched collection of data. These results have augmented knowledge of the Moon's physical and chemical characteristics and will continue, for many years into the future, to add even more to human understanding of Earth's nearest neighbor in space.

Modern space technology has produced data about comets, meteors, asteroids, and the Moon that answer questions people have been asking for centuries about these bodies. Today scientists know a great deal about the chemical composition of these objects, their orbits through the solar system, and some mechanisms by which they may have been produced. Studies that produced these data are ongoing, and even more detailed understandings of these objects can be expected in the future.

◄ CHEMICAL COMPOSITION OF CERTAIN LUNAR MATERIALS (PERCENT BY WEIGHT) ▲

COMPO-NENT	SURVEYOR			LUNAR ROCKS						
	5	6	7	70215	15545	14053	15386	62237	14321C	
SiO_2	46.4	49.1	46.1	37.8	45.2	46.4	50.8	41.9	74.2	
MgO	4.4	6.6	7.0	6.7	10.3	8.5	9.34	5.11	0.07	
FeO	12.1	12.4	5.5	19.8	22.1	16.8	10.4	5.89	5.6	
CaO	14.5	12.9	18.3	11.1	9.8	11.2	9.60	16.3	8.8	
Al_2O_3	14.4	14.7	22.3	10.4	8.6	13.6	15.0	29.6	12.5	
TiO_2	7.6	3.5	0.0	10.5	2.4	2.6	2.06	—	0.33	

(continues)

◁ **CHEMICAL COMPOSITION OF CERTAIN LUNAR MATERIALS (PERCENT BY WEIGHT)** *(continued)* ▷

COMPONENT	SURVEYOR			LUNAR ROCKS				
	5	6	7					
Na_2O	0.6	0.8	0.7	0.40	0.31	—	0.2	0.52
K_2O	—	—	—	0.06	0.04	0.10	0.61	8.1
Cr_2O_3	—	—	—	0.25	0.68	—	—	—

Source: Adapted from John S. Lewis. *Physics and Chemistry of the Solar System*, revised edition. San Diego: Academic Press, 1997, Tables IX 1a and 1b, pages 404, 405.

Conclusion

A strochemists have as little concrete matter with which to work as almost any group of scientists. Their subject matter—the stars, interstellar medium, planets, asteroids, comets, and other bodies—seldom approach within a few million miles of Earth. All these researchers have to work with, for the most part, are beams of light from tiny pinpoints in the sky or, in a few cases, a small, fuzzy ball of light.

Yet, over the centuries, astronomers have developed an impressive array of instruments and techniques with which to squeeze as much information as possible from these limited resources, and they have found ways of duplicating or, at least, simulating astronomical processes in the laboratory. As a result, by the early 1960s, astronomers had compiled a rather imposing body of knowledge about the physical and chemical structure of the universe, along with a relatively solid theoretical basis for explaining how the universe began and how it operates today.

The problem in astronomy has always been that the data available to astronomers is somewhat limited and compromised by its inherent uncertainties. So it is not surprising that, from time to time, long-held and relatively secure scientific theories about the nature of the universe are overturned or, at the least, modified to fit new and better information.

At the beginning of the 21st century, one of the most extraordinary discoveries has been that of the possible existence of *dark energy,* a force that appears to be driving particles of matter away from, rather than toward, each other. Although this concept is contrary to every physical theory that all scientists hold dear, evidence continues to accumulate that such a phenomenon may exist. If it does, it will revolutionize much of what we have come to know (or think we know) about the way the universe is constructed and the way it operates.

A quantum step forward in astrochemistry has been the development of space vehicles that can travel to any part of the solar system and out into interstellar space to take more direct measurements than have ever been available before. In addition, orbiting telescopes such as the *Hubble Space Telescope* and other detecting devices continue to provide photographs and other kinds of images of bodies both within the solar system and to the deepest recesses of space. In just two decades, astronomers have been provided with instruments to scan the skies that will keep them busy for many years in accumulating, tabulating, sorting, and interpreting the data that has come from these new sources.

The future holds bright promises for even more riches. NASA, the European Space Agency, and the Japanese Institute of Space and Aeronautical Science are planning space probes to the planets, comets, asteroids, and other bodies within the solar system and, in some cases, to the very edges of that system. Within the next decade, young people who are studying chemistry in high schools today will be using data from these voyages to make discoveries and develop theories that will transform many fields of astronomy. The oldest of all the sciences, astronomy also holds unparalleled promises for leading humankind's understanding of the origin of our world, the way it operates, and how it relates to the origin and development of human life.

GLOSSARY

absolute luminosity   The brightness a star would have if it were placed at a distance of 10 parsecs from the Sun.

aerogel   A silicon-based foam used to collect very small particles of matter, such as those that make up interplanetary and interstellar dust.

albedo   The ratio of the amount of light reflected by a body compared to the amount received by the body.

amino acid   Organic acids containing the amino group ($-NH_2$), which are the building blocks of proteins.

arcs   Optical effects in the atmosphere of Neptune that make it appear as if the planet is surrounded by incomplete rings. In fact, the planet's rings are complete, and the arcs are only regions where the density of matter is greater than elsewhere in the rings.

asteroid   A body whose orbit usually lies between the orbits of Mars and Jupiter; also called a *minor planet* or *planetoid*. Asteroids range from the size of a grain of sand to nearly 600 miles (1,000 km) in diameter.

astronomical unit   A unit of distance measurement in astronomy equal to the average distance from the Sun to Earth, or about 92,955,628 miles (149,597,870 km).

black dwarf   The final stage in the evolution of a star with a mass roughly equal to that of the Sun.

Cassini division   The largest gap in the rings around the planet Saturn, located between rings A and B.

chondrule   A small nodule, consisting of silicate materials, found in certain types of meteorites and asteroids.

CNO cycle   A series of nuclear reactions with carbon as a catalyst by which hydrogen is converted to helium.

coma   A mass of glowing gas and dust that surrounds the nucleus of a comet, produced by the vaporization and sublimation of matter from within the nucleus.

coronal gas   A mass of gas consisting of material ejected from stars, novae, supernovae, and other explosive objects in the universe.

cosmic microwave background   A form of "fossil" electromagnetic radiation that permeates the universe and is a remnant of the earliest period of the universe's history.

cosmology   The study of the universe and its history.

degenerate state   A form of matter in which electrons have been stripped of their nuclei and both nuclei and electrons are distributed randomly throughout the matter.

downwelling   The sinking of material in a planet's atmosphere toward its surface.

dust   Particles with diameters of less than a micron found in the interstellar medium.

dust tail   A stream of particles ejected from the coma of a comet by the Sun's radiative pressure. The stream is visible because its component particles reflect sunlight.

electromagnetic spectrum   The ordered series of electromagnetic radiation arranged by wavelength or frequency.

emission nebula.   A gas cloud that gives off light when excited by a nearby star.

evolutionary track   The line on a Hertzsprung-Russell diagram that shows changes in a star's temperature and luminosity during its lifetime.

5-micron hotspot   Cylinder-shaped regions on the surface of some planets that are thought to act as vents through which heat generated in the planet's interior—primarily in the 5-micron wavelength region—escapes into the outer atmosphere.

gas giants   Solar system planets that are larger and less dense than the terrestrial planets (such as Earth). They include Jupiter, Saturn, Uranus, and Neptune and are also sometimes called *gas giants* or *Jovian planets.*

Great White Spot   A prominent but relatively short-lived feature that appeared on the face of the planet Neptune, thought to be evidence of a giant storm in the planet's atmosphere.

Hayashi track The line on a Hertzsprung-Russell diagram during which a star's luminosity stays relatively constant, while its temperature continues to decrease.

helium burning A series of nuclear reactions in which helium nuclei fuse to make larger atomic nuclei.

helium flash A period of very rapid helium burning that occurs in the core of a star with low mass.

Hertzsprung-Russell diagram A graph that plots the color of stars against their luminosity.

highlands Areas of higher elevation on the Moon consisting of both igneous and metamorphic rocks.

hydrogen burning A somewhat misleading expression that describes those nuclear reactions by which hydrogen is converted to helium as a result of fusion.

interstellar extinction The reduction in the brightness of a star that occurs when starlight passes into a dense cloud of dust and gas, blocking out the star's light from viewers on Earth.

interstellar medium The material that makes up the space between stars. It consists largely of gases and dust.

interstellar reddening The alteration in the apparent color of a star that occurs when a dust cloud scatters the star's blue light, leaving a predominance of red light to reach Earth observers.

ion tail A visible stream of ions trailing behind the nucleus of a comet (relative to the Sun), formed when solar radiation ionizes atoms and molecules from the comet's coma.

Kuiper belt A region of space outside the orbit of Neptune thought to contain very large numbers of bodies of varying sizes, from which certain types of comets originate.

luminosity The total amount of energy emitted per second by a celestial object.

Main Sequence The region on a Hertzsprung-Russell diagram occupied by stars that are fusing hydrogen into helium in their cores.

major planets *See* GAS GIANTS.

maria (singular *mare,* Latin for "sea") Relatively flat, dark areas on the Moon consisting largely of basaltic materials produced during volcanic outflows.

mass defect   The amount by which the mass of an atomic nucleus is less than the sum of the masses of its constituent particles.

metallic hydrogen   A form of hydrogen in which hydrogen atoms have become ionized and exist as separate protons and electrons.

meteor   A streak of light left by a meteoroid as it pass through Earth's atmosphere.

meteorite   A meteoroid that has survived transit through Earth's atmosphere and fallen on its surface.

meteoritic fall   A meteorite whose fall to Earth is observed by some person.

meteoritic find   A meteorite that has been found on Earth's surface, although nothing is known as to how and when it fell.

meteoritics   The science that involves the study of meteors, meteoroids, and meteorites.

meteoroid   A small chunk of matter, ranging in size from a few grams to more than 10 metric tons, that travels around the Sun in an orbit close to that of Earth.

minor planets   *See* ASTEROID; TERRESTRIAL PLANETS.

monomer.   The smallest repeating unit of a polymer.

neutron capture   A nuclear reaction in which a nucleus captures a neutron, gives off a gamma ray, and becomes a nucleus with an atomic mass one greater than the original nucleus.

nucleus   The central portion of a comet's body, usually no more than a few dozen kilometers in diameter.

Oort cloud   A spherical shell of material surrounding the solar system from which certain types of comets are thought to originate.

outgassing   The expulsion of material from the inner, warmer part of a planet or satellite.

parsec   A unit of measurement in astronomy equal to 3.26 light-years.

perihelion   The closest approach of a planet or other solar body to the Sun.

photodissociation   The splitting of a molecule by radiant energy.

photoionization   The ionization of an atom or molecule by radiant energy.

photolysis   Any chemical reaction that comes about because of energy supplied by light or some other form of electromagnetic radiation.

planetary nebula   An expanding shell of gas emitted from the outer atmosphere of a red giant star during the late stages of that star's evolution.

planetoid   *See* ASTEROID.

polypeptides   Chemical compounds consisting of many (usually more than a dozen and often many hundreds or thousands) amino acids. Proteins are polypeptides.

precipitable micron   A measure of the depth of water that would form on a planet's surface if all of the moisture in the atmosphere could be made to condense out.

protoplanet   A mass of material, formed early in the history of the solar system, that grew over time by colliding with and incorporating smaller pieces of matter, eventually growing into a complete planet.

protostar   An early form of a star consisting of gas and dust with sufficient mass to permit the initiation of nuclear reactions. A protostar has a distinct, identifiable surface.

reflection nebula   A cloud of dust that reflects a portion of starlight toward the Earth.

regolith   A loose material that covers the surface of the Moon, planets, and other satellites, consisting of a wide range of materials ranging in size from tiny dust particles to large stones and rocks.

r process   A rapid neutron capture reaction in which isotopes of heavy elements are produced; *see also* NEUTRON CAPTURE.

solar nebula   The disk-shaped mass of material out of which the solar system was originally formed.

spectral class   A system for classifying stars based on the spectral lines they emit.

spectral line   A bright or dark line given off by an atom or molecule when it is exposed to radiation.

s reaction   A slow neutron capture reaction in which isotopes of many elements are produced; *see also* NEUTRON CAPTURE.

T-Tauri star   A young star that is approaching the main sequence on the Hertzsprung-Russell diagram.

terrestrial planets   Solar system planets that are relatively small and dense compared with the gas giants, including Mercury, Venus, Earth, and Mars; sometimes referred to as the *minor planets.*

triple helium process   A fusion reaction in which three helium nuclei are converted to a single carbon nucleus.

white dwarf   The remnant of a large star that has ejected its outer atmosphere and condensed to a small core that has lost its ability to carry out nuclear reactions.

ylem   A term used by Greek natural philosophers to describe the ultimate form of matter.

young stellar object   *See* PROTOSTAR.

◆ FURTHER READING

PRINT RESOURCES

Arnett, David. *Supernovae and Nucleosynthesis.* Princeton, N.J.: Princeton University Press, 1996.

Bell, Jim, and Jacqueline Mitton, eds. *Asteroid Rendezvous: NEAR Shoemaker's Adventures at Eros.* New York: Cambridge University Press, 2002.

Bevan, Alex, and John De Laeter. *Meteorites: A Journey through Space and Time.* Washington, D.C.: Smithsonian Institution Press, 2002.

Brandt, John C., and Robert De Witt. *Introduction to Comets.* New York: Cambridge University Press, 2002.

Chown, Marcus. *Afterglow of Creation: From the Fireball to the Discovery of Cosmic Ripples.* Herndon, Va.: University Science Books, 1994.

——. *The Magic Furnace: The Search for the Origins of Atoms.* New York: Oxford University Press, 2001.

Croswell, Ken. *Magnificent Mars.* New York: Free Press, 2004.

Erickson, Jon. *Asteroids, Comets, and Meteorites: Cosmic Invaders of the Earth.* New York: Facts On File, 2003.

Evans, Aneurin. *The Dusty Universe.* New York: John Wiley, 1995.

Fischer, Daniel. *Mission Jupiter: The Spectacular Journey of the Galileo Spacecraft.* New York: Copernicus Books, 2001.

Hanlon, Michael. *The Worlds of Galileo: The Inside Story of NASA's Mission to Jupiter.* New York: St. Martin's Press, 2001.

Harland, David M. *Jupiter Odyssey: The Story of NASA's Galileo Mission.* Berlin: Springer-Verlag Telos, 2000.

——. *Mission to Saturn: Cassini and the Huygens Probe.* New York: Praxis Press, 2003.

Herman, Robert, and Ralph A. Alpher. *Genesis of the Big Bang.* New York: Oxford University Press, 2001.

Irwin, Patrick. *Giant Planets of Our Solar System: Atmospheres, Composition, and Structure.* New York: Springer Verlag, 2003.

Kaler, James B. *Cosmic Clouds: Birth, Death, and Recycling in the Galaxy.* New York: W. H. Freeman, 1997.

——. *Stars.* New York: W. H. Freeman, 1998.

Kippenhann, Rudolf. *100 Billion Suns.* Translated by Jean Steinberg. Princeton, N.J.: Princeton University Press, 1993.

Kirshner, Robert P. *The Extravagant Universe: Exploding Stars, Dark Energy, and the Accelerating Cosmos.* Princeton, N.J.: Princeton University Press, 2002.

Lemonick, Michael D. *Echo of the Big Bang.* Princeton, N.J.: Princeton University Press, 2003.

Lewis, John S. *Physics and Chemistry of the Solar System.* Revised edition. San Diego, Calif.: Academic Press, 1997.

Livio, Mario, Keith Noll, and Massimo Stiavelli, eds. *A Decade of Hubble Space Telescope Science.* New York: Cambridge University Press, 2003.

Man, John. *Comets, Meteors, and Asteroids.* New York: DK Publishing, 2001.

Martin, James L., ed. *Saturn: Overview and Abstracts.* Hauppauge, N.Y.: Nova Science Publishers, 2003.

Moore, Patrick. *Venus.* New York: Sterling Publishing, 2002.

Norton, O. Richard. *The Cambridge Encyclopedia of Meteorites.* New York: Cambridge University Press, 2002.

Parsons, Paul. *Big Bang: The Birth of our Universe.* New York: DK Publishing, 2001.

Peebles, Curtis. *Asteroids: A History.* Washington, D.C.: Smithsonian Institution Press, 2001.

Prialnik, Dina. *An Introduction to the Theory of Stellar Structure and Evolution.* New York: Cambridge University Press, 2000.

Strom, Robert G., and Anne L. Sprague. *Exploring Mercury: The Iron Planet.* New York: Springer Verlag, 2003.

Van Der Hults, J. M., ed. *The Interstellar Medium in Galaxies.* Dordrecht, The Netherlands: Kluwer Print on Demand, 2001.

Weinberg, Steven. *The First Three Minutes: A Modern View of the Origin of the Universe.* New York: Basic Books, 1994.

INTERNET RESOURCES

Arnett, Bill. "Asteroids." Available online. URL: http://www.seds.org/nineplanets/nineplanets/asteroids.html. Last updated February 26, 2006.

——. "Comets." Available online. URL: http://www.seds.org/nineplanets/nineplanets/comets.html. Last updated May 1, 2003.

Department of Applied Mathematics and Theoretical Physics. University of Cambridge. "The Hot Big Bang Model." Available online. URL: http://www.solarviews.com/eng/asteroid.htm. Accessed on November 1, 2006.

Experimental Space Plasma Group. University of New Hampshire. "The Interstellar Medium: An Online Tutorial." Available online. URL: http://www-ssg.sr.unh.edu/ism/index.html. Accessed on November 1, 2006.

Hamilton, Calvin J. "Asteroid Introduction." Available online. URL: http://www.solarviews.com/eng/asteroid.htm. Accessed on November 1, 2006.

——. "Meteoroids and Meteorites." Available online. URL: http://www. solarviews.com/eng/meteor.htm. Accessed on November 1, 2006.

National Aeronautics and Space Administration. "Asteroids and Comets." Available online. URL: http://nssdc.gsfc.nasa.gov/planetary/planets/ asteroidpage.html. Last updated September 1, 2004.

——. "Cosmology." Available online. URL: http://map.gsfc.nasa.gov/ m_uni.html. Last updated September 26, 2006.

——. "Solar System Exploration." Available online. URL: http:// solarsystem.nasa.gov/index.cfm. Last updated October 27, 2006.

National Space Science Data Center. National Aeronautics and Space Administration. "Planetary Fact Sheets." Available online. URL: http:// nssdc.gsfc.nasa.gov/planetary/planetfact.html. Last updated January 22, 2001.

Space.com. "Spaceflight." Available online. URL: http://www.space.com/ missionlaunches/. Accessed on November 1, 2006.

INDEX

Italic page numbers
indicate illustrations.

A

absolute luminosity 49
achondrites 195, 196
Adams, Walter S. 94
aerogel 175
Aitken, Robert Grant
  168, 169
albedo 118
alpha decay 78
alpha particles 67–68
Alpher, Ralph 17
Altas 152
aluminum-26 25–26
amino acids 26–27, 191,
  196
ammonia 133, 136, 138,
  142, 152, 180
ammonia ice 137, 152,
  161
ammonium
  hydrosulfide ice 137,
  152, 161
anaerobic bacteria 103
anisotropy, of CMB
  18, 19
anorthosite 92
antimatter 6–7
antineutrinos 6, 7
Apollo missions 166,
  216–218, 217, 220–
  222, 224

argon 142, 156
Aristarchus 216
Aristotle 17
asteroids 154, 201–216,
  204
astronomical unit 181
ataxites 197
atmosphere
  effect on astronomy
    from Earth 108
  of Jupiter 133, 136–
    143
  of Mars 112–116
  of Mercury 91–92
  of Moon 217–219
  of Neptune 161
  of outer planets 153
  of Pluto 167
  of Saturn 152
  of Titan 155–157
  of Triton 162
  of Uranus 158
  of Venus 96–103,
    100–102
atoms, formation in
  early evolution of
  universe 11–13
aurora 153

B

basalts 222
belts, of Jupiter 136
BepiColombo spacecraft
  94

beryllium 12–13
beryllium-7 10–11
beryllium-8 68
beta decay 78
Bethe, Hans 17
big bang 1–20, 47–48
big crunch 14
Biot, Jean Baptiste 193
birth, of star 55–61
birth, of universe 1–20
black dwarf 60, 69
"black star" 61
Blank, Jennifer 192
Bode, Johann Elert 202
Bode's Law 202. See
  also Titius-Bode Law
BOOMERANG 19
breccias 222
brown dwarf 60, 61
Burbidge, Margaret and
  Geoffrey 74–75

C

Caesar, Julius 172
calcium silicate 107
Callisto 143–144
Callixtus III (pope) 173
Campbell, W. W. 112
canali 112
canals, on Mars 111–112
Cannon, Annie Jump
  50–51
carbon 66, 68, 107, 158,
  195

carbonaceous chondrites 183, 195–196
carbonaceous particles 28
carbon-based compounds 160, 183
carbon burning 69, 70, 79
carbon dioxide
and cometary nucleus 180
in Earth's atmosphere 100, 101
in Martian atmosphere 112, 114
in Urey reaction 107
in Venus's atmosphere 94, 96, 100–103
carbon ion 38
carbon monoxide 34, 42–43, 103, 114, 167
Cassini, Domenico 111
Cassini division 154
Cassini-Huygens mission 106, 130–131, 155
Ceres (asteroid) 204, 205
Chamaeleon 22
Charon 164, 167
China, ancient 172, 192
2060 Chiron 215, 215–216
chondrites 195
chondrules 195
clouds 23, 97, 136–137. See also molecular clouds
CNO cycle 65, 65–66
cobalt 60 73
coma 175
comet(s) 171–192, 175, 179, 201
Comet Borrelly 178

Comet 67P/ Churyumov-Gerasimenko 178
Comet Encke 181
Comet Grigg-Skjellerup 180
Comet Hale-Bopp 173
Comet Halley 171, 173–174, 178–179, 182
Comet Tempel 1 178
Comet Wild-2 175
Comet Wilson-Harrington 1949 III 215
CONTOUR (Comet Nucleus Tour) 178
cooling, of early universe 5–7
core, of planets/moons 103, 136, 144, 149, 156, 158
core formation 58
coronal gas 34
Cosmic Background Explorer (COBE) 18–20
Cosmic Hot Interstellar Spectrometer (CHIPS) satellite 45
cosmic infrared background (CIB) 18
cosmic microwave background (CMB) 16–20
cosmology 6, 17
COSTAR (Corrective Optics Space Telescope Axial Replacement) 109
C-type asteroids 124
cyanoacetylenes 25, 39

D

Dactyl 206
dark energy 228
Deep Impact spacecraft 178
Deep Space 1 spacecraft 178

Deimos (Martian moon) 117–118, 122–124
Descartes, René 168
deuterium 9, 141
deuteron 9, 63, 64
diatomic atoms 12
Dicke, Robert 18
Di Martino, M. 216
"dirty snowball" 180
Discovery (space shuttle) 109
downwelling 138
Draper, Henry 49, 50
D-type asteroids 124
Dunham, Theodore, Jr. 94
dust 33
and cometary nucleus 180, 183
and formation of hydrogen molecules 35–36
and formation of solar system 138, 140
in ISM 22–23, 27–29
and planetesimal formation 141
and rings of Saturn 154
Robert Julius Trumpler's studies of 30
dust tail 180
dwarf planet 164, 205

E

Eddington, Arthur 2, 3
Einstein, Albert 3
electromagnetic (EM) radiation 2, 83
electromagnetic spectrum 40, 85
electrons 4, 6
electrostatic force 12
elementary particles 3–5
$E = mc^2$ 3, 65

emission nebulae
30–31, *33*
energy 1–5
enstatite chondrites 195
erosion, on Callisto's
surface 144
Esposito, Larry 104–105
ethane 152, 161
Europa 148–149
evolutionary track 58
Ewen, Harold Irving
40, 41
expanding universe
13–14
extraterrestrial life,
search for 26–27

F

failed star 60
fault canyons 160
5-micron hotspot
137–138
Flamsteed, John
176–177
flat universe 20
fossil radiation 17
Fraunhofer, Joseph
von 83
fusion reaction 48–49,
60, 67, 69–80. *See also*
hydrogen burning

G

galaxies 13, *59*
Galilean moons 143
Galileo (spacecraft)
asteroid flybys
209–210
Jovian moons 143–
148
Jupiter orbit 129–
130, 136–137, 141
study of atmosphere
of Jupiter 142–143
Venus flybys 95, 96,
106
Galileo probe's Neutral
Mass Spectrometer
(GPMS) 142

γ, n reaction 78–79
gamma rays 2, 4, 7,
9, 66
Gamow, George 16–17
Ganymede 144, 148
gas(es)
in comets 183–188
in ISM 22–23
in Moon's
atmosphere 218,
219
gas giants 126, 156–160
Gaspra 210
gas tail. *See* ion tail
Gauss, Johann 205
Gemini telescope
system 45
giant molecular clouds
(GMCs) 31–34
giant star 53–54
Ginenthal, Charles
104
goethite 115
graphitic particles 28
gravitation
and expanding
universe 14, 48
and formation
of compound
particles 8–9
and r process 76
and star formation
48, 49, 56, 60
gravitational energy
67
gravity assist 96
Great Red Spot 136
Great White Spot 161
Greece, ancient 177,
216
greenhouse gas 102

H

half-life 73
Hall, Asaph 117, 122–
123
Halley, Sir Edmund
173–174, 176–177
Halley group 180–181

Halley's comet. *See*
Comet Halley
Harding, Carl Ludwig
205
Hartmann, Johannes
21, 23
Hastings, Battle of 171
Hayashi track 55, *55,*
59, *59*, 60
Heaven's Gate 173
heavy elements,
formation of 47–80
helium 61–69, 84,
141–142. *See also*
hydrogen burning
helium-3 9–10
helium-4 10, 15
Helium Abundance
Detector 141
helium burning 66–69
helium flash 67
Helmholtz, Hermann
von 58
hematite 115
Herman, Robert 17
Herschel, William 205
Hertzsprung, Ejnar
51–52
Hertzsprung-Russell
diagram 51–55, *53,*
54, 58, 59
hexahedrites 197
hexamethyl-
enetetramine (HMT)
188, 190
HI clouds 31–33
HII clouds 30–32
Hipparchus 49, 216
Hollenbach, David 35,
36
hotspot. *See* 5-micron
hotspot
Hubble, Edwin Powell
13, 108
Hubble Space Telescope
(HST) 108–109
Io observations 149
Martian moon
observations 124

Hubble Space Telescope (HST) (continued)
  Neptune
    observations 161
  Pluto observations 131
  Saturn observations 153
Huggins, Sir William 112
Huygens, Christiaan 111
Hydra 164
hydrocarbons 38–39, 195–196
hydrogen
  and big bang theory 14–15
  conversion into helium. *See* hydrogen burning
  and deuteron 9
  and HII clouds 30
  in ISM 23
  in Jupiter's core 136
  late arrival in universe 12
  in outer planets 141
  and protostar 61
  in Saturn's atmosphere 152
  and star formation 55–56
  in Uranus's atmosphere 158
  Hendrik van de Hulst's analysis of 40, 41
  visible spectrum *83*
hydrogen, atomic 30–34, 144, 148
hydrogen, ionized 35–36, 114
hydrogen, molecular 133, 161
hydrogen, neutral 23, 32
hydrogen-3 9–10
hydrogen burning 49, 60

hydrogen chloride 107
hydrogen deuteride 152, 161
hydrogen envelope 180
hydrogen fluoride 107
hydrogen molecules 12, 31, 35–39
hydrogen sulfide 103, 138, 142
hydronium 36

I

ice. *See* water ice
ice caps, on Mercury 93
ice clouds 114
Ida (asteroid) 206, 210
Imager for Mars Pathfinder (IMP) 124
inert gases 97, 142
infrared radiation 84, 85
infrared spectrum 41
inner planets 81–125
intercloud medium 34
International Astronomical Union (IAU) 164, 205
International Comet Explorer (ICE) 174
International Ultraviolet Explorer (IUE) 85
interstellar clouds 29–34
interstellar extinction 28
interstellar medium (ISM) 15, 21–46, *22, 27, 42–44*
interstellar molecules 23–25
interstellar reddening 29
intraconverting 32–33
Io (Jovian moon) 149–150
ionosphere, of Europa 149
ions, and ISM chemistry 38

ion tail 179–180
iron
  in Europa's core 149
  in inner planets 141
  in large stars 70
  on Mars 115, 117
  on Mercury 92, 93
  in neutron capture reaction 72
  and r process 76
  on Venus 107
iron meteorites 196–197, 202
iron oxide 115
Irwin, Louis 103
ISEE-3 (International Sun-Earth Explorer 3) 174
isotopes 10–11, 73, 79

J

James Webb Space Telescope 109, 166
Jansky, Karl Guthe 40
Janssen, Pierre 84, 112
Jovian moons 130, 143–151, *149*
Juno 205
Jupiter 126, 132–143, *133*, 174, 182. *See also* Jovian moons
Jupiter family 180

K

kamacite 197
Kaplan, Lewis 112–114
Karin group 214
Kelvin, Lord. *See* Thomson, William (Lord Kelvin)
Kelvin-Helmholtz Contraction Phase 58
Kennedy, John F. 166
kinetic energy 12
Kozlowski, R. W. H. 92
KREEP rocks 222
krypton 142

Kuiper, Gerard Peter 112, 162, 167–170, 182
Kuiper belt 131, 167, 169
Kuiper Belt Objects (KBOs) 167–170
Kumar, Shiv 60–61

L

Lassell, William 162
lava 104
Lemaître, Georges Edouard 2–3, 16
Leonid meteor shower 193
Lick Observatory 168–169
light elements 14–15
lightning, on Jupiter 137
line spectrum 83
lithium 14–17
lithium-6 10–11
lithium-7 10–11, 17
Lockyer, Sir Norman 84
long-term comet 181–182
Lucey, Paul G. 91, 92
luminosity 49
Lunar and Planetary Sciences Laboratory (LPSL) 91, 92
lunar materials 225–226
lunar meteorites 200
lunar rocks 221–224

M

Maddox, John 75
Magellan spacecraft 95–96
magnesium 117
magnesium oxide 106
magnetic field 136, 144, 148
Main Sequence 53–55, 59, 60
major planets. *See* gas giants

Manhattan Project 17
mantle 103, 115
Maraldi, Giacomo Filippo 111
Mariner 6 & 7 114
Mariner 9 118
Mariner 10 90–92
Mariner Mars Project 85, 95
Mars 85, 111–125, *117,* 200–201
Mars Infrared Spectrometer (IRS) 85
Mars Pathfinder mission 115, 118
mass defect 64–65
matter 3
matter-antimatter annihilation 7–8
MAXIMA 19
Mercury 90–94
mesosiderites 197
MESSENGER space probe 93–94
metallic hydrogen 134–136
metal silicates 28
meteor 172, 192–202
meteorites 171, 192–202, 214
meteoritic fall 194
meteoritic find 194
meteoritics 193, 197
meteoroid 192–202
methane
  and cometary nucleus 180
  formation of 38
  on Jupiter 133
  on Neptune 161
  on Pluto 167
  in Saturn's atmosphere 152
  in Titan's atmosphere 169
  in Uranus's atmosphere 158
microorganisms 103

Microwave Anisotropy Probe (MAP) project 19–20
microwave radiation 18–20
minerals 198–200, 223–224
minor planets 205. *See* asteroid; terrestrial planets
Miranda 160, 170
molecular clouds 30–34, 55–56
molecules, interstellar 23–25, 42–44
monomer 190
Moon 200, 216–226, *217. See also* lunar
moons
  of Mars 117–118, 122–124
  of Neptune 162
  of outer planets 127
  of Pluto 164
  of Saturn 151, 152
  of Uranus 156, *159*
muon 4, 6, 8
Murchison meteorite 196

N

National Aeronautics and Space Administration (NASA) 165–166
neon 142
neon burning 69, 70
nepheline 107
Neptune 126, 161–163
Nereid 162, 170
neutrinos 2–4, 7, 66
neutron 8, 9, 15, 64, 77
neutron capture 70–74
neutron decay reaction 72
New Horizons Pluto-Kuiper Belt Mission 131, 134, 167

Newton, Hubert Anson 193
Newton, Sir Isaac 173, 176, 177
Newton's theory of gravitation 173, 174, 176
n, reaction 77
nickel 73, 93, 197
nitrogen 66, 96, 100, 155–156, 162–163, 167
nitrogen-based compounds 160
nitrogen bases 196
Nix 164
nuclear instability 8
nucleus, of comet 178–179, 183

O

Oberon 160
octahedrites 197
Olbers, Wilhelm 205
Olmsted, Dennison 193
Oort, Jan Hendrick 40, 41, 181
Oort cloud 181
orbit 181–182, 193, 206, 214–215
organic molecules 26, 183, 189–192, 196
outer planets 126–170
outgassing 97, 100
oxygen 66, 68, 92, 117, 158
oxygen burning 69, 70, 79
oxygen ions 114, 149

P

Pallas 205
pallasites 197
Pandora 152, 154
parallel universe 7
parsec 49
particle decay 7–8, 64
Penzias, Arno 18
perihelion 181

Perseid meteor shower 192
p, reaction 78
Phobos (Martian moon) 117–118, 122–124
Phobos 2 space probe 113, 124
photodissociation 190–191
photoionization 190, 191
photolysis 97, 190
photons 2, 4
Piazzi, Guiseppe 205
Pillan Patera 149
Pioneer Project 127–128
Pioneer Venus program 95
plagioclase 92
planet(s) *82, 82*–90, *83, 85*
  inner. *See* inner planets
  outer. *See* outer planets
planetary nebula 69
planetesimals 140–141
planetoid 205. *See* asteroid
Pliny the Elder 172
Pluto 131, 164, 167
polonium 74
polycyclic aromatic hydrocarbons (PAHs) *27, 28*
polyoxymethylene (POM) 188, 190
polypeptides 191
Porco, Carolyn 155
potassium 91, 92
precipitable micron 113
Principia (Newton) 173, 176, 177
Prometheus 152, 154
proton 4, 10, 15, 62–64
proton capture *76*
proton-proton cycle 64–65, *65*

protoplanet 169
protostar 58, 60
Purcell, Edward Mills 40, 41

Q

quantum mechanics 63–64
Quaoar 131, *132*
quarks 4–6

R

radio astronomy 40, 41
Ramsay, Sir William 84
red giant 69
reflection nebula 29
regolith 222
ring compounds 25
rings
  of Neptune 163
  of Saturn 151, 153–155
  of Uranus 156, 158–160, *159*
Robinson, Mark S. 91, 92
Rome, ancient 172
Rosetta spacecraft 178
r process 74–78, *76*
runaway greenhouse effect 102–103
Russell, Henry Norris 52

S

Salpeter, Edwin 35, 36
salt water 143–144, 148
satellites (planetary). *See* moons
Saturn 128, 130–131, 151–156
Schiaparelli, Giovanni Virginio 112
Secchi, Pietro Angelo 111–112
SETI (Search for Extraterrestrial Intelligence) Institute 26–27

shape, of universe 14, 20
shepherd moons 158, 163
short-term comet 180–182
Shulze-Makuch, Dirk 103
silicates 92–93
silicon 117, 158
silicon dioxide 92–93, 106
slow neutron capture 73
sodium 91, 92
solar nebula 140, 141
solar system, formation of 138, 140–141
spectral classes 50, 52
spectral lines 30, 40–44, *42–44*
spectrometry 83–85, 91
spectroscope 83
speed of light (c) 3
spiral arm, of galaxy *59*
Spitzer, Lyman 108
Sprague, Ann L. 92
s process *76*, 77–78
star 15, 17, 49–55, 69–80. *See also* stellar evolution
Stardust spacecraft 175
stellar evolution 48–69
Stern, S. Alan 134–135
Stickney Crater 123–124
stony-iron meteorites 197, 202
stony meteorite 195, 202
Submillimeter Wave Astronomy Satellite (SWAS) 45
sulfur dioxide 103–105, 150
Sun
    abundance of helium in 15
    and chemical

composition of planets 141
and chemistry of short-term comets 182
effect on ion tail 179–180
formation of 140
Pierre Janssen's spectroscopic analysis of 84
supergiant HII region 31
supergiant star 53, 54
supernova 77, 79
Syrtis Major 111

T

taenite 197
tail, of comet 179–180
Tarter, Jill 61
thermonuclear fusion. *See* fusion reaction
Thomson, William (Lord Kelvin) 58
Tibullus 172
Titan 151, 155–157, 169
Titania 160
titanium 92
Titius, Johann Daniel 202
Titius-Bode Law 202–204
Tolman, Richard 16–17
triple helium process 67–68
tritium 9–10
Triton 162–163
Trumpler, Robert Julius 30–31
T-Tauri star 59–60
Turks 173
Twining, A. C. 193

U

ultracompact HII region 31
ultraviolet radiation 27, 84, 85

Ulysses spacecraft 128–129
universe, beginnings of 1–20
Uranus 156–160, *159*, 202, 203
Urey reaction 106–107

V

Valhalla basin 144
vanadium-50 78
van de Hulst, Hendrik Christoffel 40–41
Vaucouleurs, Gérard de 114
Venera program 95, 106
Venus 94–107, *100–102*, *105*, 110–111
Venus Express mission 96, 103, 107, 111
Very Large Array radio telescope 93
Vesta 205
Viking Project 114, 115, 118
vinyl alcohol 26
visible light 84
Voyager mission
    Io observations 149
    Neptune observations 161, 162
    to outer planets 128–129
    Saturn observations 151, 152, 154
    Uranus observations 157–159
vulcanism 104–105, 149–150

W

water
    in atmosphere of Jupiter 142
    beneath Callisto's crust 143–144
    in carbonaceous chondrites 195–196

water (continued)
  in comets 180, 183,
    190
  formation of
    molecule 36
  on Jupiter 133, 138
  in Martian
    atmosphere 114
  in Venus's
    atmosphere 94
water ice 137
  in cometary nucleus
    180
  on Ganymede 144
  on moons of Uranus
    160
  in Neptune's
    atmosphere 161
  on Pluto's surface 167

in rings of Saturn 154
in rings of Uranus
  158
in Saturn's
  atmosphere 152
in Uranus's core 158
water vapor
  in Earth's
    atmosphere 100–
    101
  in Martian
    atmosphere 112–
    113
  in Venus's
    atmosphere 100
Webb, James E. 165–
  166
Whipple, Fred 180
white dwarf 53, 54, 69

Wildt, Rupert 115
William the Conqueror
  (duke of Normandy)
  171
Wilson, Robert
  Woodrow 18
wind, on Jupiter 136
Witteborn, Fred C. 92

X

xenon 142

Y

ylem 17
young stellar object
  (YSO). See protostar

Z

zones, of Jupiter 136